Blackwell Cases in Human Resource and
Change Management

# Blackwell Cases in Human Resource and Change Management

Edited by John Storey

BLACKWELL
*Business*

Copyright © Blackwell Publishers, 1996
Selection and editorial material copyright © John Storey
Case 11 Manuflex plc © Linda Dickens

First published 1996

First published in USA 1996
2 4 6 8 10 9 7 5 3 1

Blackwell Publishers Ltd
108 Cowley Road
Oxford OX4 1JF
UK

Blackwell Publishers Inc.
238 Main Street
Cambridge, Massachusetts 02142
USA

*British Library Cataloguing in Publication Data*

A CIP catalogue record for this book is available from the British Library.

*Library of Congress Cataloging-in-Publication Data*

Blackwell cases in human resource and change management / edited by John Storey.

   p.   cm.
   ISBN 0–631–19752–4
   1. Personnel management—Case studies.   2. Organizational change—
Management—Case studies.   I. Storey, John, 1947–
HF5549.B614  1996
658.3—dc20
                              95–42830
                              CIP

ISBN 0–631–197524

Typeset in 11 on 13 pt Plantin
by Graphicraft Typesetters Ltd., Hong Kong
Printed in Great Britain by T.J. Press, Padstow, Cornwall

This book is printed on acid-free paper

# Contents

Copyright John Storey 1996, Blackwell Cases in Human Resource and Change Management

# List of contributors

Peter Ackers, Lecturer in Industrial Relations, Loughborough University Business School, UK.

Nick Bacon, Lecturer in Management, University of Nottingham.

Greg Bamber, Professor of Strategic Management and Director of the Australian Centre for Strategic Management, Queensland University of Technology, Australia.

Michael Beer, Professor of Business Administration, Harvard University, Graduate School of Business Administration, USA.

Christian Berggren, Professor of Industrial Management, Swedish Institute for Work Life Research, Stockholm, Sweden.

Klaus Blettner, Research Officer, University of Trier, Germany.

Harry Boer, Associate Professor, University of Twente, The Netherlands.

David Buchanan, Professor of Organizational Behaviour, Leicester De Montfort University, UK.

Linda Dickens, Professor of Industrial Relations and Organizational Behaviour and Deputy Director, Warwick Business School, UK.

Paul Edwards, Professor of Industrial Relations, Industrial Relations Research Unit, Warwick Business School, UK.

Russell A. Eisenstat, Consultant and Director of the Senior Human Resources Executive Forum, Harvard Business School.

Petra Garnjost, Research Officer, University of Trier, Germany.

Nancy Hubbard, Templeton College, University of Oxford, UK.

Henrik Holt Larsen, Professor, Institute of Organization and Industrial Sociology, Copenhagen Business School, Denmark.

Mick Marchington, Professor, University of Manchester Institute of Science and Technology, UK.

Ian McLoughlin, Senior Lecturer, Brunel University, UK.

Klaus Peter Otto, Executive Manager, Dillinger Hütte, Germany.

Tom Redman, Senior Lecturer, Teesside Business School, UK.

Graeme Salaman, Reader, Faculty of Social Sciences, The Open University, UK.

Christian Scholz, Professor, Universität des Saarlandes, Saarbrüken, Germany.

Hugh Scullion, Senior Lecturer in HRM, University of Newcastle Open Tyne, UK.

Mark Shadur, Principal Research Fellow, Centre for Corporate Change, Queensland University of Technology, Australia.

David Simmons, Research Fellow, Centre for Strategic Management, Queensland University of Technology, Australia.

Ed Snape, Lecturer, Hong Kong Polytechnic University, Hong Kong.

Doug Stace, Senior Research Fellow, Centre for Corporate Change, University of New South Wales, Australia.

John Storey, Professor of Strategic Human Resource Management, The Open University, UK.

Hartmut Wächter, Professor, University of Trier, Germany.

Adrian Wilkinson, Lecturer in Human Resource Management, University of Manchester, Institute of Science and Technology, UK.

Bob Wilson, Workforce Utilization Project Coordinator, Leicester General Hospital, UK.

Colin Whiston, Lecturer in Industrial Relations, University of Keele, UK.

# Preface and Acknowledgements

This book of case studies has been compiled as the unique underpinning to Blackwell's extensive list of books on human resource management. The idea originated with Richard Burton, Publisher, Blackwell's Business and Economics Division. It was he, and his then deputy, Claire Fisher, who convinced me that this would be an interesting and challenging project. So it has proved to be!

There are many types of 'case'. The difficulties in compiling the type which is on offer in this volume are of the most demanding kind. The (self-imposed) aim was to commission original cases from leading researchers from a number of different countries who would cover a balanced spread of contemporary issues and problems. Unlike an edited collection of textbook or discursive chapters, this aim necessitated the availability of specialist authors who would be able to call upon original, in-depth, case-based research which had reached a sufficient stage of progress to merit write-up. Timing was critical: a number of variables had to be brought into alignment within a constrained time-frame. By implication, the case research would have to be already under way. There was no time to negotiate new access to case sites and yet we wanted fresh material: work-in-progress rather than finished and previously published work.

Topics, authors, case-based research: these were the critical demands. The right authors, willing and able to commit their valuable time, currently engaged not only in research but also in the case-based mode and in a permutation which allowed a balanced spread of issues to be covered: these, when taken in combination, constitute a demanding set of requirements. I am, above all, grateful therefore to my panel of contributors for their unstinting efforts in composing material under these sorts of constraints.

John Storey
Milton Keynes
UK

**A *Tutors' Manual* which contains answers to the set questions at the end of each case is available upon application to the publishers. Please write to Blackwell Publishers, 108 Cowley Road, Oxford OX4 1JF. Use official stationery showing a telephone number by which you can be contacted.**

# Introduction

## JOHN STOREY

This is a collection of *research-based* case studies which report on real-life situations: these cases are neither anecdotes nor imaginary depictions. On the contrary, the cases to be found herein are condensed insights generated out of in-depth research by exceptionally talented analysts. The original impetus for these researchers was not to produce teaching material *per se*; our contributors were going about their scholarly pursuit of knowledge in work organizations. In this book, however, they have responded to our invitation to produce material directed primarily towards the needs of students and tutors.

The themes, issues and problematics remain broadly the same as they would be were the write-ups designed for the scholarly journals, but the treatment has been adjusted to facilitate the use of the material in the classroom. The audience for whom the book was compiled is envisaged as advanced students of personnel, human resource management, organizational behaviour and indeed students from any discipline taking a module involving the study of 'managed change' or human resource management (HRM).

The cases vary in length. The shorter ones could be read and used in a classroom situation without necessarily requiring prior preparation. The longer cases clearly require some study outside the class.

The unique admix of topic, length and treatment was designed to meet a need, which many tutors running advanced modules have expressed, to locate 'good cases'. What constitutes a 'good case' is hard to define (beyond the obvious generalities); it is almost a question of 'feel'. This 'feel' stems from sufficient depth and content, contemporary relevance, authenticity and a certain clarity emerging from complex reality. Each of these cases has been designed to meet these exacting criteria. Many of these cases have been tried and tested on MBA and similar students by the case writers in their own institutions. The cases also have an application and significance beyond teaching. For example, the Next Patient Please case has been used by the chief executive of the Leicester General Hospital Trust as part of the selection process to find his successor.

The nature and various uses of the case method have been examined elsewhere (see most notably Eason, 1992). There seems little point in repeating the argument here. Many of the students using this book will be familiar already with the case method from other modules. The same general principles concerning careful reading, diagnosis, the construction of alternative interpretations and alternative 'solutions' with an eye to costs and risks as well as benefits, all apply here.

Each case is accompanied by a selected list of recommended reading. This reading will fill out, in appropriate depth, the concepts, perspectives and current knowledge about the issues raised in the cases. Each case also ends with a list of questions. These have been designed with some care. In practice, they are likely to be the assignments set for classroom discussion. There is a tutors' manual available from the publishers which contains the 'answers' to these questions which the case writers themselves would give (subject to the usual warning that these should not necessarily be interpreted as definitive, exclusive responses, although in a certain more modest sense they could be seen as 'models' of a kind). Access to the tutors' manual is restricted.

## Content

This book of case studies is designed to have a broad coverage of themes in human resource and change management. No book can be fully comprehensive — it would be foolish to try to make it so — but one of the original objectives was to ensure that the collection met the needs of students and tutors on the kinds of modules in which we collectively are engaged. Accordingly, there is coverage of the 'core' areas of resourcing, developing, industrial relations, equal opportunities and similar staples (for sound textbook treatments see Sisson, ed., 1994; Torrington and Hall, 1991; Hendry, 1995; Beardwell and Holden, 1994; Anthony et al., 1993; Schuler, 1992).

But, in addition, we were seeking other things. First, an international perspective. The cases herein cover real-life contemporary organizational dilemmas in many countries including Sweden, the USA, Germany, Holland, Denmark and Australia. An example of an excellent text to complement these cases would be Sparrow and Hiltrop (1994).

Second, we wanted to give lively, real-life access to significant contemporary issues which do not fit easily within the conventional discipline categories. Hence, the cases cover process re-engineering (for example, see Buchanan's case), novel ways of limiting redundancies (see the cases by Wächter and Garnjost) and the human resource aspects of mergers and acquisitions (Hubbard, Case 1).

Third, there was the desideratum of good sectoral coverage. Here we have cases based in the health services, telecoms, retailing, leisure, manufacturing, computers, banking, education, offshore oil and gas, central and local government.

A particularly novel feature of the book is the inclusion of cases which report on research-grounded prescription. The cases illustrate research consultancy by leading figures of international standing. For example, in pioneering spirit, Michael Beer of Harvard Business School goes beyond conceptual clarification of Strategic HR and illustrates his work in enabling managers to learn how to *enact* strategy. Here, he takes us through the process step by step. Similarly, Doug Stace of the Centre for Corporate Change at the University of New South Wales uses cases to reveal how different types of strategic change can be managed most effectively.

This collection of cases is as much about the management of change as it is about the management of human resources – hence the title of the book. An increasing number of managers have come to express an interest in the processes of change management. There are, in some universities, separate modules of study on this subject. While the management of change goes beyond HRM, the centrality of change management is arguably one of HRM's defining characteristics. The joint treatment here of these subjects is therefore entirely appropriate. The prominence of both sets of issues in these newly-minted cases in itself reflects contemporary trends.

## Common Trends

Of the 24 cases, half are from and are located in, countries other than the UK. The wide sector spread has already been noted. Given this immense variety, the temptation to make comparisons and contrasts is quite simply irresistible. To put this point another way: what lessons can be drawn about contemporary global developments in employment and organizational management from this unique crop of contemporary studies?

The most obvious strand to be found woven through most of these cases concerns heightened competitive pressures and the far-reaching organizational changes which have been devised in order to respond to these. Whether because of deregulation, globalization of trade, structural changes or other factors, the impact of competitive forces seems all too clear in the majority of cases. The intensity of the competition for markets is reflected in cases as varied as steel and cars in Germany, hearing aid manufacture in Denmark, banking and steel tubes in Australia, diesel engine manufacture in The Netherlands, and medical equipment distribution and manufacture in the USA. To this extent at least, there are seemingly certain universal forces at play.

But what can be inferred about the responses to these forces? Among the inevitable variations and complexities, certain recurring patterns do emerge. For example, the increased emphasis on 'quality' and customer service as competitive strategies is a leitmotif in many of these cases. It can be seen most clearly in the cases described in Three Roads to Quality (case 12) and in Richer Sounds (case 20). Another pattern is the willingness to embark on radical programmes of organizational restructuring and change. This tendency is shown in Oticon (case 5), The Danish Patent Office (case 7), Indian Snacks (case 25) and Global Products (case 1). A further pattern concerns experiments in flexible working hours and flexible working practices (see, for example, Unilever (case 21), FMS at Diesel Engines plc (case 23), and ChocCo,).

Underneath these apparent commonalities lie two interesting issues. The first of these is the extent to which managers in this array of cases are merely reciting and implementing current 'recipes' which, because of modern communications and international travel, are quickly transmitted around the global marketplace for ideas. The buzzwords 'the Learning Organization' and 're-engineering' exemplify this tendency. The second issue concerns the precise way in which attempts are made to implement these mantras. This is where the case method is uniquely privileged in surfacing the real-life dynamics. Excellent examples of the 'warts and all' processes in messy, real-world situations are to be found in the cases of The Danish Patent Office, British Rail, Global Products and Contract Catering, Next Patient Please, Indian Snacks, and to one degree or another in just about every other case in this collection.

There are, however, also some marked differences which emerge from the range of cases. These are (at least) as interesting as the common trends. One marked contrast is to be found in the different approaches to managing labour surpluses in the Continental European cases compared with the UK and the USA. The Volkswagen case and also Saarland Steel reveal a profoundly different set of assumptions and institutional and legal contexts than is in evidence in the UK where redundancy is seen as a first resort in a cost-cutting drive (see, for example, case 1). The dynamic way in which legal and socio-economic institutional contexts interact with management strategies is a lesson revealed clearly in this case collection.

## The Sequence of Cases

The sequence adopted in this collection follows the structure used in the textbook Storey (ed.) (1995). Cases which concentrate on broad strategic issues are located in Part I. Then in Part II come cases which primarily illustrate lessons about the management of change. Cases which focus on separate practice areas of HRM such as recruitment and selection, managing redundancy, equal opportunities, reward management, employee development and industrial relations are to be found in Part III. Finally, Part IV brings together those cases which concentrate on the problems of international management.

This is a simple and logical structure yet one which so far has not been adopted in previous case books. It is designed to meet the needs of most students and tutors working together in the area of human resource and change management.

## Guide to the Cases

Table I.1 will assist tutors in selecting cases to meet their needs. The table lists the cases in the same numerical sequence as they are listed in the contents page of this book. The five columns of the table then give the name of each case, the author(s), the main topic dealt with in the case, the country of location, the sector, and finally the length of each case. Table I.2 is an alphabetical listing of all of the main topics dealt with in the cases.

**Table I.1**  A guide to the cases

| Case number | Short title/(Author) | Main topic area | Country location | Sector | Number of pages |
|---|---|---|---|---|---|
| 1 | Global Products and Quality Caterers (Nancy Hubbard) | Acquisitions and mergers | UK | Gas appliances and contract catering | 16 |
| 2 | BMW (Christian Scholz) | Applying scenario analysis technique to HRM policy making | Germany | Car production | 10 |
| 3 | Transition and Transformations (Doug Stace) | Integrating business and HR strategy/ change management | Australia | Banking/steel tubes and plastic pipes/ state library services | 30 |
| 4 | ChocCo (Nick Bacon and John Storey) | Decentralized HR strategy making | UK | Confectionery manufacture | 5 |
| 5 | Oticon (Henrik Larsen) | Radical organizational change | Denmark | Hearing aid manufacture | 8 |
| 6 | The Volkswagen Model (Petra Garnjost and Klaus Blettner) | Cutting labour costs without redundancies | Germany | Car production | 14 |
| 7 | Danish Patent Office (Henrik Larsen) | A failed organizational development (OD) initiative | Denmark | Government agency | 6 |

| 8 | Saarland Steel (Hartmut Wächter and Klaus-Peter Otto) | Restructuring and redundancy | Germany | Steel production | 18 |
|----|----|----|----|----|----|
| 9 | American Medical Technologies Inc. (Michael Beer) | Implementing strategic HRM | USA | Medical equipment manufacturing and distribution | 20 |
| 10 | Optus Communications (David Simmons, Mark Shadur, Greg Bamber) | Recruitment and selection – creating an enterprise culture | Australia | Telecommunications | 13 |
| 11 | Manuflex plc (Linda Dickens) | Introducing equal opportunities | UK | Electrical engineering | 13 |
| 12 | Three Roads to Quality (Adrian Wilkinson) | Total quality management | UK | Engineering, electronics, software engineering | 17 |
| 13 | Next Patient Please (David Buchanan) | Job redesign and process re-engineering | UK | Health services | 16 |
| 14 | The Ministry of Education (Henrik Larsen) | Management development | Denmark | Central government | 10 |
| 15 | British Rail (Paul Edwards and Colin Whitston) | Discipline and absence control | UK | Rail services | 12 |

**Table I.1** (cont.)

| Case number | Short title/(Author) | Main topic area | Country location | Sector | Number of pages |
|---|---|---|---|---|---|
| 16 | Leisureco (Peter Ackers) | Employee involvement and flexibility | UK | Leisure theme park | 10 |
| 17 | Royal Mail (Nick Bacon and John Storey) | Industrial relations | UK | Mail services | 3 |
| 18 | Deco, Ceco and Coco (Ian McLoughlin) | Employment practices in non-union companies | UK | Computers, consumer electronics, offshore oil and gas | 19 |
| 19 | Metropol (Nick Bacon and John Storey) | Equal opportunities | UK | Local government | 6 |
| 20 | Richer Sounds (Adrian Wilkinson, Tom Redman and Ed Snape) | Payment for customer service | UK | Hi-Fi retail | 9 |
| 21 | Unilever (Nick Bacon and John Storey) | Annualized hours/ working time | UK | Liquid detergent manufacture | 6 |
| 22 | Superco (Mick Marchington) | Employee involvement | UK | Food retailing | 15 |

| | | | | |
|---|---|---|---|---|
| 23 | FMS at Diesel Engines plc (Harry Boer) | Flexible manufacturing | Netherlands/UK | Diesel engine manufacture | 21 |
| 24 | The Case of ABB (Christian Berggren) | Local presence and cross-border learning within a transnational corporation | Switzerland/ Sweden/Canada | Power transformers and process automation/ instrumentation | 24 |
| 25 | Indian Snacks (Graeme Salaman) | Organizational change/ MNC and local influence | India | Food and drink manufacture | 12 |
| 26 | Food and Drink International (Hugh Scullion) | International staffing | Global | Food and drink | 9 |

**Table I.2**   Alphabetical listing of case topics

| Topics | Cases |
| --- | --- |
| Absence | 15 |
| Acquisition | 1 |
| Annualized hours | 21 |
| Cost reduction | 6 |
| Customer service | 20 |
| Decentralization | 4 |
| Discipline | 7 |
| Employee involvement | 16, 22 |
| Enterprise culture | 10 |
| Equal opportunities | 11, 19 |
| Flexibility | 16 |
| Flexible manufacturing | 23 |
| HRM policy | 2 |
| International HRM | 26 |
| Industrial relations | 4 |
| Integration | 3 |
| Job design | 13 |
| Learning | 24 |
| Management development | 14 |
| Managing change | 3, 5, 25 |
| Mergers | 1 |
| New Deal in employment | 17 |
| Non-unionism | 18 |
| Organizational development | 7 |
| Payment systems | 20 |
| Process re-engineering | 13 |
| Re-engineering | 1 |
| Recruitment | 13 |
| Redundancy | 10 |
| Restructuring | 1, 6, 8 |
| Selection | 8 |
| Scenario analysis | 10 |
| Strategy | 2 |
| Total quality management | 4, 9 |
| Transnational corporations | 12 |
| Working time | 24, 25 |
| | 16, 21 |

References

Anthony, W. P., Perrewe, P. L. and Kacmar, K. M. 1993: *Strategic Human Resource Management.* Fort Worth, Texas: The Dryden Press.

Beardwell, I. and Holden, L. (eds.) 1994: *Human Resource Management.* London: Pitman.

Eason, G. 1992: *Learning from Case Studies.* Hemel Hempstead: Prentice-Hall.

Hendry, C. 1995: *Human Resource Management: A Strategic Approach to Employment.* London: Butterworth-Heinemann.

Schuler, R. S. 1992: *Managing Human Resources.* 4th edn., New York: West Publishing.

Sisson, K. (ed.) 1994: *Personnel Management.* 2nd edn., Oxford: Blackwell.

Sparrow, P. and Hiltrop, J. M. 1994: *European Human Resource Management in Transition.* Hemel Hempstead: Prentice-Hall.

Storey, J. (ed.) 1995: *Human Resource Management: A Critical Text.* London: Routledge.

Torrington, D. and Hall, L. 1991: *Personnel Management: A New Approach.* Hemel Hempstead: Prentice-Hall.

# PART I

# Business Strategy and Human Resources

# 1

# Global Products and Quality Caterers

*Acquisitions: managing to motivate and the construction of new psychological contracts*

## NANCY HUBBARD

A review of a well-orchestrated acquisition implementation offers an interesting contrast to an acquisition where human issues were not taken into account. The ramifications for the respective companies were enormous – one tripled its profit margins while the other lost its customer base and competitive advantage.

## GLOBAL PRODUCTS

Gas Appliances was acquired by Global Products in 1991 in an agreed bid of £400 million which was consummated after several years of negotiations between the two companies' managements.

Global Products enjoyed a meteoric rise from a small Midlands-based company to a £1,000 million turnover public company in the span of ten years due primarily to its highly successful acquisition technique. Considered a related conglomerate, Global Products had a strong home products division in which it was considered Gas Appliances would fit nicely in terms of both product fit and customer base. Gas Appliances possessed excellent brand names, especially in the home products market, but did not have the investment to capitalize on those brand names. The operation, therefore, did not fully utilize its existing assets or systems.

A primary manufacturing site was located in central England and employed approximately 400 employees producing a range of gas appliances. Its brand name was highly regarded: in fact it had been either a market share leader or runner-up in all its major product lines. The factory, however, had not been given the resources to maintain its market leading position and thus was not run at optimum efficiency. This included overstocked finished goods and inventory stores, a disused derelict warehouse, out-of-date plant and equipment, and antiquated and compartmentalized offices and eating facilities. This was manifested in a less-than-efficient attitude to work by many of the employees. One shopfloor employee commented: 'management didn't take any pride in the place so I guess none of us did either'.

The shopfloor workforce primarily comprised long-serving employees, the majority of whom were women. It was not uncommon to find employees working at Gas Appliances for over 25 years. Because of the seasonal nature of the business the factory employed a number of subcontracted employees who worked five months of the year. When full-time jobs fell vacant these employees were given priority in hiring. This system was not ideal as it was considered that the seasonal employees were less motivated and diligent in their working practices.

The bid was accepted by shareholders on 20 February 1991. The press reports detailing the deal recounted the famous Global Products' technique of having a special acquisition unit whose job it was to enter the newly acquired business and modernize it in line with the other subsidiaries. This included a reorganization of the offices and the shopfloor.

On the day following the acquisition all the directors from Gas Appliances throughout the world were summoned to Heathrow to meet the Global Products team and hear about their futures. There, a presentation was made which was considered cold and stark; it was, however, considered highly professional and inspired a great deal of respect in those directors attending. The presentation was considered impressive because of its detailed information on Global Products and the analysis of Gas Appliances' strengths and weaknesses which clearly outlined the reasons for the acquisition. The presentation technique was also considered exemplary; the Global Products' managing director conducted the presentation with what was considered extreme professionalism. One director interviewed said, 'The Global Products MD deserved an Oscar for his performance – he talked for two hours with no notes and didn't falter once. He was most impressive'. At the close of the meeting all those attending were given a copy of a Global Products video outlining the company which they were encouraged to show to their subordinates.

Within a week of the meeting the acquisition team arrived at the initial locations to analyse the business units. The acquisition team's first job was to evaluate the company's top management. While it was Global Products' policy to retain top management, Global Products management felt that the incumbent management evaluation process was an important initial step of the acquisition implementation. The management team consisted of long-serving finance, commercial and marketing directors and newly appointed managing and operations directors. The acquisition team spent several hours grilling the directors over their previously poor performance to which they responded. At the conclusion of the meeting it was made clear that the management team would be kept intact for the foreseeable future. They would, however, be operating the 'Global Products way' and must be open to new management techniques and greater accountability, to which they agreed. This alleviated a great deal of doubt in the directors' minds. One director said: 'going into that meeting I didn't think I would have a job but afterwards I knew at least I had the opportunity to prove what I could do'.

The following day the Home Products acquisition team of five people began a formal review of the operations, a process which was to last six months. A presentation was made to all employees via both the existing management team and the acquisition team. This presentation included a video on Global Products followed by an outline of future implementation plans. This comprised four points. First, senior management were asked to complete a comprehensive post-acquisition analysis of their business. This included a full financial analysis, product and profit margin analysis and a comprehensive listing of all plant and equipment as well as copies of all building leases. Second, the site would be cleaned up including the demolition of the disused warehousing and removal of all non-essential papers and trash. Third, the offices would be refurbished and modernized including the use of open-plan offices and overhauling the central reception and meeting areas. The Global Products rationale given was that if Gas Appliances was a market leader it should look like one. Finally, the shopfloor was to be reorganized with the introduction of certain total quality and short cycle management techniques which would radically change working practices.

The information session offered no opportunity for employee feedback but instead was an information dissemination session. Those

Copyright John Storey 1996, Blackwell Cases in Human Resource and Change Management

employees attending the meeting were of two opinions when hearing about the organizational changes. Approximately half were just happy to be included in the change announcement. One employee commented, 'It was the first time that they [management] had ever told us what was going on . . . it was nice to be included.' The other half were more sceptical and were taking a 'wait and see' attitude. Another commented: 'we had heard of grandiose plans before which never materialized; I decided to see if they lived up to their talk'.

The first part of the implementation commenced immediately. The directors as well as many middle managers were highly involved with the collection and correlation of the information demanded by Global Products' head office. This time proved trying for many of those employees involved due to the long hours and workload required. One director commented: 'the workload was unbelievable; I don't know if it was intentional but they kept me so busy I couldn't even think about the acquisition'. The commercial director resigned, citing incompatible management styles. The rest of the senior and middle management team, however, remained intact.

While the information-gathering phase was occurring, all other employees were responsible for cleaning up the work areas with the acquisition team supervising. Several Gas Appliances employees in each area of the facility were assigned to help in the clean-up. Many employees were approached by acquisition team members and quizzed about the origin of unclaimed papers and items. If items were not claimed within a day or deemed important, they were thrown out. Those documents which were considered important were stored in a new archive centre on the premises. Upon completion of this phase, one employee remarked: 'the offices looked better now than they did on the day I joined Gas Appliances 20 years ago'.

When this phase was complete, the second phase of office refurbishing began. The corporate builders and decorators arrived on site and began reorganizing the layout. Several key middle managers, including the office manager from Gas Appliances, were given responsibility for the office layout and design. One manager who was heavily involved commented: 'it was hard work to organize the office layout but I would far rather be involved and busy than have it done by people who don't fully understand the office nuances'. While several employees affected by the changes complained that they did not like open plan offices it appeared to be more efficient and, in the end, even those employees grudgingly admitted that the new layout was preferable to the older style, which was likened by one employee to rabbit warrens. All office staff were given the opportunity to choose new office furniture based on their own individual requirements within some limits; this was well received by those affected.

During the second phase the communal areas were also redecorated. A plush new reception area was added in which several of the products were sympathetically displayed. A bright new canteen with seating area was also added where all employees would dine and where group meetings would be held. A product demonstration building was also erected in which all the company's products were to be displayed. The site, including the shopfloor area, was painted. The results were well received by the affected employees. One marketing manager commented: 'we always wanted to bring customers here but were too embarrassed, now we are proud to bring them here'.

It was as only after the initial stages of refurbishment were completed that the final phase of reorganizing the shopfloor commenced. In order to meet the products' seasonality the company not only employed part-time seasonal employees but also historically stockpiled appliances manufactured during the summer months thus leading to a finished goods inventory which ran into millions of pounds. Often these goods would get damaged in stock and need to be refinished prior to being sold.

The operations director had a vision for the shopfloor which was similar to that of Global Products. This included the reorganization of the floor into production cells, the introduction of just-in-time inventory and finished goods, and zero defects manufacturing. In addition, the pay schedules and the use of subcontracted labour was to come under review. The shopfloor employees, although wary of the changes, did not resist the introduction of the new working practices. As one employee commented: 'they said they were going to change the rest of the building and they did a good job, so when they said they were going to change the shopfloor, we knew they would do it and that they would do a good job on that as well'.

The first task was to renegotiate the current employment contracts with the shopfloor employees. With the help of the trade unions the employee contracts were renegotiated. The employees were previously on a variety of different pay grades based on seniority, with no element of performance-related pay. These rates were increased and levelled with no loss in wages to two different pay rates on the shopfloor, one for cell leaders and another for cell members. Because of the historical use of seasonal workers it was not necessary to make any of the existing shopfloor employees redundant. In addition, Gas Appliances had begun a delayering process two months prior to the acquisition and had made redundant or redeployed an entire layer of production management. Because of this no further redundancies were necessary.

The employees were then given the opportunity to help determine how to cope with the extreme seasonality of the products. Management, via the personnel department, asked employees for ideas on how to deal with the manufacturing seasonality. Management received a variety of responses, the majority of which were helpful although a few were sarcastic. One suggestion was that the existing workforce would work shorter hours in the peak winter summer months and longer hours in the slower summer months. This response was accepted by management and the affected employees again voted on the preferred start and finish times. There was a moderate amount of cynicism over the working hours solution. One of the employees commented: 'management knew what they were going to do before they asked us, they were just going through the motions'.

The acquisition team then began the shopfloor transformation. The directors involved were given great latitude in updating the plant and equipment which engendered a positive attitude in many of those managers involved. One director commented: 'I have to say I was wary of Global Products until I saw them talking with their money; they really transformed this place'. All those in senior and middle production management positions were involved in the process; all those managers interviewed felt involved in the process and that they had received enough information about the changes. Some of those lower-level employees, however, were wary of the process and did not feel as included as they would have liked. One shopfloor employee commented: 'they were making changes all around us and they should have talked to us more'.

The increased responsibility for cell leaders and production managers created a moderate amount of uncertainty in those individuals. The bulk of this uncertainty was alleviated by a reasonable degree of training and laxity given by management during their training phases. The shopfloor employees interviewed felt that they had sufficient information concerning the changes in their own roles and jobs, their increased responsibilities and what was ultimately wanted from them by Gas Appliances and Global Products. One employee commented: 'our production director was very understanding and encouraging in helping us learn our new roles, it wasn't easy but it was worth it'. This helped reduce any role ambiguity brought on by the change in ownership and working practices.

The shifting of the lines into production cells with greater responsibility, combined with the flatter production structure, required the promotion of certain shopfloor employees into cell leader and production manager positions. It was a management decision to promote and train current employees rather than hire externally. This engendered a degree of trust in many of the employees who had worked for years with their new cell leaders.

The objective of the cells was to achieve maximum responsiveness to production needs, including functional flexibility within their cells, which was achieved via extensive training within the cells. In addition, cells were measured on their ability to achieve zero quality defects. Finally, cells were responsible for maintaining a low finished goods' inventory. The cell requirements were well publicized by the production managers and training was given in order to facilitate the achievement of these goals.

The changes took approximately six months to implement and included the full reorganization of the shopfloor. When the acquisition team finally left the site it had been transformed by the new facilities and work techniques. While there had been some initial problems with the techniques implemented, they were minimized with time and training.

The massive changes brought on by the acquisition created a degree of uncertainty among the acquired employees. They had no reason to trust or believe Global Products at the beginning of the acquisition. In spite of this the management team lost only one director during the process and virtually none of middle management. Many employees commented that while they did not initially believe Global Products, the fact that they fulfilled employee expectations had lowered their initial concerns and enhanced Global Products' credibility. This process included accurately communicating the planned changes to employees prior to their implementation and following through with the implementation as discussed. This was enhanced by the positive leadership demonstrated by Global Products' management and the positive impact that the acquisition had on the Gas Appliances' facilities.

In conclusion, the acquisition was considered a success by employees and management by virtue of achieving the stated acquisitional objectives with the least amount of disruption to the staff and operation. In fact, Gas Appliances recently received a national business award for its quality production initiatives.

## QUALITY CATERERS

This case involved the subsidiary sale of a major contract catering company, Quality Caterers, from a British-based global conglomerate (Global Services plc) to a related conglomerate, Service Conglomerate.

Quality Caterers had its head office based in a stately home outside London and eight independent operating units throughout the UK. These units were responsible for the catering contracts and employees in their region, which totalled 1,800 and 24,000 respectively. This number of contracts held put Quality Caterers in the country's top four catering firms. By the nature of the business the organization was highly decentralized with many locations supporting only a few members of staff.

Regional managers were assigned to monitor their units' performance in their specific area, to aid in budgeting and act as client liaison. Each manager was assigned anywhere from 9 to 16 contracts depending on the unit's geographical spread, the unit size and the individual manager's capability.

The emphasis at Quality Caterers was always on retaining contracts by delivering a quality service at a slightly premium price. Staff were perceived as being of the highest quality and integrity; their loyalty to their clients was seen as being a major factor in providing a quality service. Staff were well trained by the in-house training department and, in fact, Quality Caterers had recently received a government training initiative award. Quality Caterers' employees were proud of its deserved reputation as a quality provider and its record on retaining contracts; it was not uncommon for Quality Caterers to have contracts for over 20 years.

This quality image sat well with the owners of Quality Caterers, Global Services plc, who encouraged the quality culture as it fitted with the overall company culture. It was Global Services' intention to promote steady long-term growth within the group by building market share. It was not interested in short-term profit or, indeed, on making the assets work particularly hard; Global Services management was happy with the 4.5 per cent margins generated by Quality Caterers.

There had been rumours at Global Services that management would like to expand certain business areas and that it needed to raise capital to do so. These rumours reached the attention of Quality Caterers management during one of the frequent management training courses whereupon they questioned the chief executive of Global Services. They were assured that, as one manager present said: 'we were the silver on the mantle and it was absurd that we would be sold'. This reassuring message was relayed back to the regional offices and operating units. Six weeks later, Quality Caterers was sold to Service Conglomerate. The sale of Quality Caterers came as a complete shock to its management team, even its managing director.

The acquiring organization's chief executive had a ruthless reputation in the industry, having taken a competitor and, through drastic cuts in staffing and service, dramatically increased profit margins. Press comments surrounding the subsidiary sale referred to the Service Conglomerate chief executive's reputation and track record, and he asserted in the press that a similar doubling of profit margins would occur at Quality Caterers.

Service Conglomerate moved quickly in an attempt to allay the concerns of Quality Catering's senior management by holding a general reception and presentation. They distributed a detailed question-and-answer sheet which tackled many of the acquisitional issues such as reasons for sale and outlining terms and conditions. The effectiveness of this was somewhat undercut by spelling mistakes in the presentation, a poor presentation style by the Services Conglomerate chief executive and inferior catering during the event.

A follow-up letter was sent by Service Conglomerate to all Quality Caterers staff welcoming them to the new organization. This was quickly followed by a letter from the Quality Catering managing director saying 'it is business as usual' and that employees would be informed of any future changes, and finally by a discount card which offered 10 per cent off all Service Conglomerate services.

The Quality Caterers board was told to prepare, within six weeks, a business plan for Service Conglomerate which outlined profit improvement savings.

Although no figures were actually given, the media reports gave a good indication of what was wanted, namely large-scale profit improvement and little need for structural integration with Service Conglomerate. For six weeks the three most senior directors (managing, marketing and finance) worked on a plan which was eventually accepted by the Services board. The plan's implementation was to be phased over three years with the initial reductions to occur immediately. The operational plan was drawn up, with the peripheral help of the personnel function and with the inclusion of the regional managing directors, three weeks before the actual date of implementation. They did, however, know that planning had taken place prior to their involvement. Some of the directors found this upsetting; one commented: 'I found the process divisive, there were three of them on the inside and we were on the outside yet we were all supposed to be equals'.

The bulk of the plan entailed cutting the number of managerial employees without affecting the actual catering units. Certain functions such as pay-roll and accounts were going to be centralized with the former occurring nine months hence. Two of the eight regions were to be incorporated into the remaining six regions in order to save on overhead costs.

No formal communication following on from the 'business as usual' letter was sent to employees until a date was chosen as the day on which the redundancy announcements would occur. The redundancies were to remove approximately half of operational directors, 20 per cent of regional managers and most of the regional training staff. There was an attempt to find people jobs but in most cases the options offered were not very attractive and, therefore, most chose redundancy. All employees were told to attend the meetings which were to be held individually with the regional managing directors.

This day has come to be known within the company as Black Monday, and the technique of a fast and painful execution of redundancies as the 'abattoir effect'. Although some regional managing directors were better than others, the brutality of the day shocked and appalled both employees being made redundant and those remaining. The personnel managers were appraised of the situation minutes before they were supposed to assist in the process and ostensibly help with counselling. Information concerning the affected employees' terms and conditions was collected from the centrally held personnel files which in many cases were incorrect. Thus redundancy pay calculations, job titles and even names were incorrect. Employees from the disappearing regions were told to go to other offices and were made redundant by people they had not met before. In several cases, directors interrupted meetings to re-hire employees being told they were redundant. Other employees were informed that they did not have a job at one office and were told to go to another office to see if they had a job for them there. Employees, for the most part, left the offices immediately, with little ceremony or comment to those remaining. Schedules ran late and some employees were kept waiting for up to five hours.

In one case, two operational directors were given the opportunity to take regional managers' jobs. If they were to do so, four of their managers would be made redundant; the directors chose redundancy. Later that afternoon the regional managing director briefed those remaining employees of the new organizational structure. The directors' decision had not been anticipated and therefore the organizational structure had not been amended to reflect this. The names of the four middle managers (who were present) were not on the chart; instead, the operations directors' names were still present.

In addition to the staffing reductions, further changes were made in order to further maximize profits. The training department was radically reduced, yet customers continued to pay a substantial training levy. This created both substantial role conflict and role ambiguity for the managers whose previous job performance had been based on giving a total quality service. In effect, these managers were now being required to lie to customers.

Within four months of Black Monday, a further 15 per cent of middle managers had left the company voluntarily. This was due in some cases to anger over the way in which their colleagues had been treated and in others to the disillusionment caused, and ethical issues raised, by the role conflict. As further resignations were not calculated in the manpower planning strategy, some of those made redundant had to be re-hired at above their previous salaries.

The acquisition created serious problems for Quality Caterers and those employees remaining within the organization. Most employees had to cope with a dramatically increased workload, often with new colleagues, bosses, subordinates and customers. Whereas previously there had been enough time to deliver a quality service, employees did not have sufficient time to do the job in the same way – some compensated by working 70-hour weeks. In addition, there had been very little contact between Service Conglomerate and the Quality Caterers' employees which led many of those interviewed to feel they did not understand the new company or what they wanted from their new employees. One manager said: 'I don't know if I am doing my job right any more because I don't know what Services Conglomerate expects me to do'. This was exacerbated by Quality Caterers senior management's lack of communication both prior to and after the redundancies. In addition, employees believed, despite management protestations, that another wave of redundancies was coming which would further deplete their numbers and increase their workloads.

Most employees did not fully understand or accept the changes in company culture. The changes caused real concerns over role conflict and ambiguity, especially in the middle managers. In addition, many of those remaining felt survivor guilt because they did not understand the criteria for management's redundancy selections. Employees also felt the lack of communication and management action rationale led to 'expectational dissonance' which can occur when employees are led to believe one situation and then another occurs which they do not expect. This proved to be a major problem in the Quality Caterers' acquisition.

## Discussion

Several issues are relevant in the two acquisitions: the socialization process, and the renegotiation of the psychological contract, role ambiguity, role conflict and expectational dissonance. Both acquisitions resulted in a radical change in working practices for some groups of employees: middle managers at Quality Caterers and shopfloor workers at Gas Appliances. In the latter case, the changes surrounding the working practices, namely the move towards 'soft' HR practices (Storey, 1992), were discussed in detail with the affected employees. The employees were given the opportunity to ascertain exactly what their new jobs entailed in terms of working practices and reward systems; in some cases they had some input into those changes. At Quality Caterers, the regional managers were not given any guidance as to their job changes; although they knew their jobs had altered they did not know what behaviour was considered appropriate by Service Conglomerate. This resulted in greatly increased role ambiguity for those employees. Rizzo et al. (1970) define role ambiguity as the 'lack of existence or clarity of behavioural requirements, often in terms of inputs from the environment, which would serve to guide behaviour and provide knowledge that the behaviour is appropriate' (p. 156). In such a situation employees have to rely on predictability and information accuracy. At Quality Caterers, both predictability and information were inconsistent, thus exacerbating role ambiguity.

Feldman (1981) suggests that for the first several weeks in a new job employees will 'try to define exactly what tasks they have to do, what priorities are among those tasks, and how they are to allocate their work time' (p. 312). Employees who feel that they have incomplete or incorrect information will have a much more difficult time sorting out exactly what they are supposed to be doing. This was the situation faced by many of the Quality Caterer managers but not by the Gas Appliances' employees. The latter were given sufficient information as to changes in their job performance, priorities and reward structures.

Related to this was the issue of role conflict at Quality Caterers where many of the managers felt the new client charges as well as management's behaviour on Black Monday were unethical. These led to a feeling of role conflict which can occur when, according to Rizzo et al. (1970), an employee is 'caught in the crossfire of incompatible orders or incompatible expectations' (p. 150). This can cause employees ultimately to reject the organization (Rizzo et al., 1970), a situation which was occurring at Quality Caterers. After both acquisitions, employees underwent a re-socialization process which Caplow (1954) defines as 'an organisationally directed process that prepares and qualifies an individual to occupy an organisational position' (p. 169). The socialization process at Gas Appliances was thorough: changes to working practices, organizational priorities and rewards were fully explained to all affected employees. The job changes at Quality Caterers were not addressed and, while they were not as drastic, employees felt both their roles and rewards in the new organization were not clarified satisfactorily.

Poor socialization can result in employees rejecting the organizational goals or refusing to enter into the psychological contract. Psychological contracts can be defined as a 'commitment on the part of the organisation to care for the personal and social needs of the employees who build up expectations such that those needs will be met . . . in return, the company expects that for their part, the employees will remain loyal, well motivated and hardworking' (Schein, 1980). The psychological contract determines the motivational and performance commitment of the employees based on their expectations of the result (Handy, 1976). The unclear outcome expectations caused by the increased role ambiguity only served to exacerbate employee concerns at Quality Caterers and could have contributed to employee turnover. The low employee turnover rate at Gas Appliances was due in part to employees understanding and accepting the socialization process and thus entering into the new psychological contracts with Global Products.

Finally, the acquisitions differed in management's abilities to manage employees' expectations. The ability to manage expectations is deemed as critical to acquisition success (Hubbard and Purcell, 1994) as expectations are the beliefs employees hold about what leads to what in the environment and serve as a visual map of the organization (Porter et al., 1975). If these practices are not discussed openly after a merger or acquisition, the organization cannot expect the new target company employees' expectations or behaviour necessarily to fall in line with the new organization's expectations.

The mismatch of employee and new organizational expectations can lead to a condition of 'expectational dissonance' (Hubbard and Purcell, 1994) which can occur when employees evaluate the new organizational environment in light of their previously held beliefs and find these to be in conflict. This appears to be the case at Quality Caterers where new practices and beliefs were not openly discussed and when implemented employees felt a sense of betrayal and confusion which only exacerbated the other feelings of ambiguity. This was heightened by the disparate messages received by employees, namely that it was business as usual followed by mass redundancies. This expectational dissonance was not found at Gas Appliances where the changes were openly discussed and accepted and where management's actions mirrored management's communication given earlier, thus enhancing their ability to manage expectations. Thus, there was a quicker and greater acceptance of the organizational changes.

It becomes apparent when examining acquisition that implementation is critical to the overall acquisitional success (Marks and Mirvis, 1982; Hunt et al., 1986; Hubbard and Purcell, 1994). Often it is not the implementation message which is paramount to acquisition success but the method of the message's dissemination which appears critical.

---

## Questions

1 What were the different companies' approaches to the socialization process for their acquired employees?

2 Did the socialization process affect the renegotiation of the psychological contract? If so, how?

3 Did the manner in which the acquisition process occurred affect employees in terms of role conflict and role ambiguity? What caused these feelings and what were the manifestations?

4  What role did 'expectational dissonance' play in the issues outlined above?

## References

Caplow, T. 1954: *The Sociology of Work*. New York: McGraw-Hill.

Feldman, D. C. 1981: The multiple socialization of organization members. *Academy of Management Review*, **6**(2).

Handy, C. B. 1976: *Understanding Organisations*. Middlesex: Penguin Books.

Hubbard, N. and Purcell, J. 1994: The implications of managing employee expectations during acquisition implementation. Work, Employment and Society annual conference, Canterbury: August.

Hunt, J. W., Lees, S., Gramber, J. J. and Vivian, P. D. 1986: *Acquisitions: The Human Factor*. London: London Business School and Egon Zendhor International.

Marks, M. L. and Mirvis, P. H. 1982: Merging human resources. A review of current research. *Mergers & Acquisitions*, No. 93, June.

Napier, N. K. 1989: Mergers and acquisitions, human resource issues and outcomes: a review and suggested typology. *Journal of Management Studies*, **26**(3).

Nicholson, N. and Arnold, J. 1991: From expectation to experience: graduates entering a large corporation. *Journal of Organizational Behavior*, **12**.

Patch, F., Rice, D. and Dreilinger, C. 1992: A contract for commitment. *Training & Development*, No. 114, November.

Porter, L., Lawler III, E. and Hackman, J. R. 1975: *Behavior in Organizations*. New York: McGraw-Hill.

Rizzo, J. R., House, R. J. and Lirtzman, S. L. 1970: Role ambiguity in complex organizations. *Administrative Science Quarterly*, **15**.

Rousseau, D. M. 1990: New hire perceptions of their own and their employer's obligations: a study of psychological contracts. *Journal of Organizational Behavior*, **11**(124).

Schein, E. H. 1980: *Organizational Psychology*. New Jersey: Prentice-Hall.

Schweiger, D. M., Ivancevich, J. M. and Power, F. R. 1987: Executive actions for managing human resources before and after acquisition. *Academy of Management Executive*, **1**(2), May.

Sinetar, M. 1981: Mergers, morale and productivity. *Personnel Journal*, November.

Storey, J. 1992: *Developments in the Management of Human Resources*. Oxford: Blackwell.

Vroom, V. H. and Deci, E. L. 1971: The stability of post-decisional dissonance: a follow-up study in the job attitudes of business school graduates. *Organizational Behavior and Human Performance*, **6**. March.

Wanous, J. P. et al. 1992: The effects of met expectations on newcomer attitudes and behaviors: a review and meta-analysis. *Journal of Applied Psychology*, **77**(3), March.

## Further Reading

Bastien, D. T. 1987: Common patterns of behavior and communication in corporate mergers and acquisitions. *Human Resource Management*, **26**(1), March.

Buono, A. F. and Bowditch, J. L. 1989: *The Human Side of Mergers and Acquisitions*. San Francisco: Jossey-Bass.

Davy, J. A., Kinicki, A., Kilroy, J. and Scheck, C. 1988: After the merger: dealing with people's uncertainty. *Training & Development Journal*, **42**(11), November.

Dunnette, M., Arvey, R. and Banas, P. 1973: *Why do They Leave?* Minneapolis, Minnesota: University of Minnesota (unpublished paper).

Ivancevich, J. M., Schweiger, D. M. and Power, F. R. 1982: Occupational stress, type A behavior, and physical well being. *Academy of Management Journal*, **25**(2).

Jemison, D. B. and Sitkin, S. B. 1986: Acquisitions: the process can be a problem. *Harvard Business Review*, **64**(2), March.

Kouzes, J. M. and Posner, B. Z. 1990: The credibility factor: what followers expect from their leaders. *Business Credit*, **92**(5), 101, July.

Leana, C. R. and Feldman, D. C. 1988: Individual responses to job loss: perceptions, reactions, and coping behaviors. *Journal of Management*, **14**(3).

Marks, M. L. and Mirvis, P. H. 1992: Rebuilding after the merger: dealing with 'survivor sickness'. *Organizational Dynamics*, **21**(2).

## 2

# BMW

*Using the scenario analysis technique for
HRM policy construction*

## CHRISTIAN SCHOLZ

In the early 1980s BMW, one of the leading German car manufacturers, began to focus on the systematic analysis of internal and external changes in order to construct a solid base for a future-oriented
human resource management (HRM). The central idea was to take
changes in society as the basic framework for all decisions on the
strategic level of HRM.

Up to now, two interlinked steps have been accomplished: the value
orientation programme and the scenario programme.

### The Value-orientation Programme

As the first stage of these efforts, in 1983, BMW formally initiated a
programme called 'value-oriented personnel policy' to integrate social changes in values into corporate HRM. The aim of this concept
is to obtain a fit between the corporate HRM and the values of the
employees in order to reach a stronger identification and motivation
of the employees. As a result of various workshops with the top
management, BMW identified 16 basic values as especially relevant
for the corporate HRM (Table 2.1). For each of them BMW defined
the current situation, C, the traditional value, T, the value according
to the changes in society, S, and the prior goal, G1, as well as the new
corporate goal, G2.

**Table 2.1**   The scale of the sixteen basic values

| Basic values | Less important | | | Weight | | Very important |
|---|---|---|---|---|---|---|
| | 1 | 2 | 3 | 4 | 5 | 6 |
| Orientation of leadership behaviour towards ethical objectives | C | | | T | | s |
| Humanity/dignity | C | T | G1 | G2 | s | |
| Tolerance | C | | G1 | G2 | T | s |
| Search for fairness | | | | | | |
| Property | s | | G1 G2 | C | T | |
| Performance and counter-performance | | s | C | G1 | G2 | T |
| Independence and individuality | C | | T | G1 G2 | s | |
| Self-fulfilment on the job | | C | T | G1 G2 | s | |
| Self-fulfilment off the job | T | C | G1 | G2 | s | |
| Social achievements | | T | | G2 | G1 | C |
| Social contact | C | G1 | G2 | | s | |
| Information and communication | T | C | | G1 | G2 s | |
| Freedom of speech | C | G1 | G2 | T | C | |
| Safety needs | | | | | | s |
| Social effects of work | T C | G1 G2 | | | s | |
| Democracy | C | G1 | G2 | T | | s |

Key
C  = current situation
G1 = prior goal
G2 = new corporate goal
S  = society
T  = traditional value

The values then had to be translated into day-to-day work (Table 2.2). The value 'information and communication', for example, leads to the development of new means to inform employees.

**Table 2.2**   Examples of the significance of values for day-to-day work in BMW

| Underlying values | Practical action points |
| --- | --- |
| Information and communication | New means to inform employees |
| Performance | Result-related remuneration systems |
| Self-fulfilment on the job | New working structures |
| Orientation of leadership behaviour towards ethical objectives | Appraisal by subordinates |
| Independence and individuality | New working time systems |

## The Scenario Analysis

Soon it became obvious that a strong orientation towards values was important but not sufficient to fulfil the future tasks of HRM. Not only the values, but also many other factors, influence HRM and are interdependent. Thus, dynamic aspects are the crucial point to look at. Consequently, in a second stage beginning in 1990, BMW started to examine its HRM strategy by using the scenario analysis technique, a multidimensional approach of scenarios. A multiple scenario analysis consists of two or more scenarios where every single one is a hypothetic sequence of events in order to describe possible developments in the future:

BMW had to accept that many *unpredictable* changes concerning the company's environment have influence on Human Resource Management within BMW. For that reason, BMW has to explore a range of possibilities [what happens, if] rather than attempt to plan detailed actions in order to achieve certain targets. (Walter Hell, head of the scenario project)

Scenario analysis in BMW follows two basic assumptions:

1   A broad spectrum of departments has to participate to link HRM with the other functions of the corporation and to avoid results from only the HRM perspective.

2   External support is needed to validate the exogenous situational factors by experts' opinions.

BMW decided on scheduling the process of scenario analysis for one year. It consisted of five steps.

## Step 1

The main future factors influencing HRM were evaluated by a small team consisting of members of different departments. Internal factors identified included the production process, products, administrative processes and computer-aided techniques (CA-techniques). The external factors identified were political change, social change, labour costs, demographic trends and the education system (Figure 2.1).

**Figure 2.1**   Factors influencing HRM

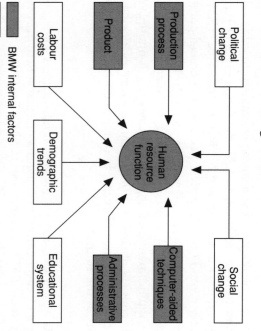

## Step 2

For each of the nine future factors, groups of six BMW employees were built up. These 54 employees had to prepare themselves intensively before discussing possible scenarios under the guidance of a moderator. In several meetings they developed nine separate scenarios.

### Step 3

In a workshop lasting two days, these separate scenarios were integrated into two holistic scenarios for the year 2000, scenario A as the probable scenario, scenario B as a contingency one (Figure 2.2).

**Figure 2.2**   Results of the integration

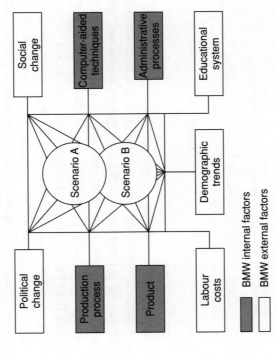

### Step 4

Derived from the probable scenario A, again in small teams, six key issues were defined. They served as information input for the general HRM strategy until the year 2000. Special theses were derived from these key issues to be the main goals of the HRM for the following ten years:

1  The qualified employee will become a self-confident entrepreneur of his own labour potential.
2  The central key to efficiency and productivity lies in corporate and leadership culture.
3  Qualification will become the key factor relevant to success for both the employees and the company.

4 The time for revolutionary changes in production is over. In the future, one will face evolutionary developments in structures of labour and organization.

5 The older employee will become a central challenge for HRM.

6 The attractiveness of BMW as employer depends more and more on its role as leader in the field of ecologically oriented innovation within the car industry.

## Step 5

Finally, three workshops involving all departments took place. Here, the central theses were specified to support the execution of the main HRM-related goals in the different fields of HRM. The cells of a specification matrix (Figure 2.3) show practical activities as results of the theses systematically combined with each field of HRM. These possible HRM-applications are ready to be implemented when they are not in contrast to the corporate strategic objectives. In the following years, the scenarios will be regularly evaluated as to whether they are still realistic or not, and adjusted to current developments. In this way, an early-warning system will be implemented which helps to

| Scenario results / Personnel policy functions | Thesis 1 'The qualified employee . . .' | Thesis 2 'The key issue for . . .' | Thesis 3 'Qualification becomes . . .' |
|---|---|---|---|
| Personnel requirement | Long-term-oriented personnel requirement forecast mainly for quality, not for quantity | | |
| Personnel supply | Long-term-oriented labour market analyses have to be more differentiated regarding qualifications and regions | | Consideration within personnel supply that there is an appropriate relation between generalists and specialists |
| Personnel development | | Reinforcement of organizational development and organizational processes (employee as co-former) | |
| Leadership | | | |

**Figure 2.3** Specification matrix

keep BMW from unexpected changes in the environment which are relevant to HRM policy.

The following three examples will show the contents and applications of the key issues.

### Example 1. The employees of the future

*Thesis*   The statement of this key issue was the thesis: 'the qualified employee will become a self-confident entrepreneur of his own labour potential'.

*Scenario background*   The background of this consideration is the fact that the employees will become more and more one of the strategic success factors of BMW. This thesis is based on central results of the scenario as the following examples show:

- The competition for qualified employees will increase, caused by the expected boom in the 1990s by the growth of European market and economic opening of Eastern Europe.

- The technological dynamism in products, production and administration causes structural adaptation and leads to new demands concerning the employees' qualifications.

- At the same time, it is expected that there will be a smaller supply of qualified employees for the car industry because of the fact that students will choose their specialities not for the needs of the labour market but for their own purposes.

- Moreover, there can be identified a change in employees' attitudes concerning their demands with regard to the conditions and contents of work. For example, employees show much more interest in ecological and ethical subjects than before, and individual needs have a great influence on their personal plans of life. This leads to a more critical selection of employers for whom they would like to work.

*Application in HRM*   The actual application on the fields of human resource management touched not only the external but also the internal sphere of BMW: personnel planning is more and more linked to the planning in other departments. There will be more flexibility concerning, for example, working time and remuneration, and the employees will have more influence on structuring their own work or the whole organization.

In external fields, personnel supply activities will be realized earlier than before concerning, for example, university contacts or presence at trade fairs.

*Example 2. The role of corporate culture and leadership culture*

*Thesis*    The thesis 'The central key to efficiency and productivity lies in corporate and leadership culture' shows the important meaning of this subject for corporate success. The employee of the future tends to have many more demands concerning conditions and contents of work (as described before) than ever before.

*Scenario background*    This thesis is derived from the following points of the scenario:

- First, the change in employees' attitudes described above directly causes the need of an appropriate corporate and leadership culture.
- Furthermore, more and more new working and organizational structures will be developed that are based on communication and co-operation. Good teamwork is only possible if previous characteristic actions are avoided.
- Moreover, it will be expected, that experts' knowledge and information will increase even more and holistic solutions will only be possible if single specialists work together constructively.

*Application in HRM*    To reach these goals, those employees will be chosen who fit into the corporate and leadership culture and who have the competence for teamwork. Concerning the organizational structures, it will be necessary to reduce hierarchies and to enforce organizational development.

*Example 3. Ecology and employer's image*

*Thesis*    The attractiveness of BMW as employer depends more and more on its role as leader in the field of ecologically oriented innovation in the car industry. This thesis rests on the consideration that employees form their opinion of how their future employer respects ecological needs.

*Scenario background*    In the scenario, this thesis was founded by the following statements:

- The increase in environmental catastrophes and their presence in the media and in daily personal experience generally lead to a greater sensitivity concerning these topics.

- At the same time, people rate ecological aspects much higher possibly on par with the production technology and the products of a corporation.
- Furthermore, legislation has an increasing influence on production conditions.

*Application in HRM*    Based on this, BMW has to enforce topics like ecology and environment protection if it intends to remain an attractive employer in the future. As a concrete means, employees have to be sensitized for ecology. Environmental points of view have to be considered when planning and developing not only single working places but also whole manufacturing sites.

The realization of the practical action points of the single-scenario results took place at different levels and in different ways. The main results were part of an executive committee paper in which the future goals and objectives of the human resource department were described. Additionally, there were many presentations of the scenario's results in the whole corporation to spread a common vision about the future development. This long-term common vision about the future is just as important as the operative and short-term oriented application. This procedure guarantees that concepts, systems and instruments developed in different parts of the large BMW corporation are congruent to the corporate philosophy.

The special advantage of the scenario analysis was the fact that the link between the HRM function and other corporate departments could be realized already by choosing the procedure. But the scenario analysis and its application means much more to BMW than just an efficient process to gain an extensive knowledge. The scenario project also characterizes essential changes in the function 'personnel and social affairs' and in the human resource function as well as the changed role of the personnel department.

The expression for this changed way of thinking is 'customer focus'. Much more than before, the customers' wishes have to be considered within long-term plans, and these must be changed, if necessary. Flexibility becomes the decisive challenge at all levels.

Concerning the human resource function, BMW judged that the data collection which is necessary to develop such a scenario was only possible by working together with the 'customers of the personnel department'. Only that way of operating was seen as carrying the potential to guarantee that the needs of those customers as well as developments in the personnel departments would be considered.

The experiences of the scenario analysis process have to be considered during the implementation process. The results have to be adjusted to corporate strategy which itself focuses on customers. Also the application activities need to be planned and practised with respect to the customers. By this method, the role of the human resource function changes from a personnel administration to a human resource development consultation in a customer-focused scenario.

To sum up, by using these results from the scenario analysis HRM policies could be evaluated for their relevance and new topics for a strategic, long-term personnel policy were identified. As one of the fathers of this system points out: 'Consistently used, the basic formula of value oriented personnel policy reveals its strengths: via value orientation towards better motivation and through this towards improved performance. That this is the best programme to increase efficiency remains unquestioned.'

## Questions

1 What is the connection between corporate culture and national culture as seen in this case?
2 Illustrate how each of the 16 values can be transformed into practical issues.
3 Which HR fields is it necessary to take into consideration when using the results of the scenario?
4 Why do you think BMW has implemented scenario analysis as an organization development process?
5 Discuss the relationship between ethical orientation in management and the economic needs of a car manufacturer.

## Further Reading

Schmaars, S. P. 1990: 'How to develop and use scenarios, in Dyson, R. G. (ed.) *Strategic Planning: Models and Analytical Techniques.* London: Wiley.

# PART II

# The Management of Change

# 3

# Transitions and Transformations

*Four case studies in business-focused change*

DOUG A. STACE

## The Parish Priest Turns Business Partner

A remarkable transformation has been taking place in the past decade or more in many corporations. Beyond the sometimes shallow words that 'people are our most important resource', executives and human resource (HR) professionals in the leading corporations are enacting strategies to ensure that the corporation's human capital ranks with, and even beyond, its financial and production capital. The role of the HR professional was once akin to the popular imagery of a parish priest – a paternalistic welfare-type role. HR professionals are now more likely to be seen as co-partners with executives and managers in delivering and enacting the business strategy of the corporation. Or so it is in some corporations – in others, HR practitioners still wear the collar!

What does it mean to be more strategic and less paternalistic about human resource management? It is certainly about learning to live with and manage the dilemmas of change in ways which sometimes cut across deeply ingrained traditional values which limit the human resource professional's potential to act decisively and incisively. No doubt most human resource professionals would have been delighted to work with a Jan Carlzon or a Sir Colin Marshall in the 1980s, in the halcyon days of SAS's and British Airways' 'people first' programmes. However, there would undoubtedly have been fewer human resource professionals volunteering to assist the Daimler–Benz executive in its 40,000 downsize of the company in 1993, or the team from Fletcher Challenge (a leading New Zealand firm) as it thrashed out the legal, financial and personnel details of a joint venture with the Datong Steel Works in the unsophisticated hinterland of mainland China. HR professionals generally prefer to concentrate on the softer developmental or the paternalistic control agenda, leaving the hard business agenda to others.

Being strategic about human resources is therefore about developing a capability to mix the soft with the hard, to choose situationally appropriate rather than personally preferred approaches to human resource management, as the business requires. Such business requirements may fall anywhere along the following continuum:

*Softer approaches*

- adaptive strategy;
- cultural change;
- continuous improvement;
- empowerment.

*Harder approaches*

- rational strategy;
- structural change;
- radical transformation;
- command and control.

The HR agenda traditionally has been focused on the softer approach, but now effective human resources business partners must be able to position their work at appropriate points along these continua. Road maps for this more situational approach to human resource management are, however, rare and at best sketchy.

## Mapping the Business – Human Resource Partnership

Some recent work at the Centre for Corporate Change in Sydney has focused on developing a situational framework for understanding the relationship between business strategy, change interventions and human resource practices. Conceptually the interactive nature of these relationships is illustrated as in Figure 3.1.

**Figure 3.1** Relationship between business and change strategies and HR practices

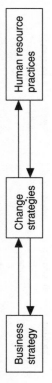

An organization development (OD) model of human resource management is not appropriate for all circumstances. There will be times when, for example, an employee empowerment programme will need to be curtailed or refocused to meet the requirements of the business. Similarly, human resource practices such as compensation systems which are appropriate in growth markets will often be inappropriate in periods of business downturn, as many businesses found to their detriment in the late 1980s.

In our research, however, we have found that the relationship between business strategy and human resource practice is not a direct relationship, but is modified by the overall orientation of, and the leadership of the organization's programmes of, change. Thus the overall approach to change being run in the organization will have a powerful impact on the appropriateness of particular human resource interventions and practices in particular divisions or strategic business units. Therefore, understanding an organization's change strategy is just as critical to its human resource practices as understanding its business strategy. The situational model of change developed by Dunphy and Stace (1990) provides focus here: this model covers not only the scale of change but also the style of change leadership, as shown in Figures 3.2 and 3.3. Figure 3.2 is the original conceptual model of change which shows four levels for the scale or intensity of change and four levels for the style of change management (that is, the way in which an organization's executive leadership or dominant elite leads the process of change).

Figure 3.3 shows the areas of the change matrix utilized by 20 sample organizations for their change strategies, based on our research. Each firm's positioning on the matrix was based on ratings by 30–50 executives, middle managers and team leaders interviewed in each organization. The interviewees rated their organizations at two time-periods.

The research results arising from data and detailed field research around this model (Dunphy and Stace, 1990; Stace and Dunphy, 1991a; 1991b), show that the predominant approach to corporate

**Figure 3.2**  The Dunphy–Stace change matrix

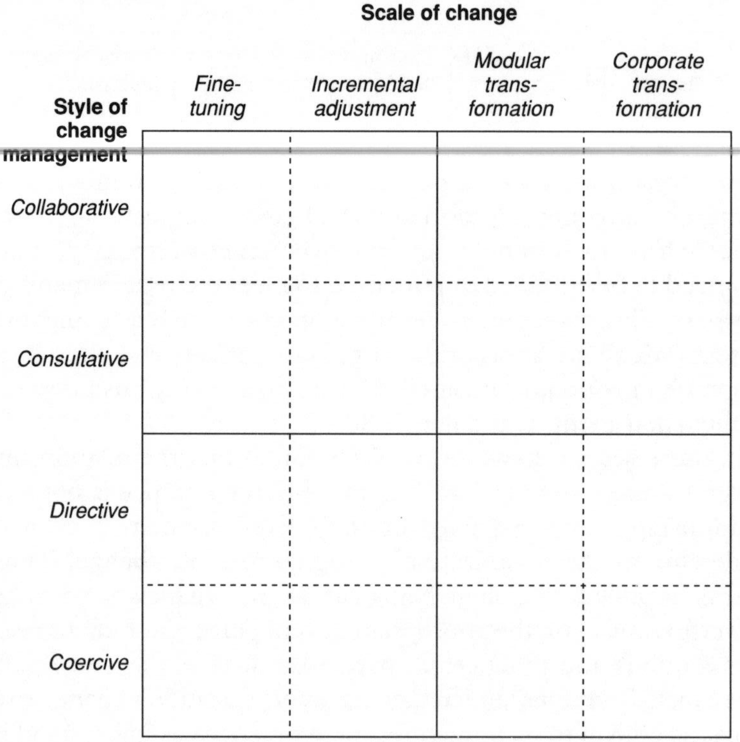

**Scale of change**

| Style of change management | Fine-tuning | Incremental adjustment | Modular trans-formation | Corporate trans-formation |
|---|---|---|---|---|
| Collaborative | | | | |
| Consultative | | | | |
| Directive | | | | |
| Coercive | | | | |

change identified was not that of participative evolution or even the charismatic transformation so widely advocated by many human resource practitioners and OD-oriented theorists; it was found that medium to high performance was maintained by leading the corporation using either a consultative or a directive management style. In the period of the initial research (1988–90) 52 per cent of the Dunphy and Stace sample organizations were in fact using transformative turnaround strategies implemented either directively or coercively. This had major implications for the choice of human resource interventions. In addition, maintaining a minimal level of change (which we refer to as fine-tuning), appeared overall to be a non-viable change strategy: the lower performing organizations in the sample were using this change strategy. Such minimal change is unable to deliver enough adjustment for the organization to sustain high performance in a rapidly changing business environment. The important point is that the style of change, and the scale of change used, must be attuned

**Figure 3.3** Dominant patterns of corporate change

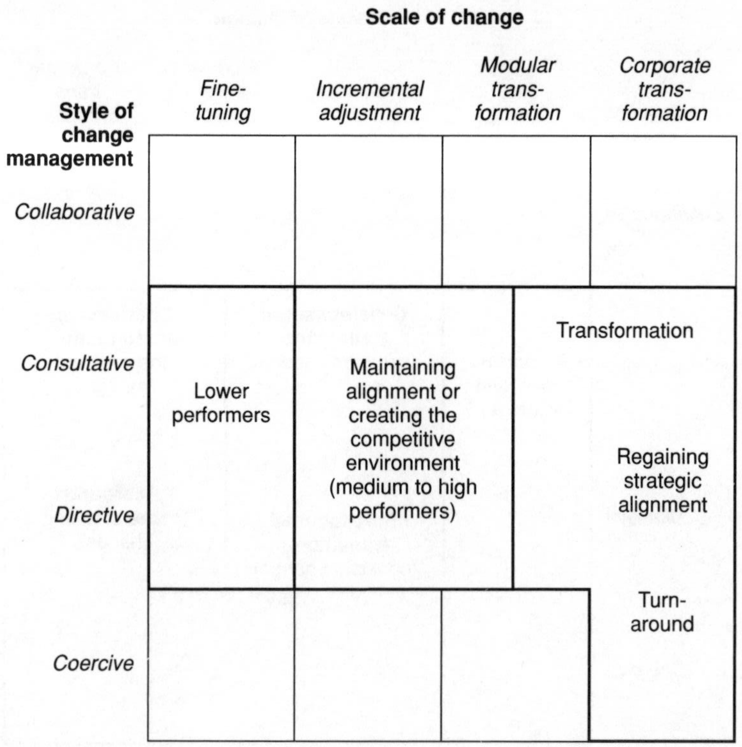

**Scale of change**

| Style of change management | *Fine-tuning* | *Incremental adjustment* | *Modular transformation* | *Corporate transformation* |
|---|---|---|---|---|
| *Collaborative* | | | | |
| *Consultative* | Lower performers | Maintaining alignment or creating the competitive environment (medium to high performers) | Transformation | |
| *Directive* | | | | Regaining strategic alignment |
| *Coercive* | | | | Turn-around |

situationally to the degree of change required to strategically reposition the organization. This creates a major philosophical issue for many human resource professionals, as the roots of much HR practice are in the tradition of careful, collaborative, 'no-big-shocks' approach to change.

During the period 1990–3 following further intensive case study analysis, the initial model was developed further. This is shown in Figure 3.4. The four categories of change successfully used by organizations to reposition themselves, or to maintain their position, are portrayed in a newer model, overlaid on the earlier model, as:

- developmental transitions (constant change);
- task-focused transitions (constant change);
- charismatic transformations (inspirational change);
- turnarounds (framebreaking change).

**Figure 3.4**    Situational approaches to corporate change

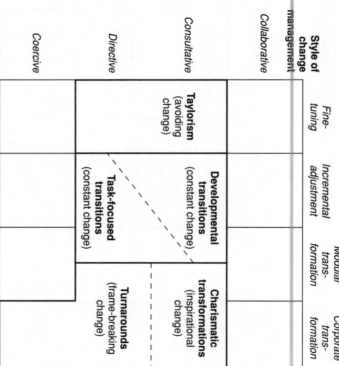

Source: Stace and Dunphy (1994)

It is this model which provides the conceptual base for our case studies and detailed treatment of different approaches to human resource management in the following pages.

## Thinking 'Business' and 'People' Simultaneously

At a practical level it is in those corporations where executives 'think people' and where human resource professionals 'think business' that a fluidity of relationship and synergy of thinking develops so that people issues become change and business issues, and vice versa. Executives and business unit managers need a 'heart' for people; human resource professionals need a 'head' for the business. Works such as Quinn's (1993) 'Intelligent Enterprise' and Hamel and Prahalad's

(1994) 'Competing for the Future' indicate that people *are* the business in advanced industrial societies. The more managers and human resource professionals work in a task-team mode, the greater the chance of human resource issues being taken into account in the key decisions of the organization. In organizations like New Zealand's Fletcher Challenge, human resource professionals are as articulate on the financial ratios of the company as on issues of workforce planning or competency analysis.

At a conceptual level, it is important therefore to realize that most human resource and change interventions will be appropriate in some business situations but inappropriate in others. What then goes with what? Tables 3.1–3.4 (see Appendix to this chapter) result from detailed research over the past eight to ten years on what are the patterns of human resource, change and business strategy which we observe in high- and medium-performing organizations. The major categories of developmental transitions, task-focused transitions, charismatic transformations and turnarounds relate to the broad categories of change illustrated in Figure 3.4. These categories and patterns are not proposed as templates for rigid application, but as guides to thinking and acting.

At times there will be lags between one part of an overall pattern of business strategy/change/human resource practices and another. However, our research suggests that in the higher- to medium-performing corporations there is in the longer term an 'intellectual coherence' between the organization's business, change and people management strategies. It is through an understanding of such patterns that human resource professionals can leverage their partnership with line managers for greater effectiveness, or at least not introduce a favourite HR intervention when the business requires something else. A fuller explanation of these patterns of relationship is developed in Stace and Dunphy (1994).

We are suggesting that the path to success varies enormously between organizations, and that implementing preferred personally or currently popular interventions may be inappropriate or even fatal for an organization. Two key principles should be borne in mind:

1   Dominant espoused ideologies of organizational change and human resource management can form into powerful practices which assist the organization in its interrelationship with the business environment in one business period, but can equally impede its business positioning in another.

2   Effective organizations and managers use 'change flex' in positioning their enterprises, sometimes instinctively, sometimes mindfully because of the frameworks of thinking provided by contingent models. They develop a capability to alternate if necessary between consultative and directive change styles and incremental and transformative scales of change, with appropriate modifications to human resource practice. In these organizations the espoused ideology of change and human resource management is therefore eclectic and pragmatic, or if any one ideology is favoured it is not so powerful that it precludes the use of other strategies which are counter-cyclical to the espoused model in the organization.

Global economic cycles are becoming increasingly important determinants of patterns of business success, and are particularly important in periods of business volatility. In such circumstances economic exigencies may force executives and human resource practitioners to act (eventually) against their espoused HR theories. An extended lag in response may have serious or fatal implications for corporate survival. In economic upturns, however, executives may be more able to indulge their favourite espoused ideology – but probably not for long periods. Favoured ideologies, and HR practice implemented as normative best practice rather than as strategically relevant processes, can lead organizations into a state of low performance.

Our research indicates that in organizational change and human resource management, 'best practice' is eclectic, pragmatic and culturally and situationally attuned. It is a matter of the human resource practitioner being a business partner, mixing the 'soft' with the 'hard', assisting in the process of relentless, productive change, rather than the softer, paternalistic, 'welfare' agenda.

## Case Studies in Business-focused Change

The four cases which follow illustrate organizations whose orientation towards change and human resource management differ substantially. While some generics may be similar: for instance all have the basics of recruitment, appraisal and such human resource interventions in place, in practice the flavour and orientation of these interventions are markedly different. Where one corporation may follow a philosophy of no forced retrenchments, others will see retrenchment as a key business tool to be used selectively and strategically. Each of these cases represent one of the four 'types' of business-focused change as characterized in Tables 3.1–3.4 (see the Appendix to this chapter) as follows:

1   Developmental transition (Table 3.1): Macquarie Bank
2   Task-focused transition (Table 3.2): Tubemakers of Australia
3   Charismatic transformation (Table 3.3): State Library of New South Wales
4   Turnaround (Table 3.4): Westpac Banking Corporation

After reading each case it is suggested that you look to the appropriate table (3.1–3.4) which provides a framework for the approach described in the case. In each case the approach described is not a recipe: the cases illustrate how organizations in different states of transition, addressing different challenges, at different stages of their history, have approached the task of change, using human resource strategies as key components of their change intervention.

## CASE 3A   MACQUARIE BANK

Macquarie Bank is an excellent example of a highly successful organization which has been able to maintain its success using an incremental adjustment process (but not fine-tuning) while operating in a rapidly changing environment. Over the period 1983–8 major changes occurred in the environment of Australian financial institutions. These included:

- Rapid deregulation of the financial services sector by the Australian Labor Government. The critical moves involved were the floating of the Australian dollar in 1983; progressive removal of restrictions on competition between banks, building societies, merchant banks and other institutions which offer financial and financially related services; approval of an additional 40 foreign exchange dealerships (1984/5) and approval of new banking licences (1984/5) including licences to 16 foreign-owned banks to operate in Australia.

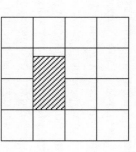

**Figure 3A.1**   (See Figure 3.2 on p. 46 for reference)

- Sydney, Macquarie Bank's home base, developed as an international financial centre.

What was Macquarie Bank's strategy in this environment? From its inception as Hill Samuel Australia in the early 1970s, the bank's strategic domain was merchant banking. In 1980 the bank commenced a process of diversification by establishing Australia's first cash management trust. But with deregulation in the 1980s it diversified further, building up strength in specialist markets, particularly in high value-added niches like corporate services, bullion and commodities. The pace of diversification quickened by the mid 1980s with the bank entering a range of new areas including retail domestic banking, equity investments, property and leasing. Growth was both by development and by acquisition. By 1995, despite the 1987 stock-market crash and the early 1990s recession, Macquarie remains one of Australia's most successful and profitable banks. So how was the needed organizational change managed by Macquarie executives?

## Change: a Matter of Values, not Revolution

Change in Macquarie has been a process of constant adjustment. One executive described it this way: 'We never stay still, but we don't change in quantum leaps – our corporate culture would preclude that – running a business on partnership concepts means that policy decisions are not dramatic, they evolve.' The rapid growth in Macquarie's product range was accompanied by a quadrupling of staff numbers in the 1980s. Business product units, or 'clusters', grew in number to almost 30 by the late 1980s, presenting an increasing problem of co-ordination in a collegial/partnership system where unit heads nominally report to the managing director.

The greater size and complexity created increased complexities of co-ordination. The obvious answer was to create additional structures, systems and controls, but this was foreign to the collegial values of the bank which is staffed mainly by highly qualified professionals. The answer chosen was to produce a 'goals and values' statement, an articulation of deeply held values about cultural and business behaviour, including how the process of change should be managed. The values statement is essentially a set of values and norms, internal controls, that substitute for external control systems. This was supplemented by developing business units into highly autonomous profit centres and then creating cross-functional synergies through more systematic communication by management across these centres. Executive responses to questions about change events in the organization indicated that these changes were basically incremental in character.

But what was the leadership style adopted at Macquarie to bring about these changes? Our study revealed increasing convergence on a consultative style of management. The consolidation of the style reflects the frequent use of the executive committee as a forum for discussion of major issues and decisions. The collegial style was symbolized by the fact that the managing director, Tony Berg, and the former managing director and chairman, David Clarke, shared the same open-plan office.

There were interesting views on the intersection of corporate management style and the ongoing process of change and innovation. As expressed by one interviewee: 'Change here is both top down and bottom up. At the macro level the Bank is run by two people, Tony Berg and David Clarke. At the micro level of products and markets, change becomes an accumulation of grass roots' initiatives at departmental level. We try to provide a managerial environment where flexibility is paramount, but the crunch comes when we have to actually build something or make big decisions.'

Interestingly enough, when 21 first-line and middle-level managers were asked for their perceptions of the bank's leadership style, they saw it as substantially more directive than consultative. All 15 respondents who rated the managerial style this way indicated that they thought this directive style was appropriate. 'We need strength and decisiveness at the top', one commented. Consistently, some who rated the leadership style as consultative believed that the style was not directive enough for the present environment. This is an interesting comment because it challenges one of the basic assumptions of the organizational development movement, which is that people want consultation about organizational strategies. In a turbulent external environment, however, they may prefer decisive leadership.

## Developing the People

Macquarie does not have the all-encompassing human resource systems typical of some organizations. It follows an organic, developmental approach, aptly summarized by one executive as follows: 'We recruit the best from the universities and graduate schools; train on

Copyright John Storey 1996, Blackwell Cases in Human Resource and Change Management

the job and pay top money – we are a meritocracy. Our policy has been to grow our own and develop and promote where possible from within. We try to provide a flexible organizational environment where people can achieve.' This policy thrust has sustained Macquarie well through years of exponential growth and a long, painful recession in Australia in the late 1980s and early 1990s. The policies are also well suited to a flat organizational structure where specialist skills can be developed within small work teams, closely related to the product-market interface. It is not expected that Macquarie will change the basic tenets of the meritocracy system. However, there was sufficient evidence during the study to indicate that the bank may need to consider more systematic approaches to its human resource policies in the future.

The priority areas in human resources practice were:

- recruitment and selection (corporate image as an employer is important; use of psychological tests, and policy of 'growing our own' from graduate trainees is a key strategy);
- performance appraisal (an essential mechanism for tracking goal achievement and to help in determining rewards);
- rewards and compensation ('We pay well');
- organization development (goals and values statement, team building, monthly newsletter).

Formal development programmes did not receive as high a priority as in some developmental transition type organizations, with much development being left to individuals and their unit managers. The bank grows further the executives will have to assess whether collegial culture in fact created an environment of on-the-job development and flexibility.

In such a dynamic environment, how was the bank able to maintain an incremental strategy and achieve such outstanding performance? Its success appears to have been mainly a function of its small size relative to other banks and its combination of diversified niche strategies with a loosely coupled flexible organization. Its short communication chains and collegial workforce culture led to considerable flexibility in responding to changing market demands. These are strengths which many larger organizations seek to emulate through the formation of decentralized, strategic business units.

Macquarie Bank has been successful operating this way so far. As the bank grows further the executives will have to assess whether these strategies can continue to work. Nevertheless the case demonstrates that participative evolution can be an effective change strategy even in a turbulent environment, at least for a relatively small, highly specialized and successful niche player such as Macquarie.

## CASE 3B TUBEMAKERS OF AUSTRALIA

Tubemakers is a fascinating example of an organization which has revolutionized the way it does business by utilizing a mixture of task-focused and developmental transition, with occasional use of turn-around change strategy. Tubemaker's predominant approach to business, change and human resource management however, is incremental – a 'no big shocks' approach. Tubemakers was formed in 1946 as a holding company to consolidate the Australian interests of BHP and two British companies, Stewarts & Lloyds and Tube Investments. It was publicly listed in 1969, and in 1992 had two large institutional shareholders, BHP (49.75 per cent) and Sumitomo (19.49 per cent). Tubemakers is built on steel products with recent diversification into plastic pipes (Vinidex Tubemakers). In 1992, 5 per cent of its profits came from off-shore operations. Its four core operations are structural and engineering, fluid conveyance, industrial merchandising and precision products.

From the 1950s to the early 1970s, Tubemakers' growth mirrored the expanding Australian economy. Large-scale infrastructure and housing developments provided reliable, often government-funded, markets for the company. It grew to be blue chip, production focused and paternalistic. At many of its sites, unions muscled their way into key decisions about production, work organization and employment conditions. Management ceased to lead.

The 1980s were a period of major refocus of the business. Changing market conditions coupled with economic difficulties led to different

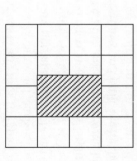

**Figure 3B.1** (See Figure 3.2 on p. 46 for reference)

structural responses within Tubemakers. Two of the major plants used contrasting methods of adaptation.

## Structural Products at Newcastle

Tubemakers' Newcastle plant adopted what might be described as a task-focused approach. In the early 1980s the Newcastle plant, employing 2,200 people suffered a debilitating six-week strike characterized by pickets, placards and vitriol. Plant management had tried to regain control of the workplace from the unions by proposing a reduction of 150 staff by voluntary redundancy. The strike demonstrated the workforce's rejection of the proposal.

By 1981 negotiations were proceeding more fruitfully, if laboriously. They resulted that year in the first Enterprise Agreement within Tubemakers – a decade before most Australian corporations had ever heard of the term.

That first agreement took over six months to negotiate. 'Now things are done differently', said a manager, who continued: 'The last agreement we negotiated in Newcastle – it took weeks, not months. That's just the way things are done now in Newcastle. We are starting the next one now. We try to give leadership, and at the end of the day, the Australian workforce is not silly. The debate has moved from industrial relations issues to business issues.'

The hard-nosed industrial bargaining model has been the approach to change used at Newcastle, initiated and carried out by local plant management with some policy help from company headquarters. The approach contrasts with the more developmentally oriented total quality management model applied at Yennora.

## Ductile Iron Pipelines Plant, Yennora

Influenced by an overseas study tour to Japan in 1981, Yennora plant manager John Burgess became an early champion of the Deming approach to total quality management (TQM). In 1983 three quality management project groups were set up at Yennora. Further groups were established the next year and staff began looking at the Deming videotapes – all 16 of them. 'Some were like tranquilizers, but it gave us a common language and philosophy', said one Yennora team leader.

During 1985 and 1986 a range of TQM-related techniques was introduced: performance analyses, statistical training packages and value-adding management (VAM). By 1989 17 quality groups were operating throughout the plant.

As with Newcastle, the approach at Yennora had been initiated by plant management. While representing nearly ideologically opposite means of change, the results at both plants clearly have been very successful.

This demonstrates that the approach used is often less important than:

- choosing a major vehicle for change and giving leadership to the change;
- analysing the directions needed and taking a pragmatic view of how to get there;
- empowering local plant managers to act with the least possible inter-ference from upper levels (both corporate and non-plant union).

The early champions of change at Tubemakers were scattered rather than cohesive, and their approaches were eclectic.

## Stirring the Corporation to 'Faith'

When, in 1987, Tony Daniels was appointed as Tubemakers' new managing director, the company began to take an overall view of how its portfolio of business interests formed a corporate vision. This led to some radical decisions to reshape parts of the business.

Tubemakers began placing more emphasis on growth markets in the water industry and on pursuing growth in Asia. Concurrently, the company rationalized its plant, closing six factories between 1990 and 1992 and reducing its overall workforce by a third. Output re-mained the same.

Change during the mid 1980s had been catalysed by the Federal Government's Steel Plan, but Daniels' leadership began a very in-tense period of management-initiated reform. 'Top management has been riding a strategic change agenda since 1988', said one execu-tive. Several processes were vital in achieving a new corporate focus in Tubemakers.

## Choosing the Vehicle for Change

Tony Daniels discovered that many US companies were using a more co-ordinated model of total quality management than was

Tubemakers. By mid 1988 the company's top management had established a project team to look at Australian and overseas organizations and identify the TQM model that best fitted Tubemakers.

A revamped TQM approach came to stand for 'Tubemakers Quality Management' and gave a common language and methodology to these businesses. 'Applying the TQM methodology has resulted in a major cultural revolution in our plants and locations – a revolution which is still in process', a senior manager said.

Process improvements in the workplace were followed by a comprehensive approach to business planning at company, plant and work unit levels. World-class operating performance was pursued by the use of key performance and process benchmarking.

Together, these methodologies form one of the most rigorous and comprehensive management overhauls seen by the author in any Australian company. The Tubemakers Quality Management approach has provided a 'system of faith' for the company.

## Strategic Intent

Tony Daniels' leadership has been crucial in giving the company a greater feeling of cohesion, but more importantly, in guiding Tubemakers along the potentially hazardous path of offshore expansion. The company's mission is qualitative and directional, but also contains some major quantitative aims: for example, 33 per cent profit from outside Australia, 15 per cent return on earnings, one of the top 50 Australian companies (by market capitalization) by 1995.

## Benchmarking

Tubemakers is moving aggressively into the area of performance benchmarking. The approach has been developing within the company for over a decade with the benchmarking of overseas sister plants occurring in the early 1980s.

Strategic benchmarking accounts for about 10 per cent of the total benchmarking process. It consists mainly of financial performance measures such as return-on-equity and returns in excess of the cost of capital. At Yennora, where benchmarking of processes has been used to help drive plant performance, the plant aims at a world-class standard of 350 tonnes per person per year, benchmarked against output from the Union City plant in the USA.

## The Planning Process

Benchmarking in Tubemakers is part of the broader process of corporate and business planning. In the early 1980s business planning was driven by the budgetary cycle. It was incremental and bottom-up in style. 'These were the days of writing a plan on Saturday afternoon, presenting it Monday and then putting it in the bottom drawer to get on with the real work', said one executive.

The planning process is now much more rigorous across all levels of the business. It was one of the new disciplines adopted when the company began introducing Tubemakers Quality Management from 1989 onwards. The process includes the following practices:

- Voice of the customer (customer surveys, focus groups, customer needs tables);
- Voice of the business (performance benchmarks, financial indicators);
- Catchball (two-way exchange of information);
- Benchmarking (against world best practice, processes and competitors);
- Tubemakers Continuous Improvement Process (TCIP).

## What Are the Gains?

Throughout the 1980s there was a relentless emphasis on rationalization across the entire Tubemakers Group. This has closed inefficient plants, reduced the workforce size, simplified and improved the company's products and improved customer focus.

Output from the Newcastle plant, for example, is now as great with about 700 workers as it was in the early 1980s with more than 2,000. Similarly Yennora, with fewer workers than it had ten years ago, has taken on the capacity of the now-closed Broadmeadows plant. This type of productivity increase is now closely tracked against international benchmarks.

Except for plant closures, the changes have been incremental, although the effects have been far reaching, if not radical. In effect, this has resulted in the gradual implementation of radical change. Tubemakers is now well placed from its consolidated domestic base to seek growth in international markets. And with only a 35 per cent gearing ratio, the company is in a healthy position for expansion.

An outstanding feature of Tubemakers is that there is not a distinct human resource discipline within the company – the corporate human resource function comprises three people, and human resource interventions are part of, and arise from, the business interventions of quality management, benchmarking, business planning, team performance enhancement and constant incremental adjustment to business structures and job designs.

Overall, the human resource professionals within the business adopt a low profile in terms of HR specialism but a high profile in terms of business partnership. To date it has been a highly successful strategy.

# CASE 3C   THE STATE LIBRARY OF
# NEW SOUTH WALES

The State Library of NSW is a clear example of the successful use of the charismatic transformation approach to change. It also demonstrates several clear principles: that a not-for-profit organization can be transformed into an entrepreneurial corporation without being fully privatized, that it is possible for the latter-day version of the organizational development model (organizational transformation) to succeed in a difficult economic environment, and that a charismatic transformation can be successful in the public sector. (Alison Crook, the chief executive, at the time of this case study was the first woman chief executive of the State Library.) It is an important case for service-sector organizations.

Alison Crook was appointed New South Wales State Librarian in 1987. She inherited a library which was highly prestigious, very traditional in its operation and primarily a book repository. Her vision was to transform the library by introducing the latest technologies of information transmission, to make it a truly state library through developing an active information exchange with other libraries throughout NSW, and to create a client-oriented corporate culture.

She moved quickly to develop a library mission statement in consultation with her senior executive group and subsequently with

**Figure 3C.1**   Library of NSW: change strategies

branch heads. This was actively 'workshopped' through the organization. She then instituted a strategic planning process to develop this mission into a rolling five-year change programme. The approach to strategic planning involved consultation at a number of levels in this 450-member organization. These approaches included:

- meetings of the executive group;
- meetings of the Advisory Committee to the State Librarian (all directors and branch heads – 25 people);
- forming focus groups (two groups of 26 and 28 first-line supervisors meeting with the state librarian on a six-weekly basis);
- holding open forums (held twice yearly with all staff).

The transformation of the State Library was fast paced, but consultation was widely used in the process.

In the process of transforming the library, structures were changed dramatically: the hierarchical structure was replaced with a flatter organizational structure, and semi-autonomous task teams were formed within units. Key entrepreneurial ventures in areas such as information search, heritage preservation, conferences and a library buildings consultancy were commenced and new technologies introduced into both the service functions and the new entrepreneurial businesses. The executive initiated job and workflow redesign, team building and leadership programmes and created a new customer service and public relations orientation.

## Education, Work Redesign and Communication

Staff development and work redesign helped realign employee skills and attitudes with the library's new strategic direction. Opting for a 'critical mass' approach to staff development, the executive asked all managers and supervisors to attend off-site management development programmes. These were also useful in building relationships within and across branches. Directors, managers and all staff were also invited to participate in a 'Managing Personal Growth' course – the full cost was met by an outside sponsor. As one manager remarked: 'There has been an enormous emphasis on training and development.' This has been necessary to support the shift to more highly skilled interdependent work.

An early experiment with work redesign and a semi-autonomous work group laid the groundwork for ongoing restructuring and team building. Margaret Coffey, Director, Management Services, explained that the semi-autonomous work group followed classic lines, in which 'every member of the team rotates through the co-ordinator's role.... Many were not used to taking much responsibility at work, and the learning curve was a sharp one to deal with group decision-making issues.' The group set its own performance standards which were negotiated with management. Job rotation has also been a significant strategy for multiskilling staff between different branches of the library.

We regard the State Library change process as a model of good internal communication, although the relatively small size of the organization and the self-contained location obviously assist effective communication. The extent of formal communication was impressive. Similarly impressive was the extent of informal feedback to staff. All senior executives attended induction sessions for new staff at which they took staff through the mission statement. Alison Crook also scheduled an individual two-hour meeting with all new middle managers to discuss implications of the latest strategic plan and clarify her expectations of management.

Communication is crucial at the library in gaining the commitment of a skilled and educated workforce to ongoing change. In Coffey's words, this requires the library to be 'a communicating organization focused on specific organizational goals.' Our research has rarely identified such a consultative style at the corporate level and consultative–collaborative approach at the business unit level particularly in organizations undergoing fast-paced, dramatic changes. It appears due to the strongly held executive ideology of 'best practice' and, in all probability, to the all-female executive team where 'the behaviours are not as combative and competitive as with males' (a senior executive).

## A Change of Pace and Approach

Charismatic transformation is a strategy which works well in growth situations. However, its downside is that the strategy is heavily dependent on the personality and style of the chief executive, and his or her capacity to articulate a vision and capture the hopes and aspirations of the majority of staff members. Charismatic leaders also frequently leave the organization abruptly, or too soon, before the transformational task has been completed. This leaves a leadership vacuum and the potential for a new leader to use a completely different and less motivating approach to change.

In the case of the State Library, the fast-paced approach was used as the early approach to change, but from 1991 onward the espoused/

realized approach lessened in pace to a developmental transition type change strategy. However, on noted occasions, Alison Crook as CEO moved quickly and incisively to a more directed task-focused approach in order to reposition the library quickly, either if the environment had moved dramatically or if the preferred approach of developmental transitions had not worked. This is shown in the Figure 3C.2. Some within the State Library say that the process of management involves constant movement between developmental and task-focused transitions: the caveat being that the rationale for such changes is always well communicated to staff. In this case the espoused 'softer' ideology does not in practice preclude the effective use of a much tougher approach when needed.

The library's strategic repositioning is clear. It has moved from a reactive strategy in the mid 1980s to a product–market innovator, a

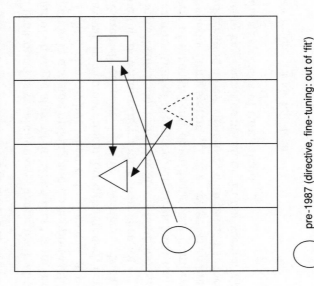

**Figure 3C.2**  State Library of NSW: change strategies

 pre-1987 (directive, fine-tuning: out of 'fit')

☐ 1987–90 (fast paced, charismatic transformation)

△ 1991–present (developmental transition: the espoused, preferred means of change)

△ 1991–present (task-focused change: the sometimes 'realized' change strategy to keep the pace of adjustment moving)

marked shift which has propelled the library to some prominence internationally. In the early to mid 1980s, Australian Airlines (now merged with Qantas) and Westpac Banking Corporation successfully used similar business approaches. What is appropriate for one era may not be useful in another, however, as Westpac has painfully discovered in the early 1990s.

The multifaceted approach used to achieve the corporate turnaround in the library was purposefully driven, and continuous. 'Needless to say it's a never-ending process', admitted Alison Crook, 'but there are lots of achievements to enjoy and celebrate along the way!' Her enthusiasm for productive change and her personal style have been powerful ingredients for successful transformation of the library to be the Australian leader, and possibly one of the world's leaders, in public libraries.

## CASE 3D   WESTPAC BANKING CORPORATION

Organizational Turnaround is revolutionary change used when the organization is out of strategic alignment, when there is no time for extensive participation in decision making and no support within the organization for radical change, but when radical change is vital to organizational survival. In its most radical form, the strategy could be characterized as extremely coercive, but the executive style can also be modified to be top-down directive rather than coercive.

This approach involves the major reshaping of corporate and business strategies, significant revision of the macro-organizational structure, stripping out layers of management, downsizing staff numbers and removing redundant operating systems. The emphasis is on breaking the old frame and creating a new structure, with particular focus on new appointments to key executive positions. In this section we look at one of Australia's key cases of turnaround.

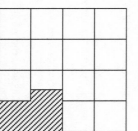

**Figure 3D.1**   (See Figure 3.2 for full details)

In late 1992 and early 1993 an unusual drama unfolded in the boardroom of one of Australia's largest banks, Westpac Banking Corporation, involving Australia's richest person, Kerry Packer. Kerry Packer's private company, Consolidated Press Holdings, had seized 10 per cent of Westpac in late 1992. Packer and his chief executive, Al Dunlap, developed a plan to slash costs and staff in an effort to turn around the banks' disastrous 1992 losses of A$1,500 million. An informal meeting of directors with Packer and Dunlap on 17 December 1992 led to the resignation of the managing director, Frank Conroy, reportedly because the change programme Conroy proposed was not considered far reaching or rapid enough for the board. Conroy's proposal involved downsizing the 45,000-person workforce by 24 per cent over 18 months.

The first official board meeting attended by Packer and Dunlap was on 15 January 1993, exactly one week after their official appointment as directors. It was widely assumed that their much more radical proposal would be accepted at this meeting. Instead, Packer and Dunlap themselves resigned from the Westpac board after what was a fiery and acrimonious discussion.

Westpac illustrates the use of different change strategies at different business stages: in this case the long history of a relatively consultative, developmental approach in the 1950s–80s did not serve the bank well after the stock market crash. In the early 1980s the bank underwent a major and successful (charismatic) transformation under the inspirational leadership of CEO Bob White. By the mid 1980s this had modified to a successful developmental transition, during which time the bank developed a very strong corporate culture and enjoyed the results and reputation of a leading bank. Its human management strategies were a much more comprehensive and systematized version of Macquarie Bank's. However, business conditions changed rapidly in the period immediately following the 1987 stock market crash, compounded by a lengthy and damaging leadership succession process within the bank.

The newly appointed chief executive, Stuart Fowler, introduced a directive, harder-nosed approach to leadership characterized by our task-focused change strategy. However, the consultative and innovative culture of the bank was so strong and the independence of some key business units so entrenched that it was difficult, if not impossible, to achieve quickly the amount of business repositioning required in radically different conditions. During this period, human resource practitioners within the bank continued to espouse and practise all the principles of the softer-type developmental incrementalism. This was one of the key factors holding back the successful repositioning of the bank in this period. In 1992–93, under the leadership of CEO Frank Conroy, extremely useful business and human resource management changes were made but they were insufficient to meet quickly key shareholder demands. This resulted in Conroy's resignation as CEO in early 1993. The key turning-points in Westpac's change strategy over the past decade are shown in the Figure 3D.2.

A key point in the Westpac case is that throughout the 1980s the bank was widely imaged as having some of the most progressive

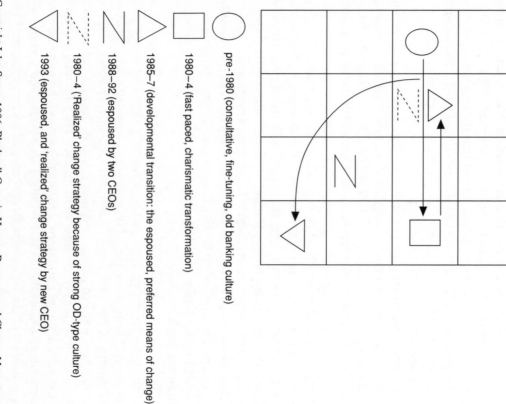

**Figure 3D.2** Westpac Banking Corporation: use of change strategies

○ pre-1980 (consultative, fine-tuning, old banking culture)

□ 1980–4 (fast paced, charismatic transformation)

△ 1985–7 (developmental transition: the espoused, preferred means of change)

N 1988–92 (espoused by two CEOs)

N 1980–4 ('Realized' change strategy because of strong OD-type culture)

△ 1993 (espoused, and 'realized' change strategy by new CEO)

human resource practices in Australia. They were built on the best principles of consultation, employee development and participative democracy. By and large they worked well in growth markets. However, the change of business conditions and bank strategies in the late 1980s were not received well by its human resource practitioners, many of whom wished the halcyon days of the developmental human resource agenda to continue. It could not in the changed business conditions, and hence the severe philosophical and management tussles which took place as the bank underwent radical reshaping in the early 1990s.

Which approach to change? To satisfy shareholders a new CEO, Robert Joss, was appointed to follow Conroy in 1993. Robert Joss moved swiftly, incisively, to challenge the power structure and culture of the bank. The effect internally was traumatic, but at the time of writing (1995) the bank's performance had improved. Westpac is undergoing framebreaking, turnaround change (35 per cent workforce reductions) and will regain a leading position in the financial services industry. We predict that the period of turnaround will continue into 1996, following which the corporate change strategy will need to move to a task-focused approach for some years. Westpac is a key example of the successful situational use of change strategies, except in the latter 1980s when a more radical, less developmental approach should have been used quickly to reposition the business. During this period its human resource strategies lagged behind its business strategies – delaying its much-needed business repositioning.

## Questions

1 Most of the texts on 'managing change' include a list of 'action points'. How relevant are such good practice lists in the light of the case research reported here?

2 Summarise the line of argument which arises from the analysis of 'dominant patterns of corporate change'.

3 What implications does this case research carry for the practice of organizational development (OD)?

4 Explain the rationale for the different paths of change followed by Macquarie Bank, Tubemakers, The State Library of NSW and Westpac.

## References

Dunphy, D. C. and Stace, D. A. 1990: *Under New Management: Australian Organizations in Transition.* Sydney: McGraw-Hill.

Hamel, G. and Prahalad, C. K. 1994: *Competing for the Future.* Boston, Mass: Harvard Business School Press.

Quinn, J. B. 1993: *Intelligent Enterprise.* New York: The Free Press.

Stace, D. A. and Dunphy, D. C. 1991(a): Beyond traditional paternalistic and developmental approaches to organizational change and human resource strategy. *International Journal of Human Resource Management,* **2**(3), 263–83.

Stace, D. A. and Dunphy, D. C. 1991(b): Translating business strategies into action: managing strategic change. *Journal of Strategic Change,* **1**, 203–16.

Stace, D. A. and Dunphy, D. C. 1994: *Beyond the Boundaries: Leading and Recreating the Successful Enterprise,* Sydney: McGraw-Hill.

## Further reading

Dunphy, D. C. and Stace, D. A. 1986: Evolution of transformation? Incremental versus transformational ideologies for organizational change. *AGSM Working Paper,* No. 28.

Dunphy, D. C. and Stace, D. A. 1988: Transformational and coercive strategies for planned organizational change: beyond the OD model. *Organization Studies,* **9**(3), 317–34.

Greiner, L. E. 1992: Evolution and revolution as organizations grow. *Harvard Business Review,* July–August, 37–46.

Hamel, G. and Prahalad, C. K. 1993: Strategy and stretch and leverage. *Harvard Business Review,* March–April, 75–84.

Levy, A. 1986: Second-order planned change: definition and conceptualization. *Organizational Dynamics,* 5–20.

Miles, R. E. and Snow, C. C. 1978: *Organizational Strategy, Structure and Process.* New York: McGraw-Hill.

Miller, D. and Friesen, P. H. 1984: *Organizations: A Quantum View.* Englewood Cliffs, NJ: Prentice-Hall.

Nord, W. R. and Tucker, S. 1987: *Implementing Routine and Radical Innovations.* Lexington, KY: University of Kentucky Press.

Pettigrew, A. M. 1985: *The Awakening Giant: Continuity and Change in Imperial Chemical Industries.* Oxford: Blackwell.

Tushman, M. L., Newman, W. H. and Romanelli, E. 1986: Convergence and upheaval: managing the unsteady pace of organizational evolution. *California Management Review,* **29**, 29–44.

Tichy, N. M., Fombrun, C. J. and Devanna, M. A. 1982: Strategic Human Resource Management. *Sloan Management Review,* Winter.

## Appendix 3.1 Four 'Types' of Change Strategy

**Table 3.1** Developmental transitions

*Case examples*
Macquarie Bank (late 1980s)
State Library of NSW (1990–3)
Tubemakers of Australia (1987–present)
Westpac Banking Corporation (mid 1980s)

| | |
|---|---|
| Business strategy | • Dominantly product-market innovator (Prospector), or<br>• Successful low-cost producer of high quality products (Defender) |
| Business planning | • Primarily 'bottom-up' planning, within corporate parameters – business units strongly influence corporate directions |
| Change strategy characteristics | • Constant, relentless mid-range change (change as a way of life)<br>• Executive leadership which operates on a collegial, consultative basis<br>• Team leadership which is sometimes directive, to balance the consultative executive style<br>• An emphasis on changing dominant values and mindsets in order to change the organization |
| Change leader type | • Coach |
| Change and HR intervention tools typically used | • Vision/mission development (consultative)<br>• Culture enhancement programmes<br>• Team building (self-managed work teams)<br>• Management and team leadership development programmes<br>• Service quality programmes<br>• Personal and professional development/skills formation<br>• Total quality management, process benchmarking programmes<br>• Building corporate competencies<br>• Radical delegation/empowerment of staff<br>• Developing horizontal organization structures |
| Communication strategies | • Widespread involvement in the communication process to develop trust<br>• Multi-directional initiatives<br>• Use of task teams/focus groups to process change issues<br>• Emphasis on face-to-face communication |
| Cultural renewal | • Normative educative strategy<br>• Creating shared experiences around development of new organizational norms<br>• Appeal to shared values<br>• Use of intrinsic rewards, sense of achievement |

**Table 3.2**   Task-focused transitions

| | |
|---|---|
| *Case examples* | MLC Life Limited (1990–)<br>Lend Lease (from 1980s)<br>Tubemakers of Australia (1987–now)<br>Pacific Power (1992–now) |
| Business strategy | • A focused strategy. Cost containment in some business areas, product-market innovation in others (Analyser), or<br>• Successful low-cost producer of high quality products (Defender) |
| Business planning | • Clear statement of corporate 'strategic intent' – implementation cascading down to business units. Mixture of 'top-down' and bottom up 'business planning' |
| Change strategy characteristics | • Constant improvement and relentless mid-range change<br>• Executive leadership which operates on a decisive/ strongly directional basis<br>• Business unit leadership is mostly consultative, but within a strong framework of well-organized systems<br>• Focus on improving structures and systems |
| Change leader type | • Captains |
| Change and HR intervention tools typically used | • Systems redesign<br>• Workforce planning/rightsizing<br>• Job redesign/business process redesign/re-engineering<br>• Productivity measurement and improvement<br>• Strategic and process benchmarking<br>• Objective setting/management by objectives/ performance contracts/appraisal<br>• Strong technical skills training<br>• Management and team leadership development<br>• TQM, continuous improvement |
| Communication strategies | • Aim is to gain behavioural alignment with the vision and key executive initiatives<br>• Use of line relationships for communication<br>• Primarily top-down communication with built-in feedback<br>• Use of technical expertise to advise teams<br>• Emphasis on formal communication, e.g. instructions, memos, e-mail |
| Cultural renewal | • Empirical/rational strategy<br>• Competence enhancement through retraining<br>• Focus on changing systems as a means of encouraging behaviour modification<br>• Constant adjustment of norms to match changing strategies<br>• Use of intrinsic and extrinsic rewards related to the task |

**Table 3.3**  Charismatic transformations

| | |
|---|---|
| *Case examples* | State Library of NSW (1988–89) |
| | Westpac Banking Corporation (early 1980s) |
| | Australian Airlines (mid 1980s) |
| | Start-Up Organizations (ongoing) |
| Business strategy | • Product-market innovator (Prospector) |
| Business planning | • Entrepreneurial, not systematized |
| | • Strong emphasis on intuitive thinking and calculated risk-taking |
| Change strategy characteristics | • Rapid, radical redefinition of the business, or creation of the new business domain |
| | • Reshaping of corporate and competitive business strategies |
| | • Executive leadership which provides an inspiring vision and generates the respect and support of staff |
| Change leader type | • Charismatics |
| Change and HR intervention tools typically used | • New vision/mission |
| | • Radical organic restructuring, rightsizing, voluntary redundancies |
| | • New executive recruits, often from outside |
| | • Top-team building programmes |
| | • Cross-functional task teams |
| | • Service excellence programmes |
| | • Symbolic communication (change of corporate name, logo and wardrobe; excellence awards) |
| Communication strategies | • Aim is to gain emotional commitment to the vision, re-examination and revision of core values and beliefs |
| | • Use of multi-media communication channels, but personalized |
| | • Top-down communication with built-in feedback and symbolic two-way communication |
| | • Use of strategic task-forces |
| | • Personalized corporate communication |
| Cultural renewal | • Paradigm shifting strategy |
| | • Creating vicarious participation and identification with new role models |
| | • Radical challenge to existing values |
| | • Infusion of a new core business culture |
| | • Use of intrinsic rewards and identification with charismatic leader |

**Table 3.4**  Turnarounds

| | |
|---|---|
| *Case examples*<br>Pacific Power (1988–91)<br>MLC-Life Limited (1984–87)<br>BHP (1984–88)<br>Westpac Banking Corporation (1993–94)<br>National Australia Bank (1982–85) | |
| Business strategy | • Dynamic refocus on the core business and selected business areas, adoption of a focused, niche strategy (Analyser) having previously been either low performers (Reactors) or medium performers and losing 'alignment' with the business environment |
| Business planning | • Top team holds frequent retreats to consider strategy<br>• Major focus on creating a new corporate plan and negotiating this with external stakeholders<br>• Business unit planning strongly influenced by the corporate plan |
| Change strategy characteristics | • Rapid, radical redefinition of the core business<br>• Divestment of non-core business areas<br>• Successive corporate and workplace restructures, downsizing and retrenchments<br>• Restructuring/abolishing traditional systems<br>• Chief executive welds together a strong top team<br>• Decision making is re-centralized |
| Change leader type | • Commanders |
| Change and HR intervention tools typically used | • Strategy and market segmentation analysis<br>• Merger/acquisition/divestment of non-core businesses<br>• Restructurings/downsizing/rightsizing/forced retrenchments<br>• Reconstruction and development of the top team<br>• Cultural and industrial confrontation strategies<br>• Radical business process redesign<br>• Human resource strategy redesign |
| Communication strategies | • Aim is to communicate a sense of organizational crisis, rationale for change and cost of non-compliance<br>• Communication put on a 'wartime' footing; frequent, total and forceful<br>• Top-down communication<br>• Use of selected change leaders as key communicators<br>• Emphasis on formal, authoritative communication |
| Cultural renewal | • Power-coercive strategy<br>• Emphasis on remoulding behaviour as approach to value change<br>• Radical challenge to existing values<br>• Recasting and reforming of core culture<br>• Use of extrinsic rewards and coercive sanctions |

**4**

# ChocCo

*Plant managers developing HR
strategies in an uncertain
organizational climate*

NICOLAS BACON AND
JOHN STOREY

As one of Britain's largest chocolate confectionery companies ChocCo made profits of £330 million in 1992–3. Its shares outperformed the UK food sector from mid 1991. Until autumn 1992 the company had impressed the City with the quality of its managers, its tight focus on core businesses and its strong commitment to product innovation and brand support. However, in 1993 the company's image and share price slipped, raising long-term doubts about its future. Key economic commentators suggested that the company had outgrown the UK but lacked a convincing international expansion strategy and that to secure future growth a bold strategic initiative would be necessary. It is within this uncertain climate that we can explore some of the difficulties managers face in developing HR strategies.

The corporate culture of ChocCo is a result of its traditionally paternalistic employment practices. From the late 1980s the company sought to distance itself from this history, adopting what senior managers regarded as a sophisticated solution to the problem of managing employees across several sites. ChocCo had traditionally adopted a common approach to employee relations across the different factories within the company. However, in an attempt to break away from this in 1990 the company decentralized collective bargaining to each factory. Senior executives believed that this would allow the different sites to recast their employment strategies more in line with their needs. Two factories in particular, AssortedChoc and BarChoc, developed very different solutions to the challenges they faced.

When Doug McCaffer took up his appointment as factory manager of AssortedChoc in 1990 he had been working at ChocCo for 26 years. In his most recent post in the buying office his role had been to 'introduce competition'. When appointed to his new job the managing director had told him, 'it's a shambles, get in there and sort it out'. In the three years before his arrival the factory had lost £7 million. In describing how he had begun to turn around the factory McCaffer admitted, 'my basic style is one of hands-on management and I tend to be autocratic rather than democratic'. His first act was to call together the factory management committee to inform them that they had six weeks to persuade him to keep them. McCaffer explained that he held managers personally responsible for permitting a situation of high earnings, high overtime and a high level of absenteeism to develop. Initially he had tried to persuade the trade unions to 'come on-board' and plan future changes. When this failed he cut the number of shop stewards from 50 to 20 and the number of convenors from five to one. The production process at AssortCo was labour intensive, employing mainly unskilled female workers with seasonal variations in the amount of labour needed. When McCaffer took over the factory there was a mixture of full-time and part-time workers frequently retained even during periods of slack demand. Overtime was high, quality low and there were piecework elements in the payment system. Historically, managers had made few attempts to involve employees in decisions. In the opinion of McCaffer the company was a deeply autocratic one and would intervene in any development it did not favour. He was unsure about the extent to which the company was serious in its statements about employee participation. In 1991, after he had informally chatted with staff, he attempted to get the company to spend £500,000 on a new air-conditioning unit for the packing department. The board rejected this and the best he could do was to prop the door open. Although ChocCo had formally decentralized pay bargaining to the factories, when he was willing to meet the union demand for a 4 per cent pay increase in 1992 the company refused him permission to make this deal. The company personnel department had taken over when the union called a strike ballot in response. McCaffer had become increasingly cynical about the company for which he worked and the job they were asking him to do. In many respects he was receiving mixed messages from the company. On the one hand it considered itself up to the mark with current progressive management ideas and practices. However, a previous attempt to launch a company-wide total quality management (TQM) programme had failed when the company had been too prescriptive in its approach. To let McCaffer speak for himself he explained his predicament thus:

We are not allowed to get on with the job. Financial benchmarking is all in this company and there is no factory manager who does anything else. My managers are performing now that I've made them bite the bullet. I'm aware that other factories have gone for different models and that they are using quality circles and the like. I'm sure we will all get these things rammed down our throats whether we like it or not. I think the people pushing these things are just on ego trips trying to advance their careers. I don't think the company is really committed to any of that. I see myself as the custodian of this job. When I leave it I hope to pass on a factory which has properly restructured itself.

McCaffer had become a harsh disciplinarian, had appointed a production manager as his personnel manager, drastically reduced overtime working and shortened the contracts and average tenure of shopfloor employees.

In contrast to AssortedChoc, the BarChoc factory was a high-technology plant employing permanent (mainly male) skilled workers. The key event that triggered change was a threat by the US distributors not to renew the company's contract due to the poor quality of some products. In response the factory manager, Jim Graves, introduced the Excellent Manufacturing Programme and sought to develop high trust relationships with employees and the trade unions. The trade unions became fully involved in developing new employee involvement programmes and the unions themselves ran a quality group on health and safety issues. Individuals tried to solve production problems in numerous newly created problem-solving groups. Although Graves himself had become firmly committed to a high-involvement route, he faced several problems. The first was in convincing the company of his approach. In the words of Graves:

I would go along to meetings with the Board and the old style managers would be obsessed with establishing control, reducing absenteeism and getting rid of shop stewards. When they asked me what we were

Copyright John Storey 1996, Blackwell Cases in Human Resource and Change Management

doing I felt I was fighting a losing battle. For the involvement approach to win you need management commitment right at the top but we didn't have it. This company is very strictly controlled by financial measures. I find it impossible to spend money so you can imagine how difficult it is for my managers no matter how much I tell them they are empowered.

A second problem occurred when the company introduced its company-wide quality programme two years after the factory's own. The company's scheme concentrated on management processes rather than shopfloor involvement. Graves received a deputation from his manufacturing managers who explained that having both systems was too much, with production variances becoming erratic. As the share price fell in the City of London in 1993, as described at the start of this case, a third problem developed. The board issued immediate instructions to reduce costs. This meant an immediate cut of 78 jobs at BarChoc. Graves found this very difficult to explain to the trade unions because it was not being forced on them directly by the performance of competitors but resulted from internal financial pressures. Thus far the unions had supported Graves in the changes he had introduced, but how could he retain their trust and a good working relationship? Graves wondered whether he would have to get tougher with the unions and follow the line set down in other factories?

## Questions

1   Give a brief summary of what you would expect the HR strategies in each of the two factories to be like. What working patterns and terms and conditions do you think are on offer? How do you think each factory organizes pay? How do they manage commitment? What roles would you expect first-line managers to be playing in each of the factories?

2   What does this case tell us about the importance of management style in how HR policies are selected and developed?

3   Armstrong (1995) has argued that it will be very difficult for the HRM approach to develop further in what he terms 'the age of management accounting'. What might he mean and how is this illustrated in the case of ChocCo?

4   What insights does this case give us into two of the ideas currently very popular with managers: decentralization and empowerment?

5   What do you think it is like to be a manager in this company considering the question of the appropriate HR strategy? What do you think it might be like to be a line manager in the two factories?

6   In developing HR strategies, who would you say was exercising most power in ChocCo? Do you think this would be a representative picture of other companies?

## Reference

Armstrong, P. 1995: Accountancy and HRM, in Storey, J. (ed.), *Human Resource Management: A Critical Text*. London: Routledge, 142–63.

## Further reading

Purcell, J. 1995: Corporate strategy and its links to human resource management strategy, in Storey, J., *Human Resource Management: A Critical Text*. London: Routledge, 63–86.

# 5
# Oticon

*Thinking the unthinkable: radical (and successful) organizational change*

## HENRIK HOLT LARSEN

Oticon is a Danish hearing aids manufacturing company which made a dramatic turn-around in 1990 (Peters, 1992; Poulsen, 1993). A project-based organization (the 'spaghetti' form) replaced the hierarchical structure, information technology replaced most of the written communication, an open-space office area with 'desks' on wheels replaced individual offices, multifunctional employees replaced unidimensional specialists and formal job structures. This case describes the background, process and consequences of this radical organizational change process.

### Background

The company was established in 1904, it has approximately 1,600 employees and is the world's third largest producer of hearing aids. The headquarters, which are located in Copenhagen, have approximately 145 employees, and is the topic for this case.

Being a fairly old, well-established and reasonably profitable company by the mid 1980s the organization had all the strengths and weaknesses of traditional, hierarchical organizations including formal procedures, a conservative culture, employee loyalty and consensus-seeking (or conflict-avoiding) behaviour. Although the company eventually achieved a position as one of the world's leading suppliers, throughout the 1980s it faced a series of serious, financial and organizational problems:

Copyright John Storey 1996, Blackwell Cases in Human Resource and Change Management

- The top management team, consisting of four elderly directors, had an increasingly reactive way of managing the company; it became clear that they preferred the status quo.
- The management board also put great emphasis on signalling consensus to various stakeholders (including the board of directors), and thus suppressing disagreement and differences of opinion.
- The company was structured around three main functional areas which had only limited interaction and communication.
- The company suffered severely from the decline in the exchange rate for US dollars as most export items were traded in dollars.
- The research and development activities were reduced during the 1980s.
- The company had great difficulties in establishing itself on the growing market for 'in-the-ear' hearing aids, and focused too heavily on the more traditional 'behind-the-ear' market.
- The employees felt an increasing need for a more proactive, open and powerful management style.

## The Change Process

These problems escalated to the point where it was obvious that radical steps had to be taken. The first was the recruitment in 1988 of a new chief executive officer, Lars Kolind, who was given full responsibility for implementing the necessary changes in the organization.

After a two-year period of rationalization and cost reduction, which reduced sales and administration costs by 20 per cent, the newly appointed CEO suggested, in early 1990, a very broad 'package' of innovative and radical initiatives in organizational structure, job design, information technology and physical layout of the company. All these recommendations were described in a seven-page memorandum called 'Think the Unthinkable' which was written by the new CEO and distributed to all staff in March 1990. The suggested changes were:

- increasing competitiveness by utilizing human and technological resources in a more efficient way, hence reducing the overhead costs which at that time exceeded the actual production costs;
- replacing a hierarchical job structure with a project-based organization where each employee is involved in a number of (often cross-organizational and cross-functional) projects at the same time, and where each project is considered a 'business unit' with its own resources, time schedule and success criteria;

- abandoning traditional managerial jobs and attributing managerial authority to the project groups or the individual employee;
- drastically reducing written paper communication by establishing electronic scanning of all incoming mail and introducing very comprehensive information technology systems, networks, and so on;
- facilitating physical mobility by creating an open-space office where each person has a cart or trolley (that is, a desk on wheels, containing the computer, the telephone and a limited space for paper) which can be moved around in the office.

The overall objective – which was stated explicitly in the memorandum of the CEO – was to increase the productivity by 30 per cent in three years. This explains the name of the development plan: Project 330.

The plan was implemented in August 1991 when the headquarters were relocated to a building which had been especially designed to support the physical, organizational and technological flexibility of the organization.

Thus, in order to maximize the physical flexibility, a fairly big open-space office makes the free movement of the trolleys possible, and the coffee bars and the café (which is not supposed to be called a canteen) create extensive opportunities for informal exchange of information and experiences. The three floors are connected by a wide staircase where people unavoidably meet each other by chance. (The elevators are used only to move the trolleys from one floor to another and require a key to be obtained from the reception desk.)

Project teams are the basic organizing unit. These teams have from two or three up to ten or even 20 participants, and the project leader can choose how to achieve the agreed objectives of the project and who should be a member of the team. Everyone can in principle be a team leader, provided he or she has the necessary technical and leadership skills.

Strong emphasis is put on providing abundant facilities for information technology and, to speed up the employees' familiarity with the computers, all staff have been equipped with a computer at home. All incoming mail is delivered to one particular room where the employees come to read it. All important mail is scanned into the electronic information system, after which the paper is shredded. Written communication within the organization is almost exclusively computerized.

Finally, funds allocated to research and development have been increased and actually tripled from 1990 to 1995 to reach 10 per cent of the turnover. The reason for this is partly an emphasis on the quality-based, upper part of the hearing aid market, partly a strategic decision to focus increasingly on the small 'in-the-ear' hearing aids. This in itself represents a huge technological challenge as it is much more difficult to obtain a satisfactory sound quality with the tiny 'in-the-ear' hearing aids.

A number of symbolic acts and psychological elements have supported the change process:

- The CEO stresses clearly and frequently that most of his ideas about managing an organization came from the Scout movement, in which he is – and for a long time has been – involved.
- The CEO does not even have an office himself, but moves around when appropriate with his trolley-desk like any other employee.
- The paper shredder in the mail-room is connected to a transparent tube which passes right through the café. The symbolic effect of seeing all the shredded paper when you have your lunch in the café is quite strong.
- The CEO has stated publicly that, when taking over the job, he bought a fairly large portion of the company's shares (and had to raise a bank loan to do this). By stressing this he has made it evident to the employees that his own financial security is at great risk if the company does not succeed.
- His entire managerial style, which is very much characterized by openness, dialogue, informality, experimentation and humility, has to a large extent influenced the culture and value system of the organization. One example is the fact that he travels economy class even to far-away destinations such as Australia.

## Results

In short, the development of the organization can be described as follows:

- from hierarchy to project organization;
- from formal information to informal dialogue;
- from managerial positions to leadership processes;
- from departmentalization to cross-functional thinking and working;
- from written communication to electronic networks;
- from supervisory control to self control;
- from extrinsic rewards to intrinsic motivation.

The very comprehensive and radical change process which the organization went through during this period supports the stereotyped perception that in the future middle managers will be fewer in number and significance. Whereas the old organization had a very top-heavy authority system and a full team of middle managers, there are hardly any middle managers left as the company has turned into a project-based organization. Top management decides which projects should be started and who should be the project leaders, but the project leaders have the proper responsibility for resources, outcome, budget and timetable for their own project. Any staff member is encouraged to put forward project proposals. A few senior specialists (mainly middle managers from the 'old' organization) have a technical, semi-managerial position. Otherwise it is a two-layer organization where titles and job descriptions have been abandoned. As mentioned above, in principle all employees can become project leaders. The project leader for one project will typically be an ordinary member of other project teams.

The human resource responsibility is undertaken collectively by the group of project leaders for whom a given employee works at any given time. This is not an ideal situation and much effort is invested in finding better ways to ensure a proper undertaking of the responsibility for human resources. A system of decentralized 'personnel managers' which was suggested in the original memorandum of the CEO has been implemented and is in constant development.

Financially, the company has improved performance significantly, as shown in Table 5.1. In the same period (1990–4) investment in research and development has tripled. The actual total costs of the organization development process are difficult to determine, but the investment in the actual change process itself was substantial: it amounted to approximately £20,000 per employee.

**Table 5.1**   Key figures 1990–1994

|                      | 1990 (DKK) | 1991 (DKK) | 1992 (DKK) | 1993 (DKK) | 1994 (DKK) |
| -------------------- | ---------- | ---------- | ---------- | ---------- | ---------- |
| Turnover             | 456        | 477        | 539        | 661        | 750        |
| Primary result       | 17         | 9          | 31         | 87         | 134        |
| Net result           | 10         | 0          | 9          | 62         | 88         |
| Net capital          | 160        | 144        | 146        | 192        | 273        |
| Return on investment | 8          | -2         | 7          | 37         | 38         |

*Source:* Oticon (1994)

In general, the project was successful and this can be attributed to the following factors (Poulsen, 1993):

1 There was a potential for development in the organization.
2 The board of directors gave the new CEO almost complete freedom of action.
3 The organization itself felt a strong need for change.
4 The changes were implemented in a radical and immediate way.
5 The existing organization was consolidated (by cost-cutting rationalization) before the radical changes were initiated.
6 A common set of values was explicitly developed and accepted.
7 The organizational change affected mainly the organizational core.
8 Structure, organization and technology were changed at the same time.
9 The new culture was given a chance to become established.
10 A consolidation of the achieved changes and results created a new balance.

The 'quiet revolution' was generally met by enthusiasm (or resignation) by the present employees. The top management team was eventually replaced or internally redeployed (which would probably have happened in any case) and all other staff were brought into the new organization. However, two years later, approximately ten employees were dismissed as part of a slimming process (not because they did not fit into the new organization). There have been only a few resignations and the turnover rate, up to the time of writing (1995) has been very low.

## Conclusion

The case shows how the 'old' Oticon got into trouble, despite (or because of?) its market success up until the 1970s. It shows how organizational and technological changes are intertwined and how important it is to have a precise strategic outlook when initiating a turn-around process. It shows how a knowledge-based organization can reveal previously untapped human resources by changing working conditions, job content and managerial style. It shows, also, how one individual (the CEO), by his own value system, his visible behaviour, his trust in people and his courage to experiment, got the company into a good shape.

As CEO Lars Kolind has said:

- 'For fifty years we have worked at making the blue-collar workers more efficient. Now, the white-collar workers are next in turn. They must be allowed to increase their productivity as well.'

- 'Up to now we have tried to find a person to fill up a given "job box". But that is wrong. Everybody has more talents than what is usually required in the job. That is why the employees at Oticon shall in the future have more than one job where they can test all their talents.'

- 'We have to get away from the traditional functionally based organization. Instead we shall have a spaghetti organization, where all employees are available to all managers. It will be up to the managers to attract the most qualified employees, and a proper market for jobs will be created. At the same time, however, the individual employee has the responsibility to find somebody to take over the job he or she wants to get out of.'

- 'If people don't have anything to do, they need to find something – or we don't need them.'

This does not mean, however, that the company no longer faces severe challenges. These include how to:

- obtain a share of the increasing market for 'in-the-ear' hearing aids;
- compete with more powerful, international competitors like Siemens (German) and Starkey (a fast-growing American company);
- maintain the spirit and enthusiasm from the 'pioneer days';
- create career possibilities in an organization which has no hierarchy and only few managerial positions.

## Questions

1　Is this a unique case which cannot be generalized to other settings? Why/why not?

2　To what extent is the process determined by the specific attitudes and behaviour of the CEO?

3　Why was the turn-around so positively received by the employees?

4　To what extent is the turn-around process and outcome influenced by the specific national (that is, Danish) culture?

## References

Oticon 1994: Annual Report, Copenhagen.

Peters, T. 1992: *Liberation management*. New York: Knopf.

Poulsen, P. T. 1993: *Taenk det utenkelige. Revolutionen i Oticon* (Think the Unthinkable. The Revolution at Oticon). Copenhagen: Schultz.

## Further reading

Hofstede, G. 1980: *Culture's Consequences*. Newbury Park, California: Sage.
Hofstede, G. 1991: *Culture and Organizations: Software of the Mind*. London: McGraw-Hill.

# 6

# Volkswagen

*Cutting labour costs without
redundancies*

## PETRA GARNJOST AND
## KLAUS BLETTNER

**Facing Hard Times – the Economic Situation in the
Car Industry**

Since the mid 1980s the situation in the car industry has been characterized by a massive production capacity overshoot. The recession
of the early 1990s put even more pressure on Western car producers
because of reductions in demand and South-East Asian expansion
strategies. Even with an economic upturn, production capacity still
exceeded, by far, the growing demand in the market (Nolte, 1994,
p. 13). In 1993 global annual sales were about 34 million cars, whereas
world-wide production capacity had reached approximately 44 million
and was growing at an annual rate of 1.2 million.

The Volkswagen Group had developed into the biggest European
car producer and was number four world wide with its subsidiaries
Audi, Seat and Skoda. New production plants in Spain, Portugal,
Eastern Europe, the new German federal states, and the recent economic decline had led to a remarkable capacity surplus within the
group. Consequently Volkswagen had very serious problems.

The company's 1993 annual report showed that Volkswagen had
suffered a 19.2 per cent reduction in turnover, a 25.2 per cent reduction in sales, a 55.9 per cent reduction in investment and a 46.3 per
cent reduction in annual results.

All this led to a crisis at Volkswagen which needed serious changes
in management in order to keep the company running successfully

over the next decade (Hartz, 1994, pp. 16–18). According to Womack et al. (1990) not only production capacity but also productivity turns out to be problematic for Western car producers. They had, and still have, to catch up with the South-East Asian standards of lean production and high quality. Compared with the leading competitors, Volkswagen were 20–30 per cent behind in terms of productivity (Kuhlmeyer, 1994, p. 31). This is not an easy task, especially for German car producers, because they also have to face relatively high labour costs, low rates of innovation, high taxes and fewer working hours compared with other European countries (Clement and Röhreke, 1994, p. 292).

Because of excess capacity and productivity improvements, in conventional terms one-third of the workforce should have been laid off between 1994 and 1995. But the company tried to avoid this solution, and the problem to solve, therefore, was how to cut down DM2 billion of labour costs, which is the equivalent of making about 30,000 workers redundant (Hartz, 1994, p. 10).

It was quite clear that traditional methods of manpower reduction would not provide the optimal solution to the problem that Volkswagen faced. One reason was that the workforce had already been reduced by 8.8 per cent in 1993 compared to 1992. New and innovative methods of manpower planning and organization had to be developed.

## Traditional Ways to Reduce Manpower

Employment policies offer different ways to deal with planned demanning. German human resource managers and theorists distinguish between the different approaches as shown in Figure 6.1.

### Production planning

As can be seen in Figure 6.1, all the instruments of production planning, for example extended stock keeping or postponed rationalization investments, bear two general problems. First, they focus on short-term success but neglect any strategic planning. Consequently they rely on a more-or-less rapid change of economic circumstances in the future. Second, they are not compatible with the task of increasing productivity. Furthermore, they tend to avoid making any productivity improvements in order to maintain the present level of

**Figure 6.1**  Employment policies of planned de-manning

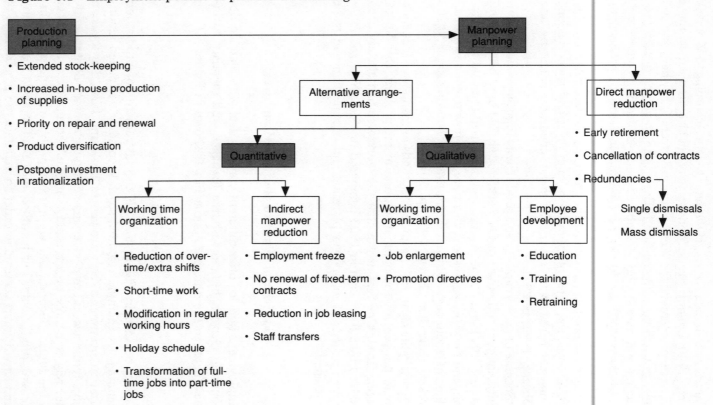

*Source*: RKW-Handbuch Personalplanung (1990), p. 206

employment. Nowadays these traditional production planning methods are not appropriate to ensure that companies can survive in the global competitive environment.

In the case of Volkswagen, the new target was to improve quality, reduce production time and the complexity of production, as well as improving environmental aspects. Innovations should also be transformed to the production line much more quickly than had been usual in the past. This led to what the company called KVP (*kontinuierlicher Verbesserungsprozeß* – continuous improvement schemes) (Hartz, 1994, pp. 96–109). The improvements were not only based on the workplace itself but also on the whole production process including production planning. Hence, Volkswagen implemented new sourcing strategies to improve its co-operation with suppliers in order to economize both at Volkswagen and at the supplier (Hartz, 1994, pp. 100–02).

The three key sourcing strategies are:

1 forward sourcing, where the research and development (R&D) department of Volkswagen co-operates with suppliers to push ahead development of new components, which leads to a reduction in internal scope of production;

2 global sourcing, where Volkswagen looks for the best supplier world-wide; and

3 strategic insourcing, where suppliers are encouraged to build new plants next to Volkswagen to manage just-in-time (JIT) production with minimal transport costs and delay.

Volkswagen forecasted a 25 per cent rise in productivity as the outcome of KVP. However, the introduction of these improvements increased the already existing manpower surplus of 10,000 workers, to 30,000 workers in total.

### Direct manpower cuts

Coming back to Figure 6.1, direct manpower cuts seem to be the easiest and most economical way to cut labour costs. From a legal point of view, making 30,000 workers redundant would have been a 'mass dismissal for operational reasons adjusted to production' (*Massenentlassung bei Betriebsänderung*). Consequently this would have been fairly expensive because of the co-determination rights of the works council (Rosdücher and Seifert, 1994, p. 4). Pursuant to paragraph 112 Betriebsverfassungsgesetz (Works Constitution Act) the works council has the right to force the company to set up a social compensation plan in order to avoid social hardship. Therefore no immediate cost saving could have been achieved, especially considering the bargaining time.

Moreover, such a mass dismissal would have damaged the company's image considerably as Volkswagen is known for caring for its workforce (Kuhlmeyer, 1994, p. 31). To continue with this tradition, managers and employees were both highly motivated to look for a more satisfying solution (Hartz, 1994, pp. 23–5).

A step in this direction could have been pre-retirement schemes, because it is a more balanced compromise between company compulsion and employees' needs than mass dismissal. However, over the previous decade 30,000 workers had already participated in a pre-retirement scheme offered by Volkswagen or benefited from other social regulations. By the early 1990s, practically no workers were left for further arrangements in this field (Hartz, 1994, p. 10).

### Alternatives to manpower cuts

It was quite clear that instruments of indirect manpower cuts such as freezing recruitment or avoiding prolonging non-permanent contracts were also not sufficient to solve the manpower problem at Volkswagen. Short-term labour cost savings and cost stagnation could have led to the need for massive investments in human capital in the future due to an ageing workforce. What remains is the reorganization of working time and the training of the workforce. As also shown in Figure 6.1, in Germany short-time work is a special instrument to handle temporary manpower overcapacity. However, there are strict legal regulations which determine its use. First, it is restricted to a period of six months unless there is a serious order gap which allows an extension for an additional 18 months. The cost effect for the company is that during short-time work the workforce is paid by the German Federal Labour Office. Short-time work is seen as a method to prevent unemployment. That is the reason why workers receive 68 per cent of the regular net wage from the State. None the less, Volkswagen has a works agreement to increase this monthly payment by up to 95 per cent, which curtails its possible costs savings (Rosdücher and Seifert, 1994, p. 4).

As we have shown, these traditional instruments were not suitable in this case: either because Volkswagen had used them already or the total savings were not sufficient due to special legal or company regulations (Bach and Spitznagel, 1994). These circumstances forced Volkswagen, and especially its industrial relations director, Peter Hartz, to find alternatives in the fields of working time organization and training.

## An Innovative Solution – the Volkswagen Model

The Volkswagen Model consists of three elements (Hartz, 1994, pp. 60–92):

1 a 28.8-hour working week for any employee;
2 part-time employment for younger and older workers;
3 qualification periods.

Only the 28.8-hour working week is covered by a collective bargaining agreement valid from 1 January 1994 to 31 December 1995. For the qualification and the part-time elements of the model Volkswagen has chosen work agreements, as these issues are more complicated and therefore more time consuming to negotiate with the trade unions.

### *The 28.8-hour working week*

The basic idea was to save 20 per cent of the annual labour costs immediately, without layoffs. This was possible by cutting working hours from 36 to 28.8 hours per week without wage compensation.

This element of the model had to fulfil different requirements to ensure its acceptance by the works council as well as by the management. First, it had to be applicable to the whole workforce including exempted workers and management. Second, it had to exclude dismissals for operational reasons during its running period. Third, it had to secure the same monthly income, avoiding pecuniary difficulties for the individual worker. Fourth, it had to facilitate the transfer of employees from one plant to another as well as from one job to another (Peters et al., 1994, p. 169).

The key to the complicated wage package was to distribute all annual special payments over a 12-month period (see Figure 6.2). In detail:

**Figure 6.2**   The new monthly income plan

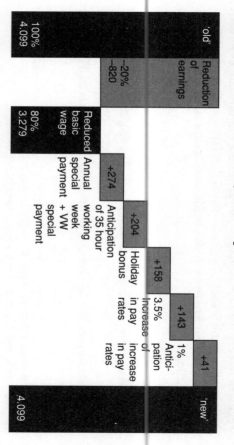

*Source:* Hartz (1994), p. 67

- the already-agreed increase in pay rates of 3.5 per cent was postponed from 1 November 1993 to 1 January 1994;
- the 35-hour working week with full wage compensation of 2.8 per cent planned for 1 October 1995 was introduced on 1 January 1994;
- the annual special payment (96 per cent of the monthly income) and holiday bonus were transformed into monthly payments;
- the 1 per cent increase in pay rates negotiated for (1 August 1994) was brought forward to 1 January 1994;
- the remaining gap of 2 per cent of the monthly gross wage was covered by a special payment made by Volkswagen.

(*Source:* Volkswagen AG, 1993)

The annual loss in net income for each worker was between 10 and 12 per cent depending on the individual taxes to be paid (Rosdücher and Seifert, 1994, p. 21). However, the cut in labour costs per car was 13 per cent compared to only 6 per cent if Volkswagen had chosen mass dismissal (Hartz, 1994, pp. 63–8).

As outlined above, the impressive cut in labour costs was partly realized because exempt employees as well as managerial employees participated in the 20 per cent income cut. This was possible without constructive dismissals because annual bonuses and special payments were also added monthly to the reduced basic income (Hartz, 1994, pp. 88–90). Despite this cut in income no respective reduction in the working hours per week was realized.

The implementation of the new four-day working week for non-exempt employees led to a variety of different shift patterns (Rosdücher and Seifert, 1994, p. 14). Only about 70 per cent of the staff work in a four-day rhythm with the Friday or Monday free (see Figure 6.3). This was primarily possible in areas which were not directly involved in production. Nevertheless, some departments had to set up a rotating system of a three- and five-day working week to ensure a regular service for customers and other departments from Monday to Friday.

Technical needs and high expenditures in such areas as painting, carcass building and along the assembly lines have meant that the five day working week is still in use. However, the shorter working time has been put into practice either through a reduction of the daily shift time or by introducing additional free shift time. In some cases they have even extended the working time which led to relatively long (five-day working) and numerous free periods, normally every fourth or fifth week (see Figures 6.4 and 6.5).

**Figure 6.3**  Four-day rhythm

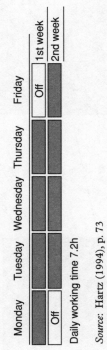

Daily working time 7.2h

*Source:* Hartz (1994), p. 73

**Figure 6.4**  Daily reduction of working hours

Daily working time 5.76h

*Source:* Hartz (1994), p. 74

As already mentioned, another element of the collective bargaining agreement to ensure temporary job security was the possibility of transferring workers from one Volkswagen plant to another. As can be seen from Figure 6.6, manpower surpluses differed from plant to plant, from 15 per cent in Hannover up to 48 per cent in Emden.

The 28.8 hour working week is not able to adjust these differences, therefore it was important to regulate the transfer of workers in the

**Figure 6.5**   Free-time model

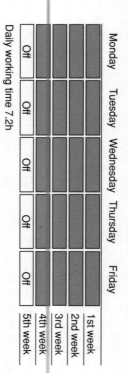

| | Monday | Tuesday | Wednesday | Thursday | Friday | |
|---|---|---|---|---|---|---|
| | | | | | | 1st week |
| | | | | | | 2nd week |
| Off | Off | Off | Off | Off | | 3rd week |
| | | | | | | 4th week |
| | | | | | | 5th week |

Daily working time 7.2h

*Source:* Hartz (1994), p. 76

**Figure 6.6**   Manpower requirements

**103.000**

| | |
|---|---|
| Rest | 15.700 |
| Salzgitter | 7.800 |
| Emden | 9.400 |
| Kassel | 14.200 |
| Braunschweig | 5.700 |
| Hannover | 14.000 |
| Wolfsburg | 36.400 |

30%
15%
34%
48%
25%
20%
15%
41%

**71.900**

| | |
|---|---|
| | 13.300 |
| | 5.200 |
| | 5.000 |
| | 10.700 |
| | 4.500 |
| | 11.900 |
| | 21.300 |

1993                1995

*Source:* Hartz (1994)

collective bargaining agreement. The agreement states that workers are obliged to accept an assigned job but only if it is suitable for them. Criteria for suitability are the former job, the qualification, income and place of residence. The works council and management both have to agree on the suitability; if they do not, the decision is made by a special committee. The conciliation board has final appellate jurisdiction.

The working time element of the Volkswagen model with all its re-gulations has already been implemented successfully. But the exist-ing manpower overshoot cannot be controlled in the long run simply by reducing the working hours. Consequently, the part-time employment and qualification elements have been introduced.

### The part-time employment element of the model

The idea behind the part-time element is a 'contract' between the younger and the older generation. It enables younger workers, after they have finished their apprenticeship, to start working step by step to gain full employment instead of becoming unemployed. They start with a 20-hour working week for the first two years. After these two years the working time changes to 24 hours per week for the following 18 months and after 42 months they are employed on a full-time basis. The part-time element for the older workers functions in the opposite way. They can reduce their working time at the age of 56 down to 24 hours and have the possibility to go down to 20 hours after their 59th birthday (Hartz, 1994, pp. 81–7).

Whereas younger workers have to accept the conditions of part-time work, older workers are free to choose if they wish to work part time or not. So far 1,500 apprentices from 1994 onwards had a chance to stay employed, although at the price of distinct income reduction. Nevertheless, their income is still double compared with their training allowance. Older workers hesitate to accept the part-time element because it has a long-term consequence on their future retirement pay. Volkswagen still has to bargain over an appropriate design of the compensation payment for legal and company pensions. But so far the incentives to work fewer hours are not attractive enough because of their disadvantages. Theoretically, more than 21,000 workers over the age of 50 years could participate in the part-time element over the next few years and provide more job opportunities for the younger generation. As a result this remains a problem for Volkswagen to solve. So far only 400 additional jobs could be offered to former apprentices starting work on a part-time basis (Rosdücher and Seifert, 1994, p. 8).

Up to now, all the elements of the Volkswagen model achieve the goal of maintaining employment and cutting labour costs. Savings with the introduction of the 28.8 working hour week amount to 1.6 billion DM and the part-time model will allow another substantial cut in labour costs (Hartz, 1994, p. 68).

The additional benefit of this element is rising productivity, assuming that shorter working periods are less tiring and enable greater efficiency despite the effect on motivation due to temporary job security. Nevertheless, the qualification element is more balanced in meeting both the need to cut labour costs and rising productivity.

### The qualification element

The qualification element of the model is based on a three- to six-month break. The main target group consists of employees between 18 and 30 years and singles, which amounts in total to 42,000 employees at Volkswagen. It is expected that advantage will be taken of this opportunity by the workforce, when offered.

The options for the individual employee are the fulfilment of private plans, the opportunity to gain further qualifications outside Volkswagen or to join a training programme in the newly founded Volkswagen coaching unit (Hartz, 1994, p. 80). The coaching GmbH is the result of outsourcing the personnel development department of Volkswagen. Its main functions are to train and develop production workers and to be a consultant for continuous improvement processes through workshops and training courses for moderators. In addition, it is responsible for management development at Volkswagen. The attached International School of Integrated Management offers training courses on various subjects for managers from different companies and branches. Besides these core activities it also runs labour economic projects, co-operates with universities, and benchmarks experiences and knowledge of other international companies (Hartz, 1994, pp. 144–61).

The concept behind the qualification programmes offered by the coaching GmbH is the so-called M4 employee – the future employee at Volkswagen (Hartz, 1994, pp. 112–27). This vision, which applies to blue-collar workers as well as managers, contains four elements:

1   multi-skilled and multi-functional (*mehrfachqualifiziert*);
2   mobile (*mobil*);
3   creative (*mitgestaltend*);
4   human (*menschlich*).

Thus changes in job design in terms of job enrichment and job enlargement ought to be expected and appreciated by the staff. In order to control personnel placement and to be able to practise advanced manpower planning, Volkswagen demands that employees are willing to change their place of residence if necessary. The company also counts on the ability to improve issues related to the job and to the production process, with supervisors being empowered to implement suggested changes. Last but not least, the workforce should be committed to the company and involved in their jobs. The individual worker is seen as a human being and should be given the possibility of improving his or her skills.

During the qualification time, workers are paid 68 per cent of their last net income by the employment service. This is due to the fact that this qualification time is formally treated as short-time work in the sense of the German Employment Promotion Act (Section 63 IV Arbeitsförderungsgesetz). On top of this the workers receive an allowance from Volkswagen which can be up to 80–95 per cent of their last monthly income depending on their wage group (Rosdücher and Seifert, 1994, p. 11).

The main advantage of the qualification element for Volkswagen is the opportunity to upgrade its workforce without any interruption in production and while also receiving governmental subsidy. Besides the positive effect of getting a flexible and highly skilled workforce, Volkswagen can also adjust the usage of this model to the economic situation – the better it is, the less qualification time will be offered. On the other hand, it is not necessarily an advantage for the workforce to be put on a qualification scheme. First, they have some loss in income and, second, they cannot expect to get a different job or any rise in pay after the training. But in the long term the model reveals advantages for Volkswagen and the employees. Through the investment in human capital the individual worker makes a contribution to his personal job security. At the same time, Volkswagen invests in its future productivity and enables the company to secure a high man-power standard.

## Volkswagen – a Special Case?

Traditionally, Volkswagen is not a typical company in the German industrial landscape. First, 20 per cent of its shares are held by the county of Niedersachsen. This is not surprising, taking into consideration that Volkswagen was in the past a nationalized company. Second, most of its plants are located in industrially weak areas. Moreover, company collective agreements are long established at Volkswagen, which is very unusual in the German industrial relations context. Industry-wide or sectoral agreements are standard in Germany. Volkswagen is not a member of the employers' association and bargains directly with the union (IG Metall). Because of a very high union density and intensive co-operation between the IG Metall and the works council the contents of the company collective agreements were always progressive (Jacobi et al., 1992, p. 247).

In contrast with the collective bargaining agreement of the IG Metall for Niedersachsen, Volkswagen provides its workers with better working conditions (for example, additional breaks), higher basic wages, skill-based pay elements and fringe benefits. Approximately 45 per cent of all fully employed workers in Germany have, on average, a lower collectively bargained income than most Volkswagen workers. In total only half the German workforce could bear a 10–12 per cent cut in net income. Therefore such massive reductions in working time could take place only in areas with income well above the national average (Rosdücher and Seifert, 1994, p. 27).

As mentioned above, a precondition for the IG Metall union to accept the Volkswagen model was the temporary job guarantee for the agreed term. Despite the fact that job guarantees are a very sensitive issue even in the German context of long employment relationships, it would be virtually impossible to settle such an agreement on a regional or sectoral scale. Considering the distinct crisis at Volkswagen, with the alternative of making 30,000 employees redundant, the work-force was willing to accept sacrifices. This had substantial influence on the bargaining process (Rosdücher and Seifert, 1994, p. 27). The massive time pressure on Volkswagen and the general will to find a common solution made such an innovative agreement possible within less than one month (Peters et al., 1994, p. 168).

To conclude, the Volkswagen model is an individual solution under special company conditions. But it points towards a more flexible, company-based approach to solve such problems. Above all, the Volkswagen model is proof that unconventional problem solutions are possible in economically tough times – if employers use personnel planning instruments in a creative way and if the employees are willing to renounce outmoded preservation of acquired rights.

---

## Questions

1  Explain what is novel and distinctive about the VW model.
2  What are the likely long-term consequences of the model for VW workers?
3  What are the likely consequences of the VW model for the operation of the local labour market?
4  Could a similar solution be adopted by other companies?

References

Bach, H. and Spitznagel, E. 1994: Modellrechnungen zur Bewertung beschäftigungs orientierter Arbeitszeitverkürzungen, *IAB-Werkstattbericht*, **2**, 25 January, 13–21.

Clement, R. and Röhreke, H. 1994: Beschäftigungsprobleme und strukturelle Fehlentwicklungen, *Wirtschaftsdienst*, **74**(6), 291–7.

Hartz, P. 1994: *Jeder Arbeitsplatz hat ein Gesicht.* Frankfurt am Main/New York: Campus.

Jacobi, O., Keller, B. and Müller-Jentsch, W. 1992: Germany: codetermining the future, in Ferner, A. and Hyman, R. (eds), *Industrial Relations in the New Europe*, Oxford: Blackwell.

Kuhlmeyer, G. 1994: Das Volkswagen-Modell, *Karriereführer*, **2**(15), 31–3.

Nolte, D. 1994: Die Strukturkrise in der Automobilindustrie – Entstehungsursachen und Perspektiven, *WSI-Diskussionspapier*, **(6)**.

Peters, J., Schwitzer, H., Volkert, K. and Widuckel-Mathias, W. 1994: Nicht kapitulieren – trotz Krise und Rezession, *WSI Mitteilungen*, **47**(3), 165–71.

RKW 1990: *RKW-Handbuch Personalplanung*, 2nd ed., Neuwied: Luchterhand.

Rosdücher, J. and Seifert, H. 1994: *Die Einführung der '4-Tage-Woche' in der Volkswagen AG*, Berlin: Schriftenreihe der Senatsverwaltung für Arbeit und Frauen, No. 4.

Volkswagen, A. G. 1993: *Vereinbarung zur '4-Tage-Woche' (28,8 Std./Woche)* Wolfsburg.

Womack, J. P., Jones, D. T. and Roos, D. 1990: *The Machine that Changed the World.* New York: HarperCollins.

# 7

# The Danish Patent Office

## How and why OD interventions can fail

### HENRIK HOLT LARSEN

The Danish Patent Office (DPO) is a government agency ensuring the industrial property rights of companies by issuing patents and registering trade marks, utility models, designs and chips (Sinding et al., 1994). Until the early 1980s the organization was very traditional and old-fashioned. So, although its domain is dealing with the latest inventions in business, it was in itself a very non-progressive organization. However, in the mid 1980s, the organization went through an intensive organizational development (OD) programme, as a result of which a system of autonomous groups with collective leadership was established. After this a number of interesting HRM processes were initiated (management development, performance appraisal, vision management, training programmes, and so on). To the great surprise of just about everybody, an organizational survey showed in 1992 that there was much dissatisfaction with the collective leadership model. Hence, it was abandoned and instead managers were appointed, a new performance-based compensation system was established and formal assessment of managers and non-managers was introduced.

## Background

In 1983 the strategic position of the DPO was very difficult. For a number of years, the Danish Government had postponed the decision whether Denmark should accede to the so-called European Patent

Copyright John Storey 1996, Blackwell Cases in Human Resource and Change Management

Convention (EPC). This agreement implies that applications can be filed directly at the central European Patent Office, thus reducing dramatically the need for a proper Danish Patent Office. This explains why for a number of years the Government had been reluctant to allocate resources (mainly manpower) to the DPO. However, this meant that applications were piling up in the DPO and the waiting-time for applications to be dealt with also increased. This created frustration among customers, and lengthened considerably the period during which applicants did not know if they would obtain a patent.

## Process

When in 1983 the Government refrained from acceding to the convention for the third time, it was decided to allocate more manpower to the organization on the condition that the organization became more effective. Consequently, a major organization development programme was initiated. It included a vast number of interviews, seminars and communication activities and created an awareness about the present situation as well as a commitment to change this. Eventually it was decided to turn the part of the organization dealing with applications into a number of semi-autonomous groups (sections). In total, approximately 20 autonomous sections were established. It was up to each individual section to choose its own leadership model, but all groups went for collective leadership and were hence sharing the managerial duties rather than having one person managing the group. As a result of this process, six to eight department heads became superfluous.

Although the autonomous group structure implied a reduction in the number of middle managers, it obviously did not make superfluous the need for co-ordination and monitoring of the groups. Hence a system of consultants and co-ordinators was established in the organization, and most of the former department heads were appointed to these jobs. The consultants were providing professional technical support in complex matters and thereby securing the *quality* of the work done. Whenever a section had a complicated technical question, advice could be achieved from one of the consultants. The co-ordinators, on the other hand, were securing the performance, that is, the *quantity* of the performance of the groups. In relation to the autonomous sections, they typically dealt with how the set objectives and work plans could be achieved. It was generally believed that this two-ladder managerial structure was rational and ensured the right balance between quality and quantity in the work of the sections.

The organization developed further, and many development initiatives were launched including radical changes in the information technology systems as well as the introduction of a dialogue-based performance appraisal system. Also, the DPO obtained status as a government enterprise, meaning that the domain of competence of the DPO increased provided that the organization made a certain minimum profit every year. The 'price' for additional degrees of freedom was the obligation to function under common, commercial conditions. Finally, the DPO relocated to a brand new and bigger building with better storing facilities for the 25 million patent specifications. This physical relocation away from an old, dark and dusty building in itself gave a kick to the organizational life and culture.

An event of significant importance was the assent to the European Patent Convention, which came into effect in 1990. As in the early 1980s, the DPO was now at a strategic crossroads. Should the DPO be reduced to a mailbox, forwarding the applications to the European Patent Office, or should it enlarge its area of business and become a technological knowledge and service centre for Danish companies? A major market research project was initiated and the result of this was a clear recommendation to turn the DPO into such a knowledge and service centre for Danish enterprises.

Unfortunately, it still took a while before the Government was convinced that it would be wise to allocate more resources to the DPO, to make the organization more visible to the business community and to market knowledge services based on the patent library, database networks and professional expertise of the DPO. In the meantime the level of frustration in the organization increased significantly. The performance decreased, some of the autonomous sections did not undertake their managerial responsibility and there was an increasing scepticism towards the managerial and organizational structure as a whole.

In 1991 an action-learning based management development programme was started. As there were only very few appointed managers in the organization the programme was open for anybody who was capable of and interested in taking part in managerial processes. It was deliberate that the target group did not consist only of appointed and/or potential managers, as a fairly large part of the organization did not have any managers and there was a strong belief in collective leadership. There were managerial processes, however, and in order to professionalize these the management development programme was initiated.

It was also decided to carry out an organizational survey, which was named 'OD 92'. Surprisingly to most groups in the organization, there was a widespread dissatisfaction with the collective management form. Hence, top management decided – after having discussed the issue with staff representatives – to abandon the autonomous group concept and appoint formal managers for all sections. The managers were all recruited internally but had to go through a comprehensive selection procedure including psychological testing by an external consulting firm. In total, about 20 middle managers were appointed. Some of these managers had been section heads in the previous hierarchical organization (up until the mid 1980s), but for most of the newly appointed managers this was their first formal managerial position.

Shortly after this the performance appraisal system was supplemented by a mutual assessment procedure between managers and their subordinates. The manager assessed the subordinates and the subordinates assessed the managers. (The above-mentioned dialogue-based ('soft') appraisal system was designed as a deliberate contrast to the 'hard' performance ratings.)

A performance-based compensation system was also introduced. These various initiatives all reflected a move towards a more hard-nosed business environment with emphasis on measuring performance, providing feedback and individualizing the work environment (quite a contrast to the previously dominant collective and egalitarian culture).

## Results

The case shows an organization which, in the first wave, changed identity from being low-key, invisible and reactive to being more outspoken, aggressive and progressive in terms of managerial practice (that is, the autonomous work groups), but which in the second phase tightened up the organization, reintroduced appointed managers, established comprehensive performance measurement schemes and became customer oriented, knowledge-based and visible. This all happened in a decade and had considerable consequences for the middle manager role. In the initial period managers were mostly appointed on the basis of their professional (functional) qualifications (mainly as engineers or lawyers). In the second phase the organization had done away with most middle managers and replaced them with collective leadership. In the third phase the middle managers were reintroduced, being appointed on the basis of their managerial skills and given wide-ranging power.

## Discussion

The case illustrates the fact that organizational change processes may mean a decrease in the number and significance of middle managers, but that this does not preclude the same organization at a later stage reestablishing a 'thick' middle management tier.

The case also illustrates the dynamics of autonomous work groups. The groups in the DPO actually fulfilled most of the requirements of self-managed teams: functionally interrelated tasks, a high degree of self-determination, collective control, distribution of tasks within the group and feedback and evaluation in terms of the performance of the whole group (Gulowsen, 1972; Wall et al., 1986; Wall & Martin, 1994). They all went for collective leadership rather than selecting a section head by peer nomination. They presumably wanted 'the real thing', that is, self management, but they ran into the following problems:

- The groups found it difficult to make unpopular decisions of a managerial nature.
- The dual management structure (with consultants and co-ordinators) did not work, and the groups suffered from this.
- The groups found it difficult to solve personnel problems within the group.
- It was difficult for the organization in general to find out who to contact in an autonomous group, and that created confusion and waste of time.
- Management development and the identification of management potential were difficult, at least in an individualized form.

These problems were felt by the organization but not considered serious enough to cause dramatic organizational changes. Also, the common belief was that the autonomous group concept was a unique feature in the DPO, based on strongly-held democratic values, which represented an advanced and future-oriented managerial style. Hence the groups were retained until the 1992 organizational survey surprisingly showed that the praise of the autonomous work groups was largely organizational rhetoric. The organizational surprise which was the outcome of the survey initiated the displacement of the groups.

Since 1992 a number of new projects have been launched: a Year 2000 strategy programme, ISO 9001, total quality management, a second-generation information technology implementation, and competence profiling for major job categories in the organization (1995 and 1999). A number of informally established teams of managers serve as *ad hoc* feedback channels for top management, as the groups are used for discussion of general managerial issues of strategic importance. By doing this, and providing feedback to the top management, the exchange of managerial experiences among the participants is greatly accelerated.

---

### Questions

1 Why was the organization taken by surprise when it was found that the general opinion was against the autonomous work groups?
2 What could have caused the autonomous group structure to survive, rather than being replaced by a hierarchical structure? Would its survival have been a step forwards or backwards?
3 How can an organization become less dependent on external circumstances?

---

### References

Gulowsen, J. 1972: A measure of work group autonomy. In Davis, L. E. and Taylor, J. C. (eds), *Design of Jobs*. Harmondsworth: Penguin.

Sinding, T., Larsen, H. H., Gironda, L. A. and Sørensen, P. F. Jr 1994: Back to the future: a pendulum in organization development, *Organization Development Journal*, **12**(2), 71–84.

Wall, T. D. and Martin, R. 1994: Job and work design. In Cooper, C. L. and Robertson, I. T. (eds), *Key Reviews in Managerial Psychology: Concepts and Research for Practice*. Chichester: Wiley.

Wall, T. D., Kemp, N. J., Jackson, P. R. and Clegg, C. W. 1986: Outcomes of autonomous workgroups: A long-term field experiment. *Academy of Management Journal*, **29**(2), 280–304.

# 8

# Saarland Steel

*Restructuring and managing redundancy*

## KLAUS-PETER OTTO AND HARTMUT WÄCHTER

A photograph from 1964 shows thousands of workers leaving the Völklinger Hütte at the end of their shift, rushing to the nearby train station. If you visited the site today, you would still see, surrounded by a still-running steel mill and rolling mills, the impressive skyline of the pig-iron production facilities but without the smoke and fumes around it. It has become a monument on the UNESCO World Heritage List. The production of pig-iron has been concentrated in one modern blast furnace further down the valley. This facility provides the raw material to all remaining steel works and rolling mills in the Saarland region: Saarstahl, producing long-products, and Dillinger Hütte, a successful producer of thick plates.

The number of steel-producing and processing units has been reduced to only a few. The number of people employed in the whole Saarland steel industry has gone down from 38,000 in 1973 to 11,800 in 1994. One high point of the crisis was reached in 1986 when traditional German redundancy measures were exhausted but around 3,500 jobs still had to be axed in order for Saarstahl to survive.

The following case describes the redundancy policy of Saarstahl, focusing on the crucial period between 1986 and 1993. The reduction of the workforce was achieved without impeding the ongoing production- and productivity-enhancing methods. What is even more important, the social stability and viability of the region has not been severely disrupted. This is exactly what Germans expect from their economic system, which has been called a 'social-market economy'.

## The social and legal framework

Production, prices, capacities and employment in the steel industry have always been of special concern to the European Coal and Steel Community (ECSC), the predecessor of the European Community (EC). The ECSC integrated the coal and steel sectors in Europe between France, the Benelux States, and West Germany. Originally it was part of the plan to prevent German remilitarization, but subsequently used its authority to control both bottlenecks and surplus in steel production. Of crucial importance in reducing capacity is the accompanying social programme. Within the framework of supranational regulation on the European level, all European countries have developed policies of job security and protection against dismissal. 'In addition to legal restrictions, the labour practices adopted by the private sector have tended to shield workers from changes in production levels to a far greater degree than is common in the United States' (Houseman, 1991, p. 2). This is particularly true for Germany. The Protection Against Dismissal Act (Kündigungsschutzgesetz) stipulates the employee's right to receive advance notice prior to dismissal, provides job security according to seniority, and encourages selection according to social criteria in case of dismissals (Sozialauswahl). For instance, an employer has to prove that there is no alternative job in his company (including the provision of retraining for a new job) prior to giving notice to an employee. This legal obligation is the more severe since it is overseen and upheld by the works council within the firm. Works council participation provides for both strong emphasis on social aspects in management decisions and a relatively flexible adjustment of this principle to situational factors in an individual firm.

Germany has also developed a sophisticated system of employment promotion (Arbeitsförderungsgesetz) and retraining (see Table 8.1). The Federal Employment Agency, a tripartite body funded by contributions from both employers and workers (social insurance principle), has developed a range of measures to re-integrate the unemployed into the work process. However, it has been reluctant to put money into protective measures which could be applied prior to unemployment actually occurring. Budgetary problems, not to mention high unemployment, forced the employment agency to withdraw active labour-market policies in favour of meeting the immediate social needs of unemployed people. The solution described in this

**Table 8.1** System of employment promotion

*Provisions of labour market policy (according to Employment Promotion Act)*

### Unemployment

Depending on the duration of previous employment, compensation payment will be granted for a certain period (maximum 52 months, or two years in the case of older employees), without means testing (unemployment benefit), and afterwards, for an unlimited time, an amount adjusted for savings and income. Availability for work is a prerequisite. In case of temporary lay-offs, short-time wages will be refunded under certain conditions equivalent to unemployment benefits.

### Further training and retraining

For full-time training courses, unemployed people, or people threatened with unemployment (those who have received notice of redundancy) can receive personal allowances slightly above the level of unemployment benefits and reimbursement of the necessary course costs. The courses duration of these courses is generally limited to one or at the most two years. Workers who are difficult to employ will be given priority allocation.

### Public works (Arbeitsbeschaffungsmaßnahmen)

For carrying out work which is supplementary and in the public interest, the Employment Agency can pay project- and employee-related grants up to 100 per cent of the staff costs at standard conditions. The courses is generally limited to one or at the most two years. Workers who are difficult to employ will be given priority allocation.

### Wage subsidies for new employment

For certain target groups of unemployed people (those who are difficult to employ, older employees, etc.), the Employment Agency grants various forms of wage supplements in the case of recruitment to a firm. This may be paid over several years and with decreasing interest rates.

case study attempts to develop an alternative, but is still bound by these restrictions.

The most striking feature of the German social market economy is the highly developed system of co-operative and corporatist industrial relations–co-determination in particular. The well-known co-determination system in Germany (for an overview, see Ferner and Hyman, 1992) has taken on a particular form in the steel industry, traditionally considered a key sector of an economy, with special importance for arms production. Here, the most far-reaching legal worker-representation system in a firm's decision making was established in 1951. Not only do worker representatives, both company employees and union officials, have an equal number of seats on the supervisory board, but also a neutral outside member of this board casts the decisive vote in case of a tie between the two factions.

Moreover, the acting board (Vorstand) must include a labour director who cannot be appointed against the wishes of the majority of the worker-representative members on the supervisory board. This has developed into a tacit understanding that the newly appointed labour director will be nominated by the union and, in fact, not infrequently comes from their ranks.

As a result, there is a special relationship between the labour director and the works council, leading to a climate of negotiating and bargaining in good faith which goes beyond the collaborative relationship already existing in most German firms.

The actual practice of co-determination in German firms has transformed their decision-making process and their culture. Co-determination is based on the legal institutions but has developed into an elaborate system of give and take, a system in which conflicts are dealt with in a relatively rational way, close to the point where they have emerged.

Figure 8.1 shows the integrated communication lines and joint committees, both on the company level and beyond, typical of all large coal and steel companies in Germany. There is a network of mutual influences between management, worker representatives and the union. Figure 8.1 is based on an internal paper from a German steel company. Although it is simplified, because worker representatives in the individual firms and the various subsidiaries complicate the picture, it represents well the self-image of this organization. Three aspects are particularly striking:

1 The intricate interlocking between works council and acting board, which demonstrates the close co-operation on all matters pertaining to employment, remuneration, social policy, and quality of work. This entails heavy works council involvement in economic issues of the firm, such as market changes, investments and new technologies, as well as direct influence on personnel policy of the firm.

2 The deep involvement of the firm's decision-making process in the wider context of the industry, the region and the union structure. This implies a strong impact of the regional labour market situation on the redundancy policy of the firm.

**Figure 8.1**   The system of co-determination in a German steel company

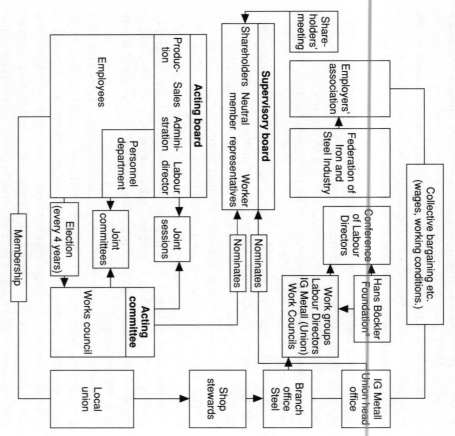

a   The Hans-Böckler-Stiftung (HBS) is a union foundation whose aim it is to foster research and consulting in the area of co-determination and problems of work

3   The perceived marginal importance of shareholders in German companies. Traditionally, in Germany, large companies are considered social institutions, not mere instruments to pursue shareholders' interests. This lack of concern for the capital market, however, has caused severe problems. The lack of a strategically operating capital owner, whether in the form of a company group or a classic owner, led in Saarstahl as well as its predecessor to a partial coalition between management and worker representatives. An over-emphasis on preserving the status quo, instead of an offensive competitive orientation, resulted from this. State subsidies increased this tendency to keep existing structures.

## The Company within the Context of the Steel Market

In order to understand the employment situation of Saarstahl it has to be viewed in the wider context of the steel market and the peculiarities of the steel production process.

The demand for steel follows the business cycle very closely. As a result, considerable changes, sometimes quite unpredictable, are symptomatic of this market. Over a longer period, however, there has been a decline in demand in the industrialized countries of Western Europe, the US and Japan since 1973. In the developing countries, on the other hand, demand has increased consistently. This increase was accompanied by a building-up of capacities in threshold countries. The production of these plants not only satisfied the increasing demand from developing countries, it also put additional pressure on steel plants elsewhere, particularly in times of economic downswing.

In the industrialized countries steel consumption is increasingly inelastic in relation to a growing GNP, the reasons being mostly structural (Kerz, 1991, p. 21). Steel is under considerable competition from substitute products, such as aluminium or plastics. Also, the efficiency of steel making and the quality of steel have been vastly improved, particularly in Japan and Western Europe. Those companies which specialized and concentrated on high-quality products were the least affected by the crises of 1974 and 1986.

The production process also accounts for specific features of the steel industry. The time-span between an investment decision and actual production is considerable. For instance, although demand dropped dramatically in 1974, capacity was still being increased due to investment decisions during the boom of 1972–3. Also, due to technological advances, the output of existing facilities grew considerably.

Also for technological reasons, it is difficult to react to shrinking demand with a continuous reduction of capacity. Low intensity production is either technologically impossible or – due to high capital intensity – extremely uneconomical. There are large-scale economies, which results in large production units and an oligopolistic market structure. Thus, decreasing demand leads either to collusive behaviour or to fierce price competition. The burden of fixed costs pressures the individual firm into a policy of maintaining a certain level of production and a reduction of prices to low marginal costs.

Apart from Dillinger Hütte, which has always specialized in high-quality thick plates and which has always been under French influence, all traditional production sites in the Saarland region experienced the fierce world-market competition in the mass production of long products. Moreover, the rivalry between the traditional owners (the 'steel barons') precluded co-operation between the sites at any one time, when it had been feasible without too much loss of capacity and jobs.

The market for mass steel products is also marked by competition from 'mini' steel plants, which are producing on the basis of electric power and which use scrap iron as a raw product. The higher flexibility and price competition of these plants put pressure on the traditional steel makers from two opposing sides: they undercut existing price levels in mass products, and they forced the traditional steel mills into making investments in new technology in order to put out more sophisticated products.

The European steel industry as a whole is affected. Since 1974–86 around 200,000 jobs have been shed. Great Britain completed this process earlier, but more radically, and France chose a parallel but more conflict-oriented path of development.

Saarstahl, the long-product producer (wire, rods, girders, and so on) in the Saarland, was hardest hit. Impending bankruptcy of some of the plants eventually forced a merger in the 1970s under the roof of the Luxembourg steel maker ARBED, with heavy financial involvement of the Saarland State and the Federal Government. Three original integrated steelworks (coke works, blast furnaces, steelworks and rolling mills) shrunk to one site with raw steel and steel production as well as sheet and forging works (Völklingen), and two others (Burbach and Neunkirchen) with only rolling trains. Despite efforts to partly restructure the production on to higher-value and therefore more profitable steel types, Saarstahl remained a mass producer under pressure to work to high capacity. The structural problems made themselves felt time and again in close conjunction with economic factors. Over the years the losses led to an excessive debt in the company. The firm only remained afloat through public funding, based on regional politics. As a result of the connection with the coal mines in the Saarland, politicians feared a total collapse of the region. With 12 per cent unemployment in the mid 1980s, the Saarland was one of West Germany's problem regions.

As a result of these different constraints, steel production and employment went down as Figure 8.2 shows. Until the start of the 1980s,

**Figure 8.2**  Rolling mill products and workforce, Saarstahl 1973–1993

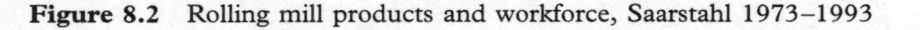

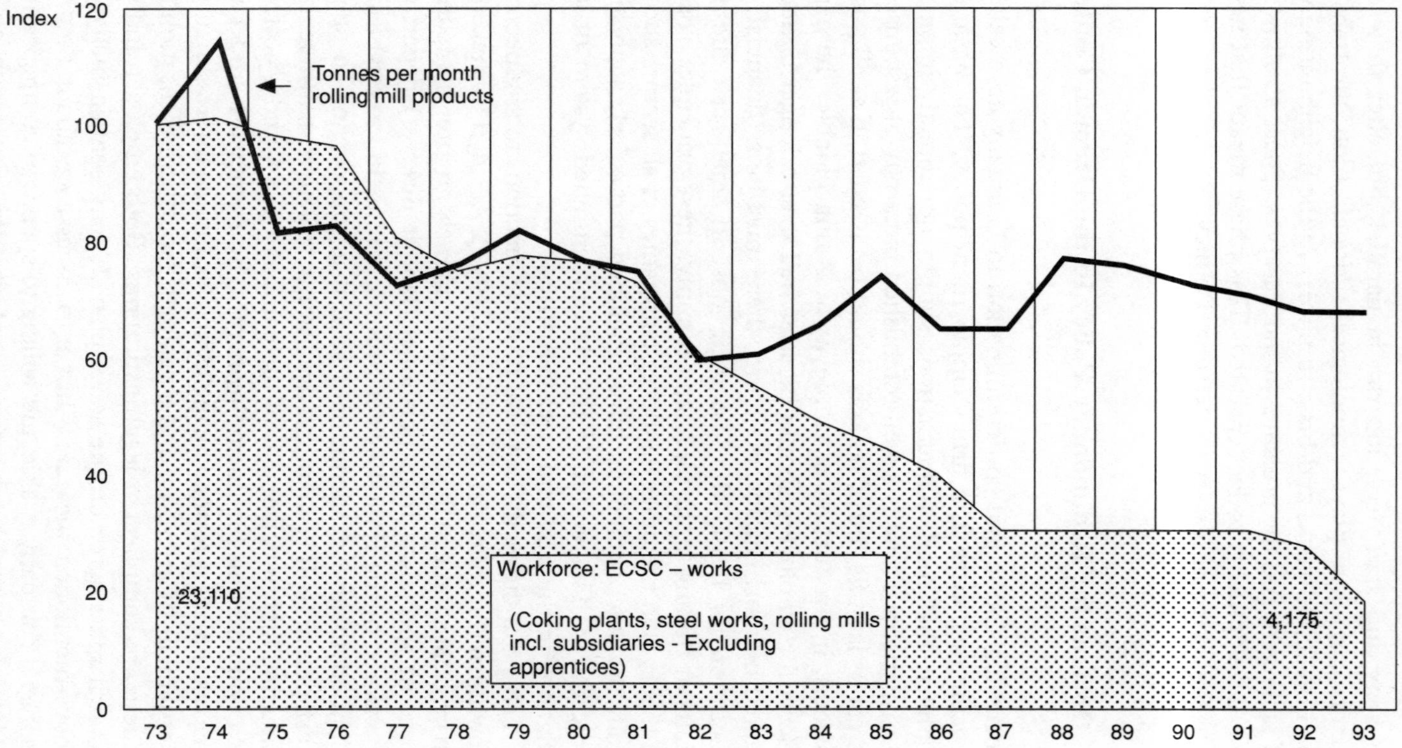

Index

120

Tonnes per month
rolling mill products

100

80

60

40

20

0

23,110

4,175

Workforce: ECSC – works

(Coking plants, steel works, rolling mills
incl. subsidiaries - Excluding
apprentices)

73  74  75  76  77  78  79  80  81  82  83  84  85  86  87  88  89  90  91  92  93

capacity and staff depletion ran in parallel, but after that several factors came into play: technological rationalization, the transfer of pig iron (coke works and blast furnaces) to the neighbouring works of Dillingen, and the pressure on staff reserves. These all allowed the two developments to be separated. This phase meant that new approaches were necessary in personnel policy.

## Options for Redundancy Policy in the German Context

Social legislation and co-determination in Germany have called for specific responses in a firm's employment policy. The basic philosophy is that market fluctuations should not directly impinge on employment. There is a well-established hierarchy of responses to a threat of lay-offs. First, lay-offs should be avoided, if at all possible. Second, if a reduction of employment is unavoidable, the negative effects for employees should be stretched over a longer period and shared by most employees. Third, there must be a (financial) compensation for those who lose their jobs. In small-scale industries, crafts or trading in the German economy, these principles exist only in theory. On the other hand, big companies in all sectors and especially the steel companies have developed particularly sophisticated procedures. This is due to the above-mentioned system of labour relations in the iron and steel industries.

Table 8.2 shows the range of possible reactions to an uneconomic downturn (for more details see Franz, 1993). Again, it was taken from an original source in the steel industry, namely an inter-company task force of specialists from personnel (labour director) departments, sponsored by the Hans-Böckler-Stiftung, a trade union establishment founded to give academic and specialist support for co-operative work practices. It is an impressive list, but still not exhaustive. It indicates the high involvement of the company in avoiding, postponing or compensating for unemployment. The framework under which this takes place is formed by the legal instruments Interessenausgleich (settlement of interests) and Sozialplan (social compensation plan). These are complicated legal institutions. Both employer and works council must agree on the social plan. It may contain many of the above-mentioned measures, but it is in essence about how much money a company is able and willing to spend on compensation for potential or actual disadvantages employees experience with job losses.

**Table 8.2** Personnel policy reactions to fluctuations in employment

**Stabilization of employment in the firm**
- job rotation and transfer to other jobs;
- creation of special task forces (for instance, for clearing up, etc.);
- anticipatory jobs, like repairs, improvement of occupational safety;
- cancellation of task-outsourcing;
- undertaking tasks from other firms, at variable costs only, if necessary.

**Temporary reduction of working time (but no lay-offs)**
- reduction of overtime work;
- anticipatory non-work shifts or holidays;
- leave for further education;
- retraining programmes, additional training;
- short-time work (partly financed by the Federal Employment Agency);
- leasing of employees to other firms;
- leave without pay;
- dismissal with guaranteed re-engagement.

**Permanent reduction of working time**
- hiring stop;
- an end to the transfer of apprentices to permanent employment;
- early retirement, using the legal possibilities;
- early retirement within an agreement with the works council;
- reduction of working lifetime for particularly burdensome jobs (in co-operation with the Social Security Agency);
- reduction of working time for shift workers (partly without compensation);
- voluntary termination of employment with compensation;
- encouragement of self-employment (outplacement).

In this way the protection of older workers is encouraged in principle by legislation, as well as through collective bargaining. In practice, this tendency is circumvented by social plans through early retirement, sometimes from the age of 50. The social programmes of the ECSC, financed from the shared costs of all steel firms, aid this instrument of redundancy policy.

In economic terms such employment practices may be deemed positive, in that they encourage the build-up of human capital. Personnel policy in a firm takes on a responsibility for employment. The practices must be considered negative in the sense of erecting barriers

to the outside labour market and thus discriminating against the unemployed. Whether internal change achieves the restructuring of a
region, or whether in fact the route via the external labour market
increases the flexibility of human resources, remains an open question.

# New Approaches to Coping with Redundancy: the Stahlstiftung Saarland and Employment and Training Company (Beschäftigungsgesellschaft)

Saarstahl found itself in a critical position in 1985–6. Falling prices,
a shortfall in demand and an excessive debt were already almost good
enough grounds for it being declared bankrupt. ARBED sold the
firm to the Saarland regional government for one DM, and then later
on put this property into a joint holding with Dillinger Hütte. In
1985 a political change occurred from the conservative to the more
labour-orientated SPD, and with it new goals for industrial policy
were formulated. The modernization of the economy was supposed
to ensue along with the simultaneous cushioning of classic coal and
steel industries.

When the new steel crisis hit Saarstahl again after a short recovery
from the downturn in the mid 1970s, most of the traditional instruments of redundancy policy were either impossible to implement
(because, for instance, since only 35 per cent of the workforce was
older than 45, there were no further candidates for early retirement)
or they were too costly. If the existing social compensation plan,
which stipulates early retirement at the age of 55, had been put into
practice, the necessary cash would have entailed bankruptcy right
away.

In order to avoid collapse, the company had to shed 3,500 jobs in
a short time and cut costs accordingly. The objectives of the company in this situation were threefold:

1   to assume its social responsibility towards its employees, even in this
    precarious situation, in order to achieve peacefully the inevitable redun-
    dancies in a short time;
2   to secure employment for core remaining employees in order to regain
    profitability and to signal to the remaining workforce that it was still
    worth working, and trying harder, for Saarstahl;

3  to stabilize the regional labour market. Since there were no alternative jobs to speak of, the labour market was not to be perceived of as a dumping ground. The state government was also much committed to this goal and indicated political and – possibly – financial support.

As a complement to the legal possibilities open to the works council in case of mass redundancies (see Table 8.2) Saarstahl was bound to a restructuring contract with the unions from 1978. This prevented redundancy for operational reasons except early retirement. The basis of future action was therefore a new agreement between the steelmakers including the Dillinger Hütte, on the one side, and the IG Metall and the Confederation of German Trade Unions (DGB), the umbrella organization of all industrial unions, on the other. Negotiations in a co-operative and consensus-orientated form took place over several weeks under the overall control of the labour director. The responsibility for personnel policy, including responsibility for those who lose their work in the industry, was defined anew. This demanded a co-operative attitude from the union, too. From management's point of view, the labour director, through his special relationship with the union and the local works council, reached an agreement which allowed for immediate cost-cutting of DM300 million and which otherwise would not have been available under similar circumstances.

A stepwise plan of measures was designed to secure the future of employees while not limiting the company's scope for action. The innovation was the Stahlstiftung Saarland. Figure 8.3 shows the construction and functions of this private foundation. Apart from repeating the traditional means of reduction (there was still an early pension scheme and short-time working when the blast furnace was closed down), it set up a sort of special 'internal labour office' for all steelmakers in the Saarland region in order to swap employees from one site to another without them becoming unemployed ('Personaleinsatzbetrieb').

Formal social selection required by the Job Protection Act was replaced by a 'policy of reasonableness' (*Zumutbarkeit*), defining the crucial aspect of what is considered tolerable for the person involved. This was agreed with the works council and was based on geographical factors (distances to a change of work of 20 to 50 km were nothing unusual), social factors (a new job which matched the worker's qualifications and status) and material factors (equal benefits for early pension or lay-off, wage continuation payment for a certain period for lower paid jobs). Social hardships could be avoided on the spot by the direct involvement of the works council.

**Figure 8.3**    Stahlstiftung Saarland

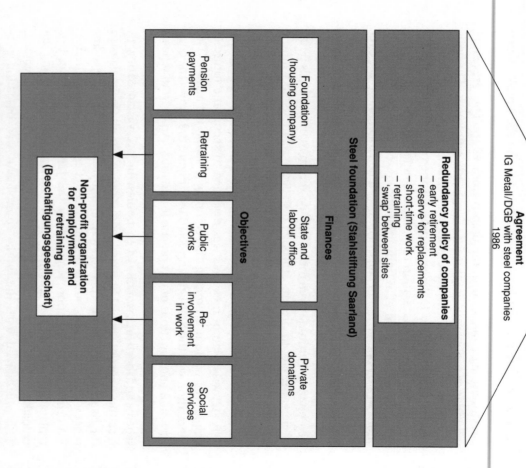

Jobs had priority. Even a change to the Dillinger Hütte, which took over the pig iron production, was reasonable. Over 500 people made use of this opportunity and replaced employees taking early retirement there.

For younger employees, qualification was the next step. However, this had to be organized and financed according to the rules of the

Federal Employment Agency (see Table 8.1), so the company could be relieved from labour costs and course fees. About 300 were put through retraining schemes, mostly using the training facilities of the steel companies. They were retrained to classic skilled jobs of the German apprenticeship system (two years) but they also took part in longer courses in automatization techniques and information technology (an extra three months to one year). The courses ended with a publicly recognized certificate which guarantees the flexibility to work in other industries. Financing the programmes was difficult enough. Qualifying individuals with little motivation and vague perspectives who worry about sitting down to study again, was even tougher. Nevertheless, the majority of those who qualified themselves found work soon afterwards.

So the most important point of the agreement was the creation of an employment scheme, which puts the company in a position to shed employees. They will, instead, be supported by this new agency. This was the creation of the Stahlstiftung (steel foundation) to coach, counsel and retrain the laid-off workers and provide them with a certain amount of compensation in addition to the unemployment benefits. The steel companies were bound to re-hire workers in the event of replacements or new openings.

Dismissals of workers under 55 was, according to the new agreement, allowed only if (1) transition to early retirement was a possibility within the five-year time-span of the agreement, and (2) the dismissed workers were eligible for unemployment benefits; that is, they were officially unemployed and available for public re-employment measures. Only under these circumstances were the union and the works council prepared to agree to dismissals. The labour contract with Saarstahl was officially terminated and, at the same time, coaching by the steel foundation began. In a complicated process of negotiations (management, works council, union, the state as owner, and the Public Employment Agency) the agreement was settled. Legally speaking, the result was the same as a dismissal. The adherence to the described formal act was necessary in order to qualify for unemployment benefits from the Employment Agency. As a result, there could not be a formal guarantee to be re-hired, because this would offset the compensation payment. This was the crucial aspect of the agreement: how can you get employees to give up social benefits (from the social compensation plan) and to trust instead a merely informal promise to be re-hired (the so-called 'moral return ticket')? In practice, a new quality of personnel work emerged, supported by the works council.

Until 1991 the foundation encompassed 2,118 persons formerly employed by Saarstahl. Almost all of them (95 per cent) gave up their job voluntarily and were willing to be taken care of by the Stahlstiftung. Most of them stayed at home, unemployed. Even part-time work is forbidden as long as unemployment money is drawn. In the short term, only a few employees in the region found new work. Subsidies for public works have long-term unemployment (at least one year) as a prerequisite. So the Stahlstiftung could 'only' provide financial security.

The Stahlstiftung is a non-profit organization. It is managed on an honorary basis by top management of the steel company and regulated by a works council representative, the labour director and the public bodies. Its capital is about DM70 million, which is the value of a housing and construction company formerly owned by Saarstahl. The benefits from these assets, donations (mostly from employees) and a large contribution from the State of Saarland constitute a five-year budget of DM78.5 million for the worst case. For the time of public subsidy from January 1987 to the end of 1991, only 45.5 million Marks were needed, however. Payments from the European Coal and Steel Community (ECSC) reduced payments from national and regional governments to approx. DM29 million.

Of that, what needed to be paid was not administrative and overhead costs – Saarstahl was responsible for these – but an increase in the means of the unemployment benefits and of the ECSC fund which the steelworks involved received. The steel foundation guarantees, according to income (a range between 50 per cent for high incomes and 95 per cent for low incomes) a percentage of previous net pay (monthly wage plus shift supplement minus taxes and social security contributions). Social security was guaranteed stepwise for up to five years.

From mid 1988 the economic situation started moving again. It was possible to re-employ about 700 persons in the remaining steel plants on all sites in the Saarland due to a commitment to fill empty positions with laid-off workers. On the practical side, this return to work was organized by the same staff employment bodies (Personaleinsatzbetriebe) which had carried out the redundancy measures. The rest of the workers aged 55 and older could not be re-employed. Until 1992 (five years after the foundation) they went into early retirement according to the existing Sozialplan. Saarstahl carried the cost for this.

The Beschäftigungsgesellschaft was originally founded as a limited company for training and job creation. Training could be realized within the steel industry and through existing external training institutes. So the new subsidy of the Stahlstiftung started two large projects of work creation schemes (see Table 8.1) in the fields of industrial archaeology and revitalization of old, contaminated sites. The projects were financed by the European Social Fund, the Employment Agency, and the State of Saarland. These projects took on mostly 'hard' cases of relatively poorly qualified persons, and developed a programme that combines work and learning. Publicly organized work instead of unemployment proved to be a feasible strategy but, in view of a restrictive job market policy, a marginal one.

The involvement of the company, through the Stahlstiftung, beyond its legal obligations, and the promise of the 'moral return ticket' which the company was able to fulfil, amount to a new quality of human resource management. Massive productivity gains in the remaining works, and the introduction of new forms of co-operation (such as total quality management) would not have been achieved without provisions for basic job security. In this respect the steel foundation can be considered as a signal to the remaining workforce that even in the worst case of impending dismissal the company is committed to re-employment or a reduction of hardship.

In terms of labour market policy, the transition from the Stahlstiftung into new jobs was limited. The wage differences between the steel industry and other jobs is still considerable. Also, the perspective of laid-off workers in the Stahlstiftung has been fixed on the steel industry as a future employer. Also, the main target of the employment scheme, that is, retraining for future jobs, was achieved only to a limited extent (for details see Bosch, 1990).

## The Stahlstiftung in the 1990s

The new idea, Stahlstiftung, helped in overcoming the employment crisis from 1985 to 1987. The employees were secured and the company was in a position once again to stand up to competition. In the middle of 1992 all those in the scheme had been provided for since the beginning. In 1989 Dillinger Hütte Saarstahl was founded as a holding company of the Saarland steelworks. The French group Usinor Sacilor holds the majority, the Saarland State Government is a minority shareholder (25 per cent), and 2.5 per cent is held by Arbed the Luxembourg steel company.

The steel foundation became an instrument for hardship cases, financed by donations and by the company. The foundation was used in case of staff cuts in the context of a general cost-reduction project. At the end of 1992 the number of new cases in the foundation rose to nearly 600, with priority to those in the queue for early retirement from the age of 55 with a maximum involvement in the scheme of five years.

At the start of the 1990s, however, there was another downturn in the economic situation. In May 1993 the losses of Saarstahl AG forced the holding company to file for bankruptcy for Saarstahl AG. The industrial co-operation with Dillinger Hütte over pig-iron production remained afloat, but for Saarstahl the connection with the French steel industry was over. The Saarland State Government assumed a large part of the responsibility. Through staff reductions and the selling off of several companies, the workforce of Saarland steel fell below 5,000. The steel foundation, however, took over a substantial role in social security in this situation. More recent staff reductions of over 2,000 employees and approximately 3,000 plans for early retirement were achieved by the foundation, even with lower performance. Again, they received public support. The Beschäftigungsgesellschaft took over the whole training from Saarstahl AG and a workshop for handicapped people. A new chapter of the foundation had begun.

---

## Questions

1  What are the overall effects of the elaborated personnel policy as shown in Table 8.2?

2  (a)  What are the reasons for the 'moral return ticket'?
   (b)  Why did employees agree to this strategy and give up their jobs voluntarily?

3  Major restructuring in the steel industry has occurred in other countries too. Using your own country (or one familiar to you) as an example, compare and contrast it with the approach adopted in Germany.

---

## References

Bosch, G. 1990: *Qualifizieren statt entlassen. Beschäftigungspläne in der Praxis.* Opladen: Westdeutscher Verlag.

Ferner, A. and Hyman, R. (eds) 1992: *Industrial Relations in the New Europe.* Oxford: Blackwell, ch. 7.

Franz, H.-W. 1993: *Handbuch Soziales Krisenmanagement für Kohle und Stahl.* Luxemburg: Amtliche Veröffentlichungen der EG.

Houseman, S. N. 1991: *Industrial Restructuring with Job Security. The Case of European Steel.* Cambridge, MA: Harvard University Press.

Kerz, S. 1991: *Bewältigung der Stahlkrisen in den USA, Japan und der Europäischen Gemeinschaft, insbesondere in der Bundesrepublik Deutschland.* Göttingen: Vandenhoek & Ruprecht.

# 9

# American Medical Technologies Inc.

*Learning the capabilities needed to implement strategic change*

MICHAEL BEER AND RUSSELL A. EISENSTAT

Such is the pace of change in global competition, rapidly changing technologies and deregulation that corporations not only face the need to realign their organizations but, beyond that, to realign *continuously*. Serial, top-down 'programmes' such as total quality management (TQM) and re-engineering will not suffice to meet this requirement (Beer et al., 1990; Schaffer, 1988). But how can an organization develop the capabilities required for this new form of strategic management? This case study reports on a real-life example of an organization learning to do just that. It is set in the context of comparative studies and interventions made by the authors in a number of American corporations.

## American Medical Technologies

American Medical Technologies is a global corporation with several relatively autonomous divisions. For many years the corporation had been a leader in strategic planning. Satisfied with the quality of its strategies, the company became increasingly concerned about the capability of its business units to implement them. The difficulties the company experienced in implementing a transnational organization, required to support their global strategy, convinced management that the company needed to turn to the fields of organization development and human resources for help. At the same time, the

Chief Executive and a Vice President of Strategy, who had been given responsibility for managing the human resource function, wanted to make the human resource function a strategic one. These forces led the company to the development of a strategic human resource management (SHRM) process. It begins with a 'profiling meeting'. The meeting is intended to spur an ongoing process of organizational diagnosis and change, for which general managers are accountable. SHRM profiles are to be repeated periodically, to measure progress and re-energize a process of continuous improvement.

The SHRM process was designed to complement the strategic profiling process. After a business unit's management team has defined its strategy through strategic profiling, it examines the organization's capacity to implement it through SHRM profiling. The stated purpose of SHRM is to 'develop a vital organization capable of implementing and reformulating business strategy'. This is done by engaging the general manager and his team in an examination of the organization's strengths and weaknesses, but always in the context of the business strategy. SHRM involves the following steps.

*Orientation and planning*

A one-day meeting led by two consultant-profilers introduces the top team to SHRM. At this meeting:

- the purpose and description of the process is presented by the profilers;
- a case study of a business unit whose organization is not aligned with strategy is used to familiarize the group with the analytic framework for assessing strategic alignment and with the problems of managing change;
- the top team re-states its strategy in terms of organizational tasks to be performed and specifies requisite co-ordination, commitment and competence;
- a task force of the unit's best employees, one or two levels below the top team, is appointed to collect data.

*Data collection*

Members of the employee task force (ETF) are trained by the profiler to conduct interviews in all functions, as well as other parts of the company with which the business unit is interdependent. Interviewees are asked to describe the specific management practices and organizational arrangements that help or hinder the business unit in achieving its strategic task(s). The profilers conduct interviews with members of the top team to obtain their views about organizational barriers to strategy implementation and their perceptions of barriers within the top team.

## Three-day SHRM profiling meeting

A three-day meeting is scheduled to enable the ETF to feed back the data it has collected. This is followed by an analysis of the organization's and the top team's effectiveness, the development of a strategically-aligned organizational vision and the development of a change plan. The profiling meeting is designed to promote personal and organizational learning.

*Day 1* The first day of the meeting is devoted to data feedback. The day begins with a presentation of guidelines for communication that will facilitate the clarification and exploration of potentially controversial information (Beer, 1980). While management listens, the ETF sits in the middle of the room and discusses their findings, organized into themes. This 'fishbowl' discussion, interrupted at the end of each theme by questions seeking clarification from the top management team, typically goes on for several hours. We have found that it provides a rich and multifaceted picture of the organization.

After the task force has finished and departed, the profiler feeds back to the top team results from interviews with each of the individual members of the top management team. Almost without exception their perception of barriers to strategy implementation are very similar to those of the task force. Issues of team effectiveness, however, though typically flagged up by the task force, are described in more detail. If the interviews suggest that the role or style of any individual team member, including the general manager, is impeding the group, these issues are discussed.

*Day 2* The second day of the meeting is reserved for diagnosis. The five-box model in Figure 9.1 is utilized in the following manner. The top team lists the patterns of capabilities/behaviour identified as barriers during the previous day (box 1). An assessment is performed – in qualitative and, if possible, quantitative terms – of how deficiencies in organizational capabilities uncovered by the task force have affected financial performance, customer satisfaction and employee satisfaction (box 2). This is followed by an assessment of how problems in co-ordination, commitment and competence might affect the organization's capacity to implement its strategic task(s) in the future (box 3). If the top team is convinced that the task force's findings are material to strategy implementation and performance, then they are encouraged to link SHRM to business issues, thereby legitimizing SHRM and increasing commitment to the process.

The diagnosis involves identifying key design levers and human resource policies within the organizational unit, including the top team itself, which are at the root of the problems identified by the task force (box 5). The top team of the division also identifies corporate policies and practices that cause them difficulty in managing their business. For example, corporate control systems and a sector president's behaviour have been identified in this analysis.

*Day 3* The third day is reserved for the development of a vision of how the organization might be redesigned to implement strategy more effectively (Walton, 1987). The same five-box analytic framework (see Figure 9.1) is used to perform this step. Typically this results in a consensus on how the top team will change its pattern of management; how critical interdependencies will be managed through *ad hoc* teams (that is, business, product development or quality teams); and what people and skills are needed to enact the organization; and what structural, measurement, information and reward systems might ultimately be put in place to support the behaviours specified. When this is complete it is intended that a philosophy of management that captures the new design will be articulated.

The final step in the meeting is the development of a plan for communicating and managing change. The plan should involve members of the task force and others in redesigning the organization and assessing progress towards the new pattern of management.

*Review with employee task force and higher management*

Following the SHRM profile, the general manager and his team meet with the task force to review what they heard and what they plan to do. The profiler is present to facilitate this exchange. The task force meets separately to evaluate the change plan and discusses their reaction with management afterwards. This step is intended to forge a partnership in managing change between management and a group of their best employees. How management reacts to the task force's critique obviously shapes the extent and nature of the partnership.

A review with higher management is the next step. The general

**Figure 9.1**   Diagnostic model of organizational effectiveness

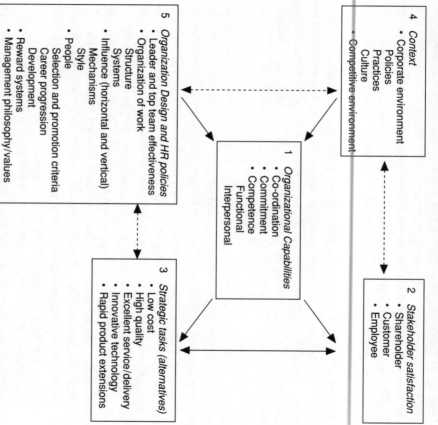

manager, with a profiler present, reviews with his/her boss the task force's finding and the diagnosis and plans for change produced in the three-day meeting. Corporate barriers to division effectiveness which were identified in the diagnosis are also discussed. Progress in organization development is reviewed by higher management, as part of its ongoing business reviews.

*Ongoing monitoring and follow-ups*

The designers of SHRM recommended that a structure and process for reviewing organizational improvement efforts be developed by each management team. A continuing role for the employee task force was envisioned. As difficulties arose, the profilers were to be available for guidance and consultation. On a periodic basis (typically every other year) another SHRM profile is to be conducted to measure progress and reinvigorate the process of renewal. Though several units followed up with a second SHRM profile, many of the organizational units failed to put in place a structure and process for managing change using the employee task force. The effects of this and the reasons for it will be discussed below. They have implications for developing ongoing learning processes in organizations.

## Research Sites and Methods

Strategic Human Resource Management at American Medical began with profiles conducted by the designers in four divisions. This led to application of SHRM profiling at the corporate level. In the last five years profiling has been applied in some 20 organizational units of the company (divisions, staff groups and one sector organization). These have been conducted by key executives from HR and Strategic Planning, trained, through apprenticeship, by the designers.

The findings in this case study are informed by the following sources of data:

- the experience of internal and external profilers who conducted the SHRM Profiles;
- interviews with the operating committee (top management team) and members of the employee task force (ETF) in five divisions and at the corporate level;
- a questionnaire survey completed by the operating committee (OC), the ETF and employees interviewed by the ETF in ten units – in all, over 1,000 employees received a questionnaire and over 500 responded;
- an analysis of barriers to strategy implementation identified by employee task forces in the ten units studied;
- feedback meetings with the top management team and the ETF where survey findings were fed back and discussed.

## Findings

All data sources were analysed to answer several research questions discussed below. Total company mean scores are provided for three groups involved in SHRM: the top team, members of the employee task forces, and those interviewed by the employee task forces. Only major findings are discussed. These are findings supported by major survey trends, interviews and consultant/researcher observations over a four-year period and the response of management to feedback of survey results.

*Did employee task forces identify common barriers to*

*strategy implementation?*

Employee task forces asked a question about barriers to strategy implementation. They then grouped their open-ended responses into themes of their own making. An analysis of these themes showed six common barriers to strategy implementation existed in almost all organizational units. These were (percentages represent frequency of mention):

- difficulties in how the top team works together (100 per cent);
- poor vertical (up and down) communication (80 per cent);
- unclear or conflicting strategic priorities (70 per cent);
- management style (70 per cent);
- poor interfunctional/divisional co-ordination (70 per cent);
- deficiencies in career development and management competence (70 per cent).

We regard these findings as significant. They suggest that underlying organization structure and human resource policies, whose design may be contingent on business environment and strategy, are core management and interpersonal processes which universally block strategy implementation and probably adaptablity. These core barriers appear to represent the organizational capability domains SHRM was intended to investigate and improve: co-ordination, commitment and management competence. Most strategic alignment interventions, structural changes and various programmes do not promote an open and direct discussion of these issues. Indeed, many are designed to avoid their discussion. These are the 'undiscussibles' in most organizations which managers zealously try to avoid, fearing a threat to relationships, careers and self-esteem (Argyris, 1990).

The six barriers are undoubtedly responsible for failure of total quality management, re-engineering, employee involvement and other programmes which fail to achieve their promise (Spector and Beer, 1994; Hall et al., 1993). Most of these sorts of interventions do not force organizational members to confront the six core barriers, or allow them to be explicitly placed on the change agenda. Although SHRM was successful in surmounting these barriers and achieving some change in many of them (see below), other data suggest that a process which requires a regular assessment and review of these inherently threatening issues faces difficulty. Organizations which can overcome these difficulties, however, will have made human resources a sustainable competitive advantage.

## Did SHRM surface previously hidden but relevant issues?

Responses of top management teams and employee task forces to the feedback process embedded in SHRM support the conclusion that SHRM makes it possible to discuss previously undiscussible data. Task force members are initially extremely nervous about discussing the barriers they identify in their interviews. There is a great deal of emotion just before the profiling meeting. Task forces typically joke about the 'messenger being shot'. The top management team also finds the feedback difficult. A general manager captured this when he recollected two years after he participated in an SHRM profile that 'we didn't know what we were getting into'.

Despite the difficulties, the process was perceived to be relatively open by operating committees and the employee task forces across the ten divisions. Survey responses showed that members of ETFs perceived management to listen and to be open to influence. Scores on listening and openness were among the highest obtained in any of the organizations we have studied (see Table 9.1).

The openness and relevance of the employee task force's findings is best captured by a division president who used SHRM to realign the division he had just taken over. A new competitor had entered the market but neither his top team nor the organization fully comprehended the implications. He was able to confirm and enrich his diagnosis, and to develop support for change, using the SHRM process:

SHRM allowed us to discuss the undiscussible; it got things on the table that would have taken me years. Getting feedback from the employees is indispensable, and putting it in a strategic context is important. We were there to discuss behaviours that were consequential; it wasn't personal. We discovered things that would help us succeed or that were preventing us from succeeding. They were strategic issues, such as delivering the goods and services to our customers better than

**Table 9.1**   Survey findings

| | Scores (Overall averages) (n = 527) | Operating Committee (n = 113) | Employee, Task Force (n = 79) |
|---|---|---|---|
| *The situation when the SHRM process began* | | | |
| The division faced business challenges that were critical to our ability to compete | 3.8 | | |
| The division president saw the SHRM process as very important in helping the division improve its effectiveness | 3.9 | | |
| All members of the division's top management team strongly supported the SHRM process | 2.8 | | |
| In initiating SHRM this division's management intended to improve business results | 3.8 | | |
| In initiating SHRM this division's management intended to improve employee welfare | 3.2 | | |
| The division initiated SHRM because it was a corporate mandate | 3.2 | | |
| *The process during the SHRM profiling meeting* | | | |
| The profiler made significant positive contributions to the overall success of the profiling meeting | | 3.9 | 3.7 |
| I felt I could be open in raising and discussing all significant issues during the profiling meeting | | 3.8 | 3.9 |
| The top management team accurately heard what the ETF reported | | 3.9 | 3.5 |
| The SHRM action plans developed by the top team effectively addressed the issues raised by the ETF | | 3.3 | 3.0 |
| The top team demonstrated openness to critique and further feedback from the ETF | | 3.7 | 3.2 |

**Table 9.1** (cont.)

| *Follow-up after the profiling meetings* | *Operating Committee (n = 113)* | *Employee, Task Force (n = 79)* |
|---|---|---|
| The results of the SHRM profile were effectively communicated throughout the division | 3.4 | 3.0 |
| The ETF and the top team worked as partners in implementing the SHRM action plans | 3.0 | 2.5 |
| The profiler established an ongoing working relationship with divisional management and helped us with problems experienced in implementing change after profiling meetings | 3.1 | 2.7 |
| The HR function in this division has played an important role in helping the division implement the changes emerging from the SHRM process | 3.0 | 2.4 |

All items about the process were rated on the following 5-point scale:

1 = to a very little extent
2 = to a little extent
3 = to some extent
4 = to a great extent
5 = to a very great extent

our competitors. Once we decided it was strategic, we had to fix it or suffer the consequences; no one is willing to suffer the consequences of gradual loss of competitive position.

We have found the SHRM process, up to and including the first day of the three-day meeting, to be extremely robust. It has never failed (in American Medical and several other companies) to elicit a similar open and constructive dialogue between the task force and management. There are several reasons for this. The process asks management to select their best employees. This raises the credibility of the feedback and makes rejection of the data difficult. Moreover, the ground rules and the 'fishbowl' method have proven to work very effectively. As the quote above suggests, because the data is collected in response to questions about barriers to strategy implementation, managers accepted the data as valid and relevant, despite the fact that many issues point to their own ineffectiveness as managers. Except for new division managers, all general managers saw SHRM as defining a personal and organizational development agenda they felt compelled to pursue, although with different levels of success.

### Did SHRM result in an improvement agenda?

In all profiles management developed an action plan for change. When purposely challenged by the researchers in survey feedback meetings about whether American Medical should continue with SHRM, given only modest change scores, the CEO and other managers responded angrily that we (the researchers) did not understand how important the process was to them in setting an agenda for change. Top management's commitment to the SHRM process is reflected by the generally higher (more positive) mean scores they had on virtually all survey items and categories.

Top management commitment to SHRM is also reflected in the fact that SHRM profiling has been conducted over the last five years in organizational units in all parts and levels of the company. This does not mean, however, that SHRM is working in the way originally conceived. Indeed, the high commitment to SHRM at the top, and less support at the bottom (see below), points to a major problem in developing an organization capable of learning.

### Did SHRM spur actual organizational change?

Interviews in five divisions, and observations of internal and external profilers, indicate that the following types of change initiatives can be attributed in whole or in part to SHRM:

- cross-functional product development and business teams;
- changes in the product development process – for example, documentation and efforts to prioritize;
- changes in structure and roles – for example changes to a sector president's role following the corporate profile;
- changes in top team functioning – types and quality of meetings, more open communication and cohesion;
- changes in the general manager's behaviour;
- changes in staffing – hiring, transfer and replacement of people;
- strengthening of functional organizations, such as engineering or quality;

- re-examination of strategies and allocation of resources where barriers between functions and businesses previously precluded effective discussion;
- improved interfunctional, interdivisional and line-staff co-ordination;
- improved vertical communication.

Survey responses showed, however, that those surveyed saw only modest change in the barriers the ETFs identified, and only modest progress in accomplishing the strategic tasks identified at the start of the SHRM profiling process. In response to a set of standardized items about the extent of 'corporate revitalization' (used in previous research on corporate change by Beer et al., 1990), employees perceived a modest amount of change. Compared to six other companies responding to competitive pressures with a corporate revitalization initiative, American Medical ranked in the middle.

An examination of items most and least changed 'since SHRM began' showed two erstwhile barriers to strategy implementation (the top team and poor cross-functional co-ordination) were perceived to have changed the most. But little or no change occurred in perceptions that people are promoted on the basis of skills in managing others, that employees can raise difficult issues with higher management, that American Medical policies and practices encourage hard work, or that the company has an interest in the welfare and satisfaction of employees.

It is significant that employees perceived little or no change in issues relating to their welfare and motivation. We believe this reflects both the character of the company and, therefore, the character the profiling process acquired. The company's focus on strategy meant that issues about the employment relationship, such as career development, did not get the attention they deserved. Our previous research suggests that, unless employees perceive that the change is intended to increase their welfare, they do not support it (Beer et al., 1990). We have concluded that the process must be modified. As opposed to being content with allowing issues of management philosophy to emerge from SHRM, as it did in many SHRM profiles conducted to date, management should state their philosophy in advance. The employee task force can then investigate the extent to which the management's espoused philosophy is in fact practised in the organization. Mohrman and Cummings (1989) recommended that 'valuing' should occur early in the process of self-design, and our research supports that belief.

### Did SHRM lead to reformulation of strategy?

One of the objectives of SHRM was to develop an organization capable of not only alignment with strategy but also reformulation of strategy. Several SHRM profiles identified that strategy was not clear to lower levels. Often, lack of clear priorities indicated underlying disagreements about strategy. In other instances, lower-level people who interface with customers or other external constituencies raised questions about strategy. When these were discussed by the top team, lack of agreement or understanding about strategy was revealed. In several instances management developed plans to engage in a strategic profile to develop a new strategic consensus. We discovered, however, that more focus was needed on how the organization identifies new threats and opportunities, and propose that this question be addressed directly by the task force. Finally, the data-collection process will be expanded to include interviews of customers.

### Did a partnership between management and lower levels develop?

Without exception, top teams perceived more progress on strategic tasks, barriers to strategy implementation and organizational revitalization than did ETF members. ETF members, in turn, saw more change than did the employees they interviewed. Interviews and observation lead us to conclude that the problem lies in management's assumption that SHRM profiling, like strategic profiling, is a tool for the top management team. In almost all divisions the operating committee did not use the employee task force to help them in redesigning the organization and in assessing progress, something the consultants recommended. Only one division is an exception to this, and in that division the gap in perception between the operating committee, employee task force and those interviewed is much smaller.

When top management was confronted with this data, and our conclusion that they had not created a partnership with employees, their response was revealing. They saw it as management's role to make decisions based on the agenda set in SHRM. They regarded it as a challenge to management's role to maintain the employee task force as an active redesign team. Consider the following thoughts articulated by a division manager who had not yet gone through SHRM profiling:

I have two concerns about the process: first the danger of diffusion of accountability – now the team is accountable not the general manager; second, delays in decision making, given the need to create consensus. When the chips are down, it is an individual that is responsible to the shareholders – one individual is responsible. Once you get this in place, it is a new religion. You can't take away that responsibility for results. It is religion that the group owns it, and the group makes decisions.

While we may not have been as clear as we might about the partnership philosophy underlying SHRM, the discussions with managers about this issue convince us that a self-design process, intended to promote ongoing organizational learning, is limited by hierarchical assumptions about where design decisions should be made. We believe that the assumptions we uncovered exist in many companies. The good news is that discussions of our research findings has provoked the company to reconsider its assumptions, although it is too early to know the final outcome.

*How much support is there for SHRM?*

A mixed picture emerged regarding SHRM. Employees perceived that various parts of the top team are divided in commitment to SHRM and saw only 'some' consensus among key managers about the ongoing need for SHRM. Considerable differences existed in perceptions of support between top teams, ETF members and those interviewed by the ETF. Top teams perceived a great deal of support, while those interviewed by the ETF saw only some support. Considering that SHRM is a mechanism for giving voice to lower levels in redesigning the organization, this finding is both surprising and important.

*Why is support mixed?*

Survey responses and discussions with management and the ETFs of several units revealed some potential answers to this question.

According to many at lower levels, SHRM is 'invisible' at the grass-roots. Some attributed this to the inability of employees to connect changes in the organization to the SHRM profiling process. Top management, as mentioned above, was not surprised at this. SHRM was an agenda-setting process to them. They did not understand or commit to making employees 'partners' in the process. These managers assumed that, like strategic profiling, SHRM is a tool to inform management so they can analyse and decide. It is now becoming clear to them that SHRM has embedded in it assumptions and values which they must embrace if they want more than an episodic tool for correcting strategic alignment problems. Whether SHRM should be more than this is a question the company is struggling with now.

Some thought that the SHRM profile put so much 'on the table' that much of it had not been worked through. Therefore follow-up was difficult, and that in turn led to ambivalence about the process at lower levels. Still others thought that SHRM did not receive more support because it was perceived as an additional burden – not a business improvement process. This perception directly contradicts one of the design objectives of SHRM – to be a business improvement process that also develops the organization and its human resources. Both survey responses and interviews suggest that the assumptions about degree of follow-up required, and the extent of actual follow-up, may partly explain the invisibility of SHRM to many employees. The fact that most management teams could not or did not want to work out how to involve the employee task force in ongoing change is consistent with these findings.

Survey findings indicate that profilers and the HR function were perceived to be relatively uninvolved in helping division management implement action plans. In discussions at feedback meetings some wondered whether HR should be involved in follow-up. These problems must be solved if a good follow-up process is to be developed. In general, items relating to follow-up were lower than other items about the SHRM process. This is consistent with the experience of the external profilers, who were unsuccessful in convincing management of the need for follow-up to support team formation. Mohrman and Cummings (1989) recommend that a project manager be appointed to co-ordinate a large-scale change process of the kind SHRM is designed to promote. Our experience suggests how important the commitment of this resource is, but also how difficult it is for management to accept the need for such a resource and to develop the role and skills needed for the job.

*Does SHRM develop a learning organization?*

The findings regarding the 'invisibility' of SHRM at lower levels suggest that, while SHRM may have opened a window for improved communication and change, the window did not remain open. It is essential that the SHRM process involves as wide a circle of employees as possible, and that they understand how energy invested in the three-day profiling meeting is connected to action in the organization. Without making that connection, SHRM will slowly lose its credibility and effectiveness as a tool for organization and management development.

As we concluded above, part of the problem with follow-up lies in management discomfort with the collaborative process we envisioned. That discomfort could have been overcome, however, if higher-level management had systematically reviewed the results of SHRM and held managers accountable for developing organizational and managerial effectiveness – one of the design objectives for the process. That did not happen in most instances.

Higher management did not review SHRM results and follow-up for several reasons. It is not yet part of their formal management control process. Time pressures may be partially responsible. The main reason, however, appears to be their own discomfort and lack of skill in discussing difficult issues with subordinates. In effect, the review is an organizational performance appraisal which provides insight into the general manager's effectiveness. Handling this discussion requires interpersonal competence and management values that the process itself is designed to develop. Hence this is a difficult problem to solve. Management has now committed itself to reviewing results, and we are developing training to enable them to do it.

There is an even more fundamental reason why SHRM has not yet become a continuous organizational learning process. Survey respondents reported that their capacity to 'raise with higher management difficult issues (such as concern about the effectiveness of other managers or the strategic direction of the business)' had not changed materially. Though SHRM creates an opportunity for open dialogue, it apparently does not develop interpersonal and organizational capability to sustain that dialogue. Without that capability lower levels cannot confront higher levels with inconsistencies between what they said they are going to change and what in fact they are changing. Without the capacity to discuss difficult issues the organization cannot self-correct the self-designing process.

Our experience suggests that we should have made much more explicit and clear that SHRM requires interpersonal enquiry skills and a culture to support it (Argyris and Schon, 1978; Senge, 1992). Unless employees can raise difficult issues in real time, lack of follow-through by management must wait two years before another SHRM profile is conducted. Unable to surface their growing cynicism, employees become reluctant to raise issues and lose commitment to engage in improvement efforts. We have discussed these issues with top management and have recommended that the development of enquiry skills and an enquiring culture should become an explicit objective of the SHRM process.

## Conclusions

The SHRM project at American Medical has revealed the difficulties corporations face if they want to institutionalize an organizational learning process aimed at developing an organization capable of implementing strategy and learning. We discovered that the knowledge and skills required to manage a process of diagnosis and change, which appropriately involves members of the organization, are not widely distributed in the management population. Therefore we conclude that an implementable organizational learning process will have to be specified in more detail than the current SHRM process, and over the full cycle of learning.

We consistently erred on the side of under-specifying the process. As a result, managers avoided doing some things they should have done or made errors in actions they did take. How do you handle negative data about a manager or department in a way that is fair but responsive to a task force that has raised this issue? When and how do you replace someone whom you have decided does not fit and cannot learn the 'new way'? How does top management hold managers accountable for improving their own effectiveness, and that of their organizations, while also providing a supportive environment for development and learning? How does one create a partnership without abdicating decision rights and responsibilities? How does one create a role and skills for HR personnel or others inside the organization to co-ordinate and catalyse an organization renewal process? Specifying a process that guides managers through dilemmas and, as a byproduct, also teaches them how to manage those dilemmas is the only way we know to develop learning that does not become a failed training programme. Of course, over-specifying runs the danger of creating a cookbook that loses the larger meaning.

A competitive world requires management processes and skills that have not yet been invented. Waiting for them to occur in the environment and studying these innovations as distanced researchers is not, we believe, the best or the fastest way to develop usable management knowledge. Collaboration between knowledgeable organizational researchers and managers is much more likely to yield superior interventions, particularly when those interventions require interpersonal behaviour regarded by many managers as an unnatural act. Action research enables the development of specifications for processes that do not come naturally, given history and social context. Engaging management in a co-investigation provides the means for developing those specifications over time. Researching the SHRM process collaboratively with management has allowed us to confront management and ourselves with underlying assumptions and values that neither we or they were aware of. For example, we became co-opted by the culture of the company when we failed to recognize that the process became so focused on strategy that it missed engaging the organization in deeper issues of management philosophy and values.

Despite early confrontation with management about the importance of potentially painful feedback from lower levels, we did not push hard enough on the importance of developing interpersonal enquiry skills because we sensed resistance from management. Finally, we believe that the profiling process itself is a powerful organizational research tool. The data is collected by organizational members relatively economically, and it provides a rich understanding about the dynamics of the organization. Perhaps more important than defining precisely specific relationships between a few variables, we are better off learning about the direction of relationships among many variables.

One of the most difficult aspects of a developmental change process is the requirement to engage in discussion of difficult and often painful issues. We argue that underlying the core barriers identified by employee task forces is the inability of organizational members to engage in an open, fact-based dialogue (see also Argyris and Schon, 1978; Argyris, 1990). While processes like 'Work Out' at General Electric and SHRM at American Medical create a window for an open, fact-based dialogue that leads to error correction, as currently designed these processes in themselves do not develop an organization capable of learning.

Perhaps the most important conclusion concerns what we call 'psychological fitness'. By this we mean managers' capacity to engage in an open, fact-based conversation. That fitness involves, among other skills, learning how to receive feedback without loss of self-esteem, to collaborate without feeling out of control and to own up to weaknesses without feeling incompetent. A process like the one we developed requires these skills and also indicates how to develop them. That is one of its greatest promises but also one of the biggest challenges.

Without psychologically fit managers, an organization is prevented from becoming a high-performing learning organization. It remains to be seen whether these skills can be developed and/or whether organizations must obtain them through selection. If these skills are to be developed, an institutionalized process like SHRM is probably the only way. The managers we have been working with describe SHRM as a powerful tool precisely because it does engage the organization in tackling underlying capability deficiencies blocking effectiveness and also because SHRM shows how to develop these capabilities or identify those who cannot develop them. But to survive, the tension between its role as a developmental process and an assessment process must be managed. Our experience suggests that the capabilities SHRM identifies are the core skills in an effective organization. They will be in greater demand as organization adaptability becomes important in a more competitive world.

---

## Questions

1  Describe, in your own words, the methodology for developing strategic capability as outlined in this case.
2  To what extent could other organizations emulate this process?
3  What is the theory of human resource and change management which underlies 'SHRM profiling'?

---

## References

Argyris, C. and Schon, D. A. 1978: *Organizational Learning*. Reading, MA: Addison-Wesley.

Argyris, C. 1980: Strategy implementation: an experience in learning. *Organizational Dynamics*, **8**.

Argyris, C. 1990: *Overcoming Organizational Defenses*. Boston, MA: Allyn and Bacon.

Bartlett, C. 1988: *Management Across Borders: The Transnational Solution*. Boston, MA: Harvard Business School Press.

Beer, M. 1980: *Organization Change and Development: A Systems View*. Santa Monica, CA: Goodyear.

Beer, M., Eisenstat, R. A. and Spector, B. 1990: *The Critical Path to Corporate Renewal*. Boston, MA: Harvard Business School Press.

Biggadike, R. 1990: Research on managing the multinational company: a practitioner's experiences. In Bartlett, C. A., Doz, Y. and Hedlund, G. (eds), *Managing the Global Firm.* London: Routledge.

Hall, G., Rosenthal, J. and Wade, J. 1993: How to Make Reengineering Really Work. *Harvard Business Review*, November–December.

Mohrman, S. A. and Cummings, T. G. 1989: *Self Designing Organizations: Learning How to Create High Performance.* Reading, MA: Addison-Wesley.

Schaffer, R. 1988: *The Breakthrough Strategy: Using Short–Term Success to Build the High Performance Organization.* Cambridge, MA: Ballinger.

Senge, P. 1992: *The Fifth Discipline.* New York, NY: Doubleday Dell.

Spector, B. and Beer, R. 1994: Beyond TQM programs. *Journal of Change Management*, **1**(2), 63–9.

Walton, R. 1987: A vision-led approach to management restructuring. *Organizational Dynamics*, **15**.

# PART III
# Key Practice Areas

# 10

# Optus

*New recruitment and selection in an enterprise culture*

DAVID E. SIMMONS, MARK A. SHADUR AND GREG J. BAMBER

## Background on the Australian Telecommunications Industry

Telecommunication services in Australia were provided by government-owned monopolies. In the 1990s, however, the Australian Government sought to deregulate the market to increase competition as a means to improve services and cut prices. There are close parallels between the Australian experiences in telecommunications and those in other countries, including the UK.

The former telecommunications monopoly, now known as Telstra, was a large, bureaucratic organization operating like a government department. Several reforms were introduced to increase competition, including the awarding of a long-distance and international telecommunications licence to Optus in 1991; and the sale of Aussat (formerly a public-sector enterprise that operated the Government's communications satellite) to Optus.

In contrast to Telstra, Optus was more or less a start-up company with a much smaller workforce and without a history of unionization (except in the former Aussat section). Optus aimed at taking market share from Telstra by competing in terms of price and customer service. To this end Optus directors sought to develop a company that was efficient, customer focused and dynamic. As it was mainly a greenfield enterprise, Optus management paid close attention to the recruitment and selection of employees in an effort to mould an enterprise culture that would engender high employee commitment in a union-free environment. In the words of the human resources (HR) director of Optus, 'the mainstay of developing the culture that we want is recruiting the right people'.

Optus is owned by a consortium. The Australian share is 51 per cent and comprises two insurance companies: the Australian Mutual Provident Society and National Mutual; and a transport company, Mayne Nickless. Bell South (USA) and Cable and Wireless (UK) together own the other 49 per cent.

Since deregulation in 1991 the Government has maintained control of Telstra; however, further deregulation, culminating in the privatization of Telstra by the end of the 1990s, is expected for several reasons, including political pressure and the opportunity to raise funds from the sale. The Telstra–Optus duopoly will remain only until June 1997, with the Government committed to open competition from then. An independent industry watchdog, AUSTEL, attempts to monitor the market. However, it appears to have less influence on the industry than its US or UK counterparts.

Some businesses favoured Optus as they had an impression that Optus would offer lower prices and better customer service. The unions assumed that Telstra's reductions in its employment would be correlated with the success of Optus in winning market share. One senior union official commented that the competition 'was fabricated', with the playing field 'sloping' to provide 'obvious advantages for the new player'.

By the mid 1990s Optus had won approximately 14 per cent of the long-distance market and a third of the mobile phone market. Optus had spent more than A$ 1,000 million establishing its fixed and mobile networks; however, due to the start-up costs, Optus had not yet realized a profit but was expected to do so by early 1996.

## Industrial Relations and Union Involvement in the Industry

Unions have had a strong presence in Telstra and have had an important role in the industry. There are currently two major unions in the industry: the Communications, Electrical and Plumbers Union (CEPU) and the Community and Public Sector Union (CPSU). The CEPU generally covered technicians while the CPSU covered office personnel.

Australian industrial relations (IR) is in a period of reform. There is an increasing decentralization of collective bargaining, although there is still a centralized framework (see Davis and Lansbury, 1993, pp. 100–26). The Australian Industrial Relations Commission (AIRC) is encouraging the adoption of enterprise-based agreements to supplement the centralized framework, while the national framework provides a safety net of minimum entitlements. Unions have sought to use enterprise bargaining to their advantage, by increasing union participation at the workplace while maintaining the protection of the safety net. Many employers have attempted to increase the flexibility of their employment relations and to distance themselves from the centralized award system. Telstra and Optus have each adopted enterprise agreements. However, the experience of both companies was very different. Telstra maintained extensive union involvement, with agreements in 1994 between Telstra and the unions which provided for increased management–union consultation.

Optus chose another path. Legislation provided for a new type of agreement: the Enterprise Flexibility Agreement (EFA). EFAs can be negotiated with employees without direct union involvement (for example, through a ratification process in which employees vote on the agreement). Optus management won the consent of its employees and the AIRC endorsed an Optus EFA. The agreement recognized the CEPU as the sole union to have coverage in Optus, but in practice the CEPU had little role in arranging the EFA and actively campaigned against the EFA.

## Getting Optus Started

Before analysing the issues relating to recruitment and selection in Optus it is necessary to understand the organizational context, including the attempts by key executives to focus on human resource management (HRM) and organizational culture and the adoption of the EFA. The outline of this HR/IR context provides the basis for the subsequent discussion.

Despite the legacy of the initial Aussat employees, Optus executives aimed to redefine the organization as a 'start-up venture' without a traditional organizational culture or structure. According to Optus management, this enabled Optus 'to start from scratch, unencumbered by an existing network base consisting of several generations of technologies' (Optus, 1992, p. 3). Several strategies were adopted to develop what Optus executives argue is a unique culture. Optus's espoused values include leadership, achievement, teamwork, empowerment and customer satisfaction.

The initial Optus executives decided to break from more traditional IR arrangements, such as those found in Telstra. Optus attempted to develop HRM systems that would provide above-average working conditions and pay and would foster a direct productive relationship between management and employees; the implication being that if such a model was successful then unions would have only a minimal role at Optus.

Pay at Optus was initially higher than average rates at Telstra. However, the union claimed that while average rates at Optus were initially higher than Telstra they had not kept pace with productivity improvements in the industry or wage increases at Telstra. There were differences between Telstra and Optus; for example, regarding working hours (Telstra 36.75, Optus 38 hours per week) and leave provisions (family leave provided by Optus but not Telstra), but the general view of the union is that conditions between Optus and Telstra were reasonably comparable.

One substantial difference between the two companies, is that there is a performance-based pay system for all levels of employees at Optus, and not at Telstra. Employees in all job categories at Optus are appraised on a five-point rating system and this is used to calculate annual salary increases and bonus payments. Optus management sees this as rewarding high performance and as a major factor in facilitating a positive work culture. However, the union argues that there are several problems with this reward system. They claim that there is a forced distribution following a bell-curve, so only a minority can receive the highest ratings (for example, about 5 per cent receive a rating of 5 and 25 per cent receive a rating of 4). The union adds that the rating system places pressure on employees to perform beyond normal work levels (for example, arriving early, finishing late, working through lunch), and encourages a compliant workforce since those who speak out tend not to be rewarded. Management disputes these points.

Despite these claims the union has had little success in organizing Optus employees. Estimates of union membership vary, with union officials claiming a higher involvement than estimated by Optus Management who put the figure at less than 5 per cent, but the level is probably about 10 per cent.

Several factors help to explain the low level of union involvement. First would be the success of the Optus executives at building what Kochan et al. (1991, p. 105) call a 'sophisticated nonunion human resource model'; one in which employees feel they have very little need for collective representation. Other factors include the advertising campaign that the union ran against Optus. Consequently, many Optus employees saw the union as being hostile to their best interests and therefore did not join it. Another factor is the relatively low average age of the Optus employees. Younger employees (for example, less than 25 years of age) are less likely to be union members than are older ones (Australian Bureau of Statistics, 1992).

In the absence of a strong union presence Optus executives argue that they are successful at developing a cohesive and positive corporate culture and point to the employee survey and the EFA to support this claim. Optus managers inferred from a 1994 employee opinion survey that Optus employees were generally satisfied. Some of the key findings are in Tables 10.1 and 10.2.

The consultant who undertook and analysed this survey concluded that there was a high level of consistency between the responses of managers/supervisors and those of staff; between men and women; and between departments. The consultant argued that this suggested a 'strong overall culture and set of work practices have been achieved which influence all employees'.

## Customers without Employees

Recruitment and selection at Optus was an early and major issue. The shareholders began the recruitment process by selecting an enthusiastic senior management team. The Optus CEO had formerly worked for McDonald's and was described by senior managers as a charismatic and people-oriented leader. The Chief Operating Officer (COO) of Optus was from Cable and Wireless. He had been involved in the start-up of Mercury Communications, the new entrant when the British telecommunications industry was deregulated in the 1980s. The COO brought two other Cable and Wireless executives with him and recruited four executives from Bell South. Another four Australian executives were recruited to make up the top team of executives.

In addition to the original 300 Aussat employees another 130 managers in total were recruited from Cable and Wireless (60) and Bell South (70). These managers came to Australia on two-to three-year

**Table 10.1**  1993 employee opinion survey[a]

| Question | Unfavourable responses % | Neutral responses % | Favourable responses % |
|---|---|---|---|
| I am pleased with the degree of success Optus is having in the marketplace | 2 | 6 | 92 |
| Optus as a service provider relative to other service companies in Australia | 1 | 10 | 90 |
| I feel proud to tell other people I work for Optus | 2 | 11 | 87 |
| I feel comfortable to express a view which is different from other team members | 7 | 10 | 83 |
| Rating your team at meeting the commitments they make to other teams | 2 | 18 | 80 |
| The level of commitment made by Optus to training | 9 | 12 | 79 |
| I am clear on my individual responsibilities and performance objectives | 11 | 12 | 77 |
| The commitment of Optus people to go the 'extra mile' to get a result | 5 | 19 | 76 |
| Your team members at meeting commitments they make to you | 4 | 20 | 76 |
| Senior management takes an active part in communicating the Optus vision and values | 16 | 21 | 63 |
| Optus operates in a manner which is aligned to its stated vision and values | 15 | 27 | 58 |
| The quality of my work is overly compromised by trying to achieve too much too quickly | 31 | 30 | 39 |
| Other departments take the time to understand our needs and requirements | 36 | 36 | 29 |

**Table 10.1**  (cont.)

| Question | Unfavourable responses % | Neutral responses % | Favourable responses % |
|---|---|---|---|
| The policies and processes I need to do my job are appropriately defined | 33 | 30 | 37 |
| The decision-making processes enable the organization to respond quickly to business needs | 30 | 29 | 42 |

[a] There were 2,103 useable responses from 2,460 employees, representing an 85 per cent response rate

**Table 10.2**  The Optus employee opinion survey: questions relating to the employee's understanding and the perceived application of the Optus Values

| The Optus Values | Understanding U:N:F | Application U:N:F |
|---|---|---|
| Ethical standards | 4:15:81 | 8:22:70 |
| Leadership | 6:19:75 | 20:30:50 |
| Achievement | 3:15:82 | 9:24:67 |
| Teamwork | 4:12:84 | 17:27:56 |
| Empowerment | 10:21:69 | 27:31:42 |
| Customer satisfaction | 1:9:90 | 4:18:78 |

*Note:* Responses are grouped according to the percentage of employees who answered Unfavourable (U): Neutral (N): Favourable (F)

contracts to assist with the start-up. Bell South tended to provide more of the sales and marketing people, while most of the Cable and Wireless expatriates were on the engineering side. Most of these executives were replaced after about four years.

Optus recruited heavily in its first 18 months: over 100 employees per month. Employee numbers then remained relatively stable for a year before starting to rise again. These recruitment efforts occurred when many other companies (for example, Telstra and IBM) were downsizing in a recession. Consequently, one advertisement might elicit over 2,000 applications.

In discussing the specifics of the early recruitment process, the COO argued that the Aussat personnel provided a good engineering and technical talent base. He stated that 'what we had to find quickly were the sales, marketing and administration managers and staff. But most people assume we've recruited all the fallout from Telstra. That is not the case' (quoted in Plunkett, 1993).

In total, about 20 per cent of Optus technical service employees had worked for Telstra at some stage, but in customer service less than 2 per cent had done so. Optus did, however, recruit extensively from the information technology (IT) industry. In the words of the HR director:

We are on guard to ensure that we don't fall into the trap of just whole-sale recruitment . . . especially of groups that have worked together. We see that not as an advantage but as a distinct disadvantage. They come in with preconceived ideas, generally closed minds in terms of how you do things. So we have a very diverse workforce and we see that as a strength.

Optus attempted to recruit employees first, on attitude and, second, on technical competencies. In most fields, therefore, it was not important to recruit employees from the telecommunications industry. One manager argued that attitude is especially important in customer service sections, where you can train people in technical skills but you cannot train them to be 'nice'. Potential Optus employees must be deemed during the selection process to possess a high degree of enthusiasm and empathy, values that the company wished to be reflected back to the customer. Also important was the ability to hire a group of employees who had personal values which corresponded with the Optus corporate culture.

## Recruitment and Selection

The structure of the recruitment and selection process for customer service personnel is sketched below. The case shows how the different stages of recruitment and selection developed from years one to four. This process was used for mass recruitment during a phase of rapid growth.

## Consultants

During the start-up Optus used consultants to assist in the recruitment and selection process. This was necessary because: (1) employee requirements were higher than forecast; (2) there was a large number of candidates to process; and (3) Optus HR resources were preoccupied with internal HR issues. By year four, Optus had attempted to internalize much of the recruitment process.

Optus attempted to limit the number of consultants to three or four at most. The consultants were assessed through a process involving interviews, presentations and reference checks. Optus aimed to employ consultants who were, of course, highly skilled, but also preferred those that had a corporate culture similar to the espoused values of Optus. The successful consultants then participated in the Optus Challenge, the induction programme for new Optus recruits (discussed below). Optus wanted the consultants to have background information on the company and what was expected of new employees. Optus expected that such information would aid the consultants in choosing the most appropriate employees for Optus.

## The stages in recruitment and selection

*The consultancy approach*  In year two, the recruitment and selection process involved five stages. It took up to six weeks for successful candidates to proceed through this process.

*Stage 1*  Although the advertisements tended to elicit a large number of responses, typically as few as ten were chosen. Those who replied to the advertisement were sent an information pack and were asked to participate in a group meeting.

*Stage 2*  Group meetings involved 20 candidates who worked on 'value-based activities'. These included designing an advertising campaign for Optus and dealing with a simulated customer. A selection panel (including consultants) observed the group, watching for such attributes as the ability of the candidates to work effectively in a team, leadership qualities and empowerment (the last gauged by examining how well candidates could work without instructions).

*Stage 3*  Candidates who were successful through the group stage then had a one-on-one interview. This was a standardized interview with a consultant who examined their attitudes and skills.

*Stage 4*  The company saw reference checking as 'absolutely critical to Optus in terms of checking the values of the employees'.

Stage 5   If successful through stages 3 and 4, candidates then had a panel interview. The panel interview was the final hurdle before being offered a position with Optus. Three candidates were interviewed by two Optus managers (an HR manager and another relevant manager). All three or none of the candidates could be successful in the panel interview.

*The Optus approach*   By year four most of the recruitment and selection process had been brought in-house. A team leader was selected and trained to manage the process. In two years the total processing time for candidates had shrunk from six weeks to ten days. The Optus approach then involved six stages.

Stage 1   A position was advertised and people were asked to call at the weekend, making it easier for potential candidates.

Stage 2   Those interested had a brief telephone screening. Candidates' phone manner and some background information was assessed.

Stage 3   If successful in stage 2, candidates had a half-hour telephone interview that assessed their background, attitude and values.

Stage 4   Optus maintained the group exercise process used by the consultants, but by year four the group process involved two exercises. The first involved a team-working activity (similar to the consultancy approach) and the second was a multi-skilling test (for example, candidates had to speak with someone while doing some task with their hands).

Stage 5   A candidate was interviewed by an HR staff member and a line manager (the line manager with whom the successful candidate would be working).

Stage 6   Reference checking occurred concurrently with stage 5 and was the last hurdle for candidates.

If they survived this process, recruits were offered positions. The HR team attempted to develop an induction programme that reinforced the values, such as teamworking and empowerment, that were stressed in the recruitment and selection process.

## Induction

The primary method for inducting new recruits was the Optus Challenge. Initially the Challenge was a two-day programme in which groups of 25 new employees participated in team and personnel development programmes with at least one Optus director. But under the Optus approach, Challenge was changed to a one-day course.

The course occurs within a few weeks after new employees have been with Optus. It introduces employees to its vision and values, so they have an initial feel for the culture. Managers discuss Optus and explain what is expected of recruits. The Challenge is expected to reinforce the recruitment process. In addition, recruits are given positive and negative examples (in the view of senior management) of past practices. Recruits are also told who they should speak with in relation to problems they might have. A union organizer argued that the Challenge encouraged employees not to go to the union with problems. Instead, the Challenge reinforced the goal of senior management to deal directly with their staff on all issues. A senior CEPU official also criticized the Challenge programme for not including unions in the process. When Mercury commenced operations in the UK, the unions were uncooperative in relation to interconnecting Mercury to the existing network. To avoid the problem that occurred in Mercury, Optus obtained an agreement from the unions that ensured smooth interconnectivity but, in return, Optus agreed to allow the union 'to participate in an agreed sector of the orientation period'. This involvement would have allowed the union to put forward their case to encourage union membership during the Challenge but, according to a senior CEPU official, 'Optus never honoured that agreement'.

## Who was selected

Approximately 90 per cent of Optus's new employees were between 20–25 years old, with a high percentage of these being recent university graduates. This age group was not specifically targeted; however, candidates from this age group tended to be more successful in the selection process. There are many possible explanations. The selection process focused on attitudes rather than skills, with the notion that Optus wished to attract enthusiastic people who could be developed as employees. Younger candidates would be less likely to carry cultural baggage from another enterprise. A senior HR manager also argued that younger candidates were more proficient in many areas of the selection process including the teamworking and multiskilling activities.

Subsequently Optus recruiters attempted to target more mature people. However, Optus managers found that the younger university graduates were more successful once they had joined Optus. It is probable that university graduates were more accustomed to learning several different tasks and adjusting to changing systems. Optus, especially during its start-up, was continually changing its systems (systems which, even when stable, were based on multiskilling). Senior management accepted that for the first few years of operation, until the systems became stable, Optus would remain a young organization.

Labour turnover was approximately 10 per cent throughout the company in year four, with higher levels in customer service areas. The HR director argued such turnover levels reflected the lifestyles of the average 20–25 year old who did not remain in one position for a long period of time. Absenteeism, on the other hand, was 'below average'.

## Discussion

The CEPU had several reservations about the selection process. A senior union official stated that, initially, Optus recruited young, tertiary-qualified employees, who would 'accept rapid change in an unquestioning way'. Many were placed in customer service positions and were led to understand that they could move fairly quickly into more challenging positions, such as in marketing or through promotion. However, Optus has a flat management structure and scope for vertical advancement is consequently limited. Accordingly, the CEPU claims there has been a high rate of attrition, with labour turnover in the customer service area between 17–20 per cent in years three and four.

Notwithstanding these claims by the union, Optus management considers that the recruitment and selection process has been one important strategy that helped to create a positive work culture and that Optus has made enormous achievements in moving from a start-up operation to a substantial and dynamic telecommunications company. Management points to the success of Optus at fielding large teams in sporting events and other outings as an implicit indication of the cohesion of the workforce (for example, the team of 400 in the popular Sydney 'City to Surf' road race was the largest corporate team). Optus executives also stress the high marks on the employee survey and the acceptance of the EFA as tangible indicators of employee commitment to the enterprise.

## Questions

1   What were the pros and cons for Optus in having recruited young, tertiary qualified staff for lower level positions such as customer service?

2   Should Optus management have involved the union more closely in its selection and induction processes? Explain your answer. What are the advantages and disadvantages for Optus of closer union involvement?

3   How appropriate were the steps in the recruitment process of: (a) the consultancy approach; and (b) the Optus approach? Justify any changes that you would recommend.

4   How important is it to recruit and select employees with the values that match those of the organization? Explain your answer.

5   What are the special considerations involved in recruiting and selecting employees for a greenfield enterprise compared to those for a well-established organization?

## References

Australian Bureau of Statistics 1992: *Trade Union Members Australia*. Canberra: Australian Government Publishing Service, August, Cat. No. 6325.0.

Davis, E. and Lansbury, R. D. 1993: Industrial relations in Australia. In Bamber, G. J. and Lansbury, R. D., *International and Comparative Industrial Relations*, London: Routledge.

Kochan, T. A., Katz, H. C. and McKersie, R. B. 1991: Strategic choice and industrial relations theory: An elaboration. In Katz, H. C. (ed.), *The Future of Industrial Relations, Proceedings of the Second Bargaining Group Conference*, Ithaca, NY: Institute of Collective Bargaining, Cornell University.

Optus 1992: *The Power of Choice*. Sydney: Optus Communications.

Plunkett, S. 1993: Optus, building Rome in a day. Australia's new telecommunications carrier fourteen months on. *Business Review Weekly*, 2 April.

# 11
# Manuflex plc

*Introducing equal opportunities*
LINDA DICKENS

Manuflex plc is an electrical engineering company based in the English Midlands, employing around 350 people. It is family owned and control has recently passed to Chris, the 34-year-old son of George whose own father started the business.

George sees the handover to Chris as a good opportunity to modernize the company, something which they both consider vital to its continued success. Manuflex managed to survive the recession, although with some job losses, and currently has fairly good order books. To remain competitive in the industry, however, both father and son recognize that Manuflex needs to respond to increasing quality demands from customers.

Having lost their major customer two years ago, Manuflex is having to compete for business from a number of different companies and to become more responsive to different requirements. This is thought likely to involve some changes in work organization. Until recently Manuflex did not have what might be called a 'training culture' but the structured development of training is now seen as a key part of the changes required in the organization.

Chris feels that personnel systems as well as production systems should be brought up to date at this time and wants to try to change the culture in Manuflex to one where all people are encouraged to contribute fully rather than just do their job. A new personnel and training manager, Sue Bains, has been appointed to play a key role in this. Sue has worked in the personnel function in the car industry since graduating nine years ago and is professionally qualified in personnel management.

Chris has told Sue that he is keen that Manuflex takes this change opportunity also to do something about equal opportunities (EO) and he is looking to her to provide direction here. He has strong personal views concerning social justice and equality. He feels that women get a raw deal generally in manufacturing industry, certainly compared to the finance sector where his wife is a manager. She was able to take a three-year career break when they had their first child. Chris also wishes the organization to be a good 'corporate citizen' in the local community, which has a higher-than-average proportion of people from ethnic minority groups.

George has some reservations about all this but has agreed that now his son is in charge he will not interfere. However, he does spell out two of his main reservations to Chris:

1  The traditions of the engineering industry cannot be overturned in one company and equal opportunities, however commendable in theory, would be a distraction from the real job of gaining competitive advantage through quality while trying not to increase costs.

2  The management and supervisors have been persuaded of the need to change aspects of work organization in order for Manuflex to survive successfully. George thinks they would resent having to take on the additional burden of worrying about equal opportunities and may even feel their own positions might be threatened: 'we can't afford to jeopardize the goodwill of these people'.

This applies too to the workers. George points out that the union has never raised any grievances about the position of women in Manuflex nor the relative absence of blacks in the company. He reminds Chris of the saying 'if it ain't broke, don't fix it'. The union has been very co-operative in the proposed change programme and George is worried 'that the equality thing might cause problems'.

Chris has a meeting with Sue at which he outlines these reservations, which he recognizes are genuine concerns. He reiterates his own desire that Manuflex should be doing something positive in respect of improving the position of ethnic minorities and women as part of the more general changes which are going to be taking place, but warns that they have to proceed carefully and will need to ensure they gain support for any initiatives rather than simply assume it. He suggests that she should present her ideas to him once she has done three things:

1  Obtained a feel for the current position and the views of some key managers in Manuflex;

2 Reviewed the 'good practice' guidance on equality of opportunity and assessed its relevance for Manuflex;

3 Ascertained what legal requirements there are and what Manuflex might need to do to avoid being found to have acted unlawfully.

This will help provide a basis for deciding key areas for action in Manuflex and for setting objectives (with short- and longer-term priorities). Chris recognizes that they need to have realistic ambitions and a viable strategy for implementation of any ideas.

## Sue's Initial Thoughts

Sue feels that the support of the managing director is of great importance but appreciates that they will not get far if any EO initiative in Manuflex is seen as simply imposed from above.

In her previous company an equal opportunity statement and policy had been developed and handed down from head office but it had had little positive impact. In the plant EO was seen as something owned by the central personnel department and was generally regarded as irrelevant to day-to-day operations. Some line managers had made it clear that they regarded the new requirements and procedures as unwarranted interference by a personnel department concerned with boosting its own importance.

Sue's experience in the car plant was that the very term 'equal opportunities' seemed to get a negative reaction and was equated with preferential treatment or 'positive discrimination'. A number of managers also resented what they took to be an implication that they were prejudiced or had discriminated unfairly in the past.

The car company, however, had succeeded in introducing more formal procedures for recruitment and selection, with proper job descriptions and person specifications and a requirement to monitor applications and appointments. The monitoring data, however, had revealed that the formalization of recruitment and selection procedures had not changed the nature of those being appointed.

## Ascertaining the Current Situation

*Workforce composition and distribution*

The personnel records would allow separate identification of male and female employees by grade but this information is not currently available. No statistics are available on the ethnic composition or distribution of the workforce. Sue forms a rough overview of the position by walking round the plant.

Women appear to make up around a third of the total workforce but, as is common in engineering, there is clear job segregation, with easily spotted 'women's jobs' and 'men's jobs'. Women are working as packers (packing finished components for onward delivery) and as packer-checkers (a higher-graded job which involves quality control functions in addition to packing). All packer-checkers work full time but the packing is done by women employed on a part-time basis who do either a morning or an afternoon shift. Women are also found performing some unskilled production tasks, particularly in connection with what are known as the 'light' products.

Men fill the other production jobs (the majority), doing work generally classified as semi-skilled and skilled, and they also work in the stores.

There is a female supervisor for the packing and packer-checking section; all other production supervisors are men.

In the offices (in a separate building on the same site) there are two male accounts clerks working to the finance manager, otherwise all secretarial, clerical and non-managerial administrative posts are filled by women.

All middle and senior management positions (apart from Sue's own) are filled by men.

It is noticeable that there are very few black or other workers who are visibly from ethnic minorities. The only exceptions are some Asian women who work on the morning packing shift.

*Recruitment and promotion*

Recruitment decisions are made by the relevant line manager. Where vacancies have occurred among the manual workers in recent years they have generally been filled through recommendations made by existing staff or by placing a notice on the gates of the works. Some skilled staff (who are harder to obtain) were recruited directly from other companies in the locality which were shedding staff in the recession. Office staff have been obtained by advertising in the local press as well as by recommendation from existing staff.

Shopfloor supervisors are promoted from among reliable workers. In the past some supervisors have gone on to fill higher management positions.

In a number of cases (for example the production manager) people have worked their way up from the shopfloor, although more recent managerial vacancies (for example the finance manager and the personnel and training manager) have been filled through outside recruitment. The managing director himself normally takes managerial recruitment decisions.

### *Union representation*

The company recognizes the AEEU (the electrical and engineering union) for collective bargaining in respect of its shopfloor workers. The majority of the full-time staff are thought to belong. The long-standing convenor, a craftsman who had worked for the company for 31 years, has recently retired and as yet no one has replaced him. Union full-time officers have rarely been involved in the company.

There was an agreement with a white-collar union in respect of non-managerial office staff but membership was always very low (around 5 per cent) and in practice the agreement has lapsed following the departure some 18 months ago of the woman who had been the union representative.

### Some Management Views

Sue has some informal meetings with management colleagues. The meetings are not about equal opportunities but she takes the chance to introduce the issue into the discussion. She makes the following notes:

*The production manager*  Promoted to the post from within Manuflex five years ago. Welcomes the new developments because they offer a chance of securing jobs in the future; felt that Manuflex risked getting left behind and becoming uncompetitive. Thought that some of the supervisors might not be so enthusiastic, however, since they seemed to see any change as threatening.

Feels that the company already has equal opportunities and that 'to make a big thing of it would be disruptive'. Pointed out that women have good jobs in the office; that the women working part-time in the packing section find the work fits in with their main jobs of looking after their families; that women don't want to do men's jobs on the shopfloor which can involve heavy work and the need sometimes to work overtime.

Noted that management is a male preserve at Manuflex but said that was 'normal for the industry' and 'Manuflex must be OK on sex equality otherwise we wouldn't have appointed you'. He also pointed out the fact that black workers don't apply to the company can hardly been seen to be Manuflex's fault. Mentioned that when they put a notice on the gates announcing a vacancy in the stores recently no black person applied. He thought this was a pity since they hadn't had a lot of response and were now going to put an advertisement in the local paper. It had been difficult to fill some jobs recently 'despite all this unemployment we hear about – it seems the good people already have jobs, certainly reliable workers'.

He feels that they may have to think a bit more about the people they recruit and how they recruit them: 'want to get people who can respond to changing demands'.

*Finance manager*  Appointed from outside Manuflex five years ago. Has been persuaded that the cost of additional training will pay off but wants to keep an eye on training spend: 'you'll have to show it contributes to the bottom line'.

Says his job isn't to worry about 'moral issues like EO' but rather the cost-effectiveness of anything the company does. Suspects any EO initiative is likely to need resources which could be better used elsewhere and perhaps it could wait until the financial position of the company is more secure.

*Employee relations manager*  Has been in post for 25 years and is also responsible for health and safety at the plant. Gets much credit for the relatively good relationship which the company has with the union and workforce. Had a good personal relationship with Jim, the senior union convenor who has recently retired: 'the two of us sorted things out, he kept the lads under control and I made sure that we did not do anything too stupid. Manuflex pays a bit better than what you'd expect to get in this area and we tried to see to it that our good people were looked after when the going got rough in the recession. We had to cut overtime working, of course, and we cut back on some of the indirect staff and discontinued the mum's shift as we called it – evening packing – but generally we came through the recession without too much blood on the floor.'

Thinks a new, younger union convenor might want to push things which Jim had little time for: 'trouble with the new lot is that we let them have time off to go on union training courses!'

Copyright John Storey 1996, Blackwell Cases in Human Resource and Change Management

Recognizes that his focus has been mainly on industrial relations negotiation and fire-fighting as well as 'coping with the mountain of health and safety regulations'. Personnel policies and practices have tended to emerge rather than be developed. He is keen to see this area professionalized and he supported the creation of Sue's post, and her appointment, for this reason.

Made some fun of the 'newspeak' of the MD (noted he uses words such as 'commitment' and 'good citizenship') but recognizes that Manuflex needs to move with the times and thinks Chris will be good for the company.

'Not opposed' to doing something about women and ethnic minorities but 'you can't change society'. Thought that there were some important personnel issues to be looked at first such as high turnover among clerical and administrative staff 'who seem to leave just as they've got to know the computer systems – an exaggeration but it seems like that sometimes'.

## 'Good Practice' Advice

Having gained a feel for the current situation at Manuflex and the views of some key managers, Sue then set about compiling a synopsis of good practice guidelines from various external sources. These included the material published by the Equal Opportunities Commission (EOC) and the Commission for Racial Equality (CRE). The following are highlighted extracts from documents and some notes which Sue made.

An equal opportunity policy aims to ensure:

that no job applicant or employee receives less favourable treatment than another on racial grounds; that no applicant or employee is placed at a disadvantage by requirements or conditions which have a disproportionately adverse effect on his or her racial group and which cannot be shown to be justifiable on other than racial grounds, and that, where appropriate and where permissible under the Race Relations Act, employees of under-represented racial groups are given training and encouragement to achieve equal opportunity within the organisation. (Commission for Racial Equality, 1984)

The Equal Opportunities Commission (EOC) Code of Practice takes a similar line with respect to women. Some companies have equal opportunity policies (EOPs) which include groups other than women and ethnic minorities, for example those with disability, and may also cover religion, sexual orientation and age.

On implementation of EOPs, the CRE advocates:

allocation of responsibility to a suitably qualified member of senior management;

consultation with trade unions or employee representatives;

a statement of the policy and publicity to all employees and job applicants;

training and guidance on law and company policy to supervisory staff and other relevant decision makers;

an examination of existing procedures and criteria for indirectly discriminatory effect, implementing change where this is found;

monitoring of policy through analysis of the composition of workforce and job applicants;

and positive action/remedial action (e.g. language training), as permitted under the legislation.

The EOC gives similar advice in respect of women. Positive action for women could include so-called family-friendly policies, such as workplace nurseries and flexibility in working patterns.

Recent material (and American literature) tends to use slightly different language, talking about the 'management of diversity' rather than 'equal opportunities', with an emphasis on making EO part of business strategy and on the positive benefits to the organization of having and valuing different types of people in the workplace. Business case arguments for taking EO initiatives are emphasized by Opportunity 2000, a campaign for improving the quantity and quality of women's participation in the workforce, and by the CRE in its publication *Racial Equality Means Business* (Commission for Racial Equality, 1995). These arguments concern the way in which organizations benefit from drawing on the skills and talents of a diverse workforce, attracting and retaining good workers, and being more attractive to customers, clients, and so on, as well as avoiding the financial and other costs of unlawful discrimination.

Finally, Sue undertook her third task and summarized the legal situation.

## Legal Requirements and Sanctions

Sue copied tables from one book (Dickens, 1994a) which summarized key aspects of UK legislation and European law (Tables 11.1 and 11.2). There was also a guide to how direct and indirect discrimination are defined in the legislation (Figure 11.1).

**Table 11.1**  Key aspects of UK legislation

*Equal Pay Act 1970 (amended by Equal Value (Amendment) Regulations 1983)*  Equal pay and other contractual conditions for men and women where engaged on same or similar work; work rated as equivalent by job evaluation, or where work is of equal value.

*Sex Discrimination Act 1976, SDA 1986*  Prohibits direct and indirect discrimination in all areas of employment on grounds of sex or married status. Sex may be a genuine occupational qualification (GOQ) in specified circumstances (including for reasons of authenticity, decency and privacy; delivery of a personal welfare service; certain employment in a single sex establishment). Special treatment permitted in respect of pregnancy and childbirth; and to encourage applications from, and to provide training for, under-represented sex. Discriminatory terms in collective agreement or employers' rules rendered void.

*Social Security Act 1989*  Equality in occupational benefit schemes (including health insurance and pensions).

*Employment Protection (Consolidation) Act 1978 (as amended)*  Maternity rights (maternity leave, with pay; right to return after leave); time off for ante-natal care.

*Race Relations Act 1976 (not applicable in Northern Ireland)*  Prohibits direct and indirect discrimination in all areas of employment on grounds of race, colour, nationality, ethnic or national origins (includes some religious groups, e.g. Sikhs and Jews). Race may be a GOQ in specified circumstances (including authenticity, delivering welfare service). Special treatment permitted to encourage applications from, and to provide training for, under-represented group. Particular action allowed by local authorities.

*Fair Employment (Northern Ireland) Act 1989 (not applicable in Great Britain)*  Outlaws discrimination on grounds of religious belief or political opinion. Employers required to register with Fair Employment Commission, to monitor religious composition of their workforce and, in the case of employers of over 250 people submit

**Table 11.1** (cont.)

monitoring returns annually. Required to take 'affirmative action' where imbalances are evident, such action enforceable by the Commission.

***Disabled Persons (Employment) Act 1944*** Duty on employers with 20 or more staff to employ a quota of 3 per cent registered disabled people. Registration is voluntary. Provides for reserved and sheltered employment.

***Companies Act 1985*** Requires employers with over 250 staff to state in the directors' annual report how their policy has operated with respect to people with disabilities, registered or not.

**Table 11.2** Relevant key European provisions

***Article 119 of the EEC Treaty*** Directly applicable. Equal pay for equal work between men and women

***Equal Pay Directive 1975 (75/117/EEC)*** Extends Art. 119 to include equal pay for work of equal value

***Equal Treatment Directive 1976 (76/207/EEC)*** Outlaws sex discrimination in all aspects of employment

***Equal Treatment Directive (state social security) 1978 (79/7/EEC)*** Equality of treatment in all state benefits except pensions

***Equal Treatment Directive (occ. social security) 1986 (86/378/EEC)*** Equality in occupational benefits except pensions (now overridden by the *Barber* case where ECJ ruled definition of pay under Art. 119 includes pensions)

***Equal Treatment Directive (self employed) 1986 (86/613/EEC)***

***Protection of Pregnant Workers Directive (92/85/EEC)*** Requires 14 weeks' paid maternity leave, right to return and protection from dismissal for all pregnant workers, regardless of service, and special health and safety provisions.

*Sue's summary notes on the law*

European law is very important for sex discrimination and equal pay – some recent cases involving disadvantageous treatment of part-time workers (indirect sex discrimination to treat women part-timers worse than full-time male workers).

**Figure 11.1**  Discrimination: definition and remedies

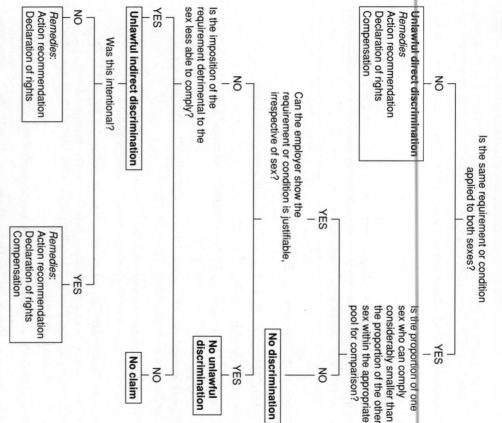

*Note:* The same approach applies to determining direct/indirect race discrimination

Indirect discrimination is a key concept: employers need to be able to show (justify) that it is necessary and appropriate for some business reason to do things which in practice adversely affect women or ethnic minorities, for example justify a requirement, explicit or imposed in practice, for particular qualifications or characteristics which fewer women will have than men, or which fewer people from some ethnic or racial group will be able to show compared to white workers. Enforcement of the law: the EOC and CRE have legal powers to undertake a formal investigation. These do not seem to be used very often. Individuals who think they have been discriminated against can complain to industrial tribunals.

Around 4,000 tribunal cases about discrimination in 1993–4; under half won by the applicants. Compensation awards include compensation for actual loss and for injury to feelings, with interest. Currently awards are about £3,000 on average. No maximum on amount of compensation that can be awarded – some very large awards mentioned in press reports of cases recently.

## Questions

Imagine you are Sue. Having undertaken the three tasks (and reflected on your previous experience), you are about to have another meeting with Chris to report and to suggest a way forward. In preparing for the meeting you should consider:

1 What is the nature of the 'equality problem' in Manuflex? (What groups are affected, in which occupations and in what ways? Are the people you spoke to aware of this situation? Do they see it as a problem?)

2 What would you identify as the potential barriers (institutional and human) to EO in Manuflex and where are potential allies to be found? What arguments might be helpful in winning support for any initiative or overcoming resistance (for example, are there ways in which greater equality at Manuflex might help solve any current problems)?

3 'Good practice' suggestions often centre on improved personnel management practices, especially in relation to recruitment and selection. How successful would you expect this approach to be at Manuflex and why?

4 What approach should be developed and what steps should be taken in the short term and longer term, and with what objectives? What realistically can be expected to have been achieved in terms of equal opportunities in Manuflex in five years and in ten years?

### Note to tutor

Questions 1 and 2 can be addressed on a reading of the case. The other two questions require more extensive reading in order to be answered fully.

In more advanced courses, or where greater exploration of some theoretical issues are required, students might also be asked:

5 What are the key differences between an approach based on 'diversity' and one based on 'equal opportunities', and which would be more effective at Manuflex?

## References

Commission for Racial Equality 1984: *Race Relations Code of Practice*. London: CRE.

Commission for Racial Equality 1995: *Racial Equality*. London: CRE.

Dickens, L. 1994: Wasted resources. Equal opportunities in employment. In Sisson, K. (ed.), *Personnel Management: A Comprehensive Guide to Theory and Practice in Britain*. Oxford: Blackwell.

## Further reading

Cockburn, C. 1989: Equal opportunities: the short and long agenda. *Industrial Relations Journal*, autumn.

Cockburn, C. 1991: *In the Way of Women*. Basingstoke: Macmillan Education.

Collinson, D., Knights, D. and Collinson, M. 1990: *Managing to Discriminate*. London: Routledge.

Dickens, L. 1994: The business case for equal opportunities: is the carrot better than the stick? *Employee Relations*, **16**(8).

Dickens, L. and Colling, T. 1990: Why equality won't appear on the bargaining agenda. *Personnel Management*, April.

Greenslade, M. 1991: Managing diversity: lessons from the United States. *Personnel Management*, December.

Hammond, V. 1992: Opportunity 2000. A culture change approach to EO. *Women in Management Review*, 7(7).

Holland, L. 1988: Easy to say, hard to do. Managing an EO programme. *Equal Opportunities Review*, (20), July/August. (This publication is a useful source of general guidance and information and practical examples.)

Jewson, N. and Mason, D. 1986: The theory and practice of equal opportunities policies: liberal and radical approaches. *Sociological Review*, **34**(2), 307–33.

Jewson, N. and Mason, D. 1992: Race, equal opportunities policies and employment practice. *New Community*, October.

Ollerearnshaw, S. and Waldeck, R. 1995: Taking action to promote equality. *People Management*, **23**, February.

## Additional reading for question 5

Copeland, L. 1988: Valuing diversity, Part I and part II, *Personnel*, June, July.

Kandola, R. and Fullerton, J. 1994: Diversity: More than just an empty slogan. *Personnel Management*, November.

Liff, S. 1993: From equality to diversity in Wajcman, J. (ed.), *Organizations, Gender and Power: Papers from an IRRU Workshop*. Coventry: Industrial Relations Research Unit, University of Warwick.

## 12

# Three Roads to Quality

*Variations in total quality management*
ADRIAN WILKINSON

### Recent Developments in Total Quality Management

In recent years changes in product markets, technology and legislation have led organizations to search for new approaches to managing organizations. Product and service quality are now high on the agenda for both private and public-sector organizations, with quality certification and total quality management (TQM) emerging as key issues (Bank, 1992). Under these conditions, enhanced quality is no longer seen as an option for management, but essential if market share is to be retained, let alone developed. The quest for quality can be seen as a search for a competitive advantage (Porter, 1980).

The quality movement is now regarded as having had a major impact on UK management practice (Drummond, 1992). Although some writers see it merely as the latest in a long line of management fashions (Gill and Whittle, 1993), Juran (1991), one of the quality gurus, describes it as a major phenomenon of this age. According to Grant et al. (1994), 'TQM is a challenge to conventional management techniques and to the theories that underlie them. Therefore it cannot be simply grafted on to existing management structures and systems' (p. 25). Hill (1991a) has examined the implications for the workforce and suggests that TQM exemplifies the ways in which firms are restructuring working relations in 'high trust' ways for managers as well as labour.

There is considerable evidence which points to the spread of TQM initiatives (see, for example, Cruise O'Brien and Voss, 1992; Economist Intelligence Unit, 1992). A survey carried out for the Institute of Management suggests that TQM is becoming more widespread, with 71 per cent of respondents claiming to have a quality campaign, although as yet appearing to be more well developed in manufacturing and in production industries such as gas, water and electricity than in services (Wilkinson et al., 1993).

## Total Quality Management and Human Resource Management

TQM has evolved from its engineering origins and its primary association with tools and techniques. In the 1980s it was taken up as a general management philosophy concerned with the attainment of continuous improvement in all processes by all staff. Quality is seen as becoming a way of life which permeates every part and aspect of the organization (Oakland, 1993, pp. 2–3). For the most part, however, the principal contributions to the analysis of TQM and its operation have come from people in the production management/operations area. With backgrounds in operational research and statistics, many of the leading gurus sought to develop 'objective' means of gaining 'hard' information about processes of production and service delivery. Much attention and effort has been directed at the measurement and documentation of procedures and outcomes through the use of flow-charts, scatter diagrams, control charts, and so on. Less consideration has been given to the 'softer' process of managing human resources in a manner likely to be consistent with the TQM philosophy of continuous improvement (Wilkinson et al., 1991; 1992). This is partly a reflection of the total quality guru's view that the system is the key and the effectiveness of individuals is largely determined by that system rather than by individual characteristics (Waldman, 1994). Yet there is increasing evidence that TQM has not fulfilled its promise, and a number of reports (by, for example Cruise O'Brien and Voss, 1992; The Economist Intelligence Unit, 1992; Wilkinson et al., 1992) suggest that human resource issues are critical to success.

One problem facing those attempting to analyse the TQM phenomenon is that TQM is not a single unified entity. However, while varying definitions and approaches are articulated, there are a number of common themes. First, quality can be defined as 'fitness for use', including both quality of design (how a customer's requirements are translated into a set of specifications) and conformance to the design (how an operation conforms to the specification of the design standard). Second, quality management emphasizes not only the external customer but also the internal customer. Hence the concept of a quality chain is central, with every member of the organization linked ultimately to the final customer via a series of internal customer-supplier relationships, each of which can be evaluated in quality terms. Third, the aim of TQM is to have quality 'built in' rather than inspected. Quality becomes the responsibility of all employees rather than of a specialist department. Associated with this is the notion that prevention rather than detection is the key, with 'continuous improvement' as the ultimate goal (Juran, 1991). Fourth, rather than assuming that quality improvements necessarily lead to increased costs, it is anticipated that they will fall due to a decline in failure rates, warranty costs, returned goods and a fall in the costs of detection. Finally, management is charged with ultimate responsibility for quality since 85 per cent of failures are regarded as the fault of inadequate management systems (Ishikawa, 1985; Lillkrank and Kano, 1989). Thus, any TQM initiative must be seen to be enthusiastically endorsed by the top management; they are the role models and must actively participate and promote quality by example.

Most writers on TQM (such as Crosby, 1979; Ishikawa, 1985) agree that the success of TQM is dependent on a people orientation, illustrated through initiatives such as teamworking, training and development, and participation (Dale and Cooper, 1992). However, apart from assumptions that these are essential to the success of TQM (for example, Aubrey and Felkins, 1985; Juran, 1988; Deming, 1982), there is little guidance on how the people side of TQM should be developed. Research (whether academic or business led) tends to mirror this. Most work *asserts* the importance of human resource issues, but does not go beyond general references to a need for training, motivation and changed cultures (Wilkinson, 1994). In other words, many of these writers (without specialist knowledge of HRM), although formally recognizing the importance of utilizing human resources, fail to appreciate the true complexities of such issues. Yet until recently TQM had received scant attention from HRM academics, partly because it was seen as a revamped version of quality circles (deemed to have failed) and was identified with production and operations issues (associated with BS 5750 certification). However, there is a growing body of literature from a human resource management/industrial relations perspective which addresses TQM (for example, Dawson, 1994; Hill, 1991a, 1991b; Giles and Williams, 1991; Hunter and Beaumont, 1994; Wilkinson et al., 1991, 1992).

Guest (1992) has also recently taken up the TQM banner. He argues that TQM is inextricably linked to HRM through the vehicle of training, because of the need for a quality and committed workforce, because the credibility of the initiative is partly governed by management's treatment of the workforce and, finally, because quality with its emphasis on involvement and flexibility, implies a high-trust organization. He suggests that 'the need for total quality management linked to and integrated with HRM is increasingly recognized' (p. 111).

## Case Studies

In this section three case studies are presented. There are two reasons for examining multiple cases here; first, it is obviously more difficult to generalize from a single case, and it is particularly important when discussing TQM to be aware of the diversity of experience; second, providing a comparative case study allows students to compare and contrast TQM in different environments. The three cases which have been chosen are from engineering, electronics and software engineering. They show quite different journeys on the road to TQM. Mactool is a story of TQM failure, with total quality (TQ) structures bolted on to an existing culture which proved infertile ground for the concept of involvement which the company espoused. In contrast Electron provides an altogether more positive note with the TQM initiative driven by the HR manager, taking account of the existing culture and appearing to be successful in a number of areas, not least in gaining staff commitment. At Software Ltd one sees how quality is embedded into existing structures, with TQM principles being part of the way the company does its business. Indeed, TQM principles are applied to each department, including the personnel function, which is seen as providing a specified service to 'customers'. The HR function also played a quite different role in each of these cases. At Mactool its role was virtually non-existent, while at Electron it played an important change agent role, and at Software Ltd it carried out the role of an 'internal contractor' applying TQ principles to itself but not guiding or shaping the actual form of the initiative.

## MACTOOL CO.

Mactool is a light engineering tool company located on the south coast of the UK which employs over 300 staff in both manual and white-collar jobs. Numbers have fallen dramatically since the mid 1970s when it employed over 1,000 staff. Various schemes were used to reduce workforce size, including compulsory redundancy, although not last in, first out (LIFO) as management wanted to retain the skills required for the remaining product range. However, at the time of the research, employment was stable.

In the early 1980s, in the face of intense Japanese competition, the company suffered heavy losses and subsequently redesigned its product range to high-cost (and higher value-added), high specification, multi-machine systems selling to blue-chip companies. Mactool is a market leader in its niche of flexible manufacturing cells. Machines are sold on technical excellence, many being unique orders, supported by production engineering packages. Warranty/sales support are important elements of the package, for example, the service department responds within 24 hours for 95 per cent of customer service calls.

Industrial relations had also changed considerably since the 1970s; the senior managers described this period as 'desperate days' when the convenor was regarded as operating as the 'joint managing director' and it was a period described by a current steward as one of 'regular overtime bans, work to rules, strikes, the lot'. However, the wave of redundancies removed many of the activists, with survival becoming the priority. Union organization does not compare with that in the 1970s, and the centrality of the union to daily work has declined, with one manager describing it as operating as a 'backstop'.

As the production system shrank in the 1980s, more flexible working arrangements were introduced and demarcations both within trades and between trades was eroded. Flexibility occurred not so much as a conscious strategy of multiskilling but a reaction to the declining size of the company and a reduction in specialist departments. The production system itself is based on sophisticated technology and the workforce is highly skilled, although there are Taylorist elements such as preprinted cards to be filled in at the end of each task. Products constructed are serviced by a 'team' of workers with different skills (fitters, electricians, hydraulic engineers, and so on) and performing different tasks.

Team briefing and consultative committees had been introduced by its parent company in the early 1980s to communicate and explain the 'hard times'. In the late 1980s there was a management buy-out which incorporated the establishment of an Employee Share Ownership Plan (ESOP). However, the ESOP did not actually give employees any real influence in the running of the company despite top management exhortations based on the principle of co-ownership. These participative schemes appeared to have been merely grafted on to a pre-existing engineering culture which emphasized hierarchical and power relations. One union representative described participation at the company as the managing director explaining 'why he wanted to do things'. This is not to say that the relationship between workforce and management was uncooperative. Indeed, as the personnel director argued, 'we can't run the operation we do here without people putting themselves out'. Nevertheless, much of the shopfloor contribution was interpreted by union representatives as loyalty to their trade, rather than any identification with the company. Thus discretion at shopfloor level was seen as relating more to management neglect and omission than to any positive policy of employee involvement (Wilkinson et al., 1994).

The adoption of TQM took place against this background and was seen as a vehicle for the achievement of 'world-class manufacturing'. A mission statement was introduced to distinguish the company from its previous identity and owners, as well as to provide staff with a long-term view of the future.

The mission, defined as 'to function as a profitable world class manufacturing company producing both stand-alone machines and cells that satisfy our customer requirements in all respects', was to be achieved in a series of steps with the first including the achievement of quality objectives through employee involvement. Employee involvement had acquired greater importance in recent times with changes in the product range and with the emphasis on service becoming a significant part of the package. For example, most production workers have visited customer sites on a regular basis for installation or to perform repair and maintenance work. Furthermore, as the organization shrunk over the years and specialist departments declined, the shopfloor remained a key base of knowledge, often modifying machines for customers on an individual basis. 'Tapping' this knowledge was identified by management as an important aspect of future activity.

The first part of the TQM programme incorporated BS 5750 certification which involved following procedural guidelines and the routine monitoring of work. This attempt to get workers to take on greater responsibility for quality, in particular inspecting their own work, has meant that the quality auditors who have replaced the inspectors perform their task within two days rather than a week, and the old ritual of calling up fitters to repair poor-quality work has virtually disappeared. This new procedure was negotiated with the union with a pay increase as a quid pro quo. However, there was a dispute concerning responsibility for customer demonstrations (a job for operators, according to management) which was seen by workers as additional responsibility and therefore warranting more pay. The personnel department played only a limited facilitating role during the introduction of TQM.

The second stage in the TQM initiative was to achieve a problem-solving structure 'to remove obstacles to improving performance'. An infrastructure was established with the formation of problem-solving groups (PSGs) reporting to a review committee, which in turn reported to a management committee. The PSGs were designed 'to offer everyone the opportunity to participate' with the benefits arising from improved productivity 'leading to increased profitability and gain for all'. PSGs were based on work groups and voluntary participation, and these met weekly. Their aims were twofold – to identify problems originating within their own work area and propose solutions, and to identify problems originating outside their own work area and refer to the review team. Group leaders – who were typically supervisors – were trained in how to set up and run a group, and both they and group members were trained in problem-solving techniques. Group members and managers also attended an appreciation seminar. The trade unions were initially suspicious, fearing that 'men would be set against men', and some stewards refused to get involved in the process.

While the PSGs started off in a 'blaze of glory', initially involving 40 per cent of the hourly-paid workforce, within two years only a handful remained active and there was some uncertainty as to whether they had been abandoned. As one manager said, 'they haven't died, they have just faded away . . . and faded on a pretty regular basis'. There did not appear to be many quantifiable benefits arising from their work.

The failure of TQM can be attributed to a mix of technical and more fundamental flaws. In relation to the former, there is no doubt that many supervisors were uncomfortable with their role as leaders – they were told that they would lead the groups and then found themselves bombarded with problems. Second, the training had stressed techniques (for example, Pareto analysis, fishbone diagrams) rather than the teamwork skills which were essential to the operation of these groups. Third, the context of meeting end-of-year production targets clearly limited the time available for PSGs. Finally, the review committee (comprising the top tier of management) vetoed almost all the suggestions coming through on the grounds of cost, which consequently demoralized the groups.

However, there were also more fundamental problems. It was apparent that the PSGs were focused on the wrong area – with the emphasis on internal problems rather than cross-functional issues.

Among line managers there was a belief that the company was good at specific task-oriented jobs within the work group and indeed production methods demanded this. However, production managers pointed out that problems originated further up the line (for example, materials shortage). However, this was outside the PSG remit and there was a lack of managerial will to tackle interdepartmental issues. Second, according to the new managing director, the PSGs had failed because they were approached in a non-participative way. The attempt to graft on teamwork to a pre-existing traditional and hierarchical culture by stating that 'there will be 14 PSGs, they will meet once a week' was simply doomed to failure. Thus TQM, like all the other management initiatives introduced at Mactool, simply ran out of steam.

## ELECTRON

Electron is part of a large Japanese-owned multi-divisional company. The factory in the south-east of England is the sole producer of Electron portable digital oscilloscopes (test and measurement instruments used in industries ranging from electronics, auto manufacturing, aerospace, defence computing and telecommunications). The company operates in a highly competitive market with business-to-business sales, and customers include major international companies. The company operated a worldwide direct order entry system which overnight downloads orders from Electron sales offices to the site's own order book. Ordered products are shipped directly to the customer from the factory ready for use. The company employs 200 workers at this site (one-third of whom are graduates or graduate equivalents), which is over 100 fewer than in the early 1990s. The AEEU is the recognized union but this is confined to grievance and disciplinary issues. Union membership has steadily declined over the 1980s from 30 per cent to no more than 10 per cent at the time of the research. An employee council meets on an ad hoc basis to discuss non-substantive issues and to share information.

The quality initiative originated in the late 1980s when developments in 'quality' in the manufacturing area meant they were beginning to come into conflict with other departments. A particular concern was the company's very segmented approach to the manufacturing process. Futhermore, market research found that the perception of the company was still shaped by its early history, and it had a 'cheap and cheerful' reputation. At the same time, a customer survey found that quality issues, such as reliability, support, warranty and maintenance costs, were at least as important as performance and technical specification. Finally, a particular incident relating to a converter problem resulted in a considerable amount of cost in recall and re-work activities.

After visits to a number of suppliers the MD became convinced that TQM was needed as a vehicle for organizational change. HR issues were seen as central to the development of TQM from an early stage. Electron had a number of long-serving staff who had experienced over the years a variety of short-lived initiatives (including quality circles) introduced by several different managers. To highlight TQM as something different and long lasting the MD interviewed all staff (then over 300) on a one-to-one basis, with meetings ranging from half an hour to over two hours. Following this the MD decided to appoint the HR director to champion the TQM initiative. There were a number of reasons behind this. First, given that the company was emphasizing the key role of communication, it made sense to place responsibility within the HR function. Second, it was necessary that TQM should not be seen as simply quality assurance, and it was felt that the wrong message would be given if the quality department were given the responsibility for TQM's introduction. Third, given that there was conflict and friction between different departments, it was important to have 'quality' led by a 'neutral' body.

A central steering committee, the quality improvement team (QIT), comprising senior management and chaired by the HR director oversaw the TQM process. In addition, there were standing teams on recognition and communication, both chaired by the HR director, and several corrective action teams. Central to Electron's approach to TQM is an error identification form (EIF) (see Figure 12.1). This report sheet can be filled in by any employee who has a problem with their work and allows them to communicate, if necessary, with the senior management team to obtain a resolution. The EIF starts with the statement, 'the following is preventing me from performing error-free work'. Problems highlighted by this system range from bad

**Figure 12.1**  Error identification form

FROM _____  DEPARTMENT _____

The following is preventing me from performing Error Free Work

_____

_____

_____

(If you wish to suggest a solution please          Signed _____
do so, although this is not essential)             Date _____

Keep bottom copy and mail the other two to the          Thank you for your help
TQ co-ordinator in the envelope provided

Supervisor/Manager's reply

_____

_____

Responsibility assigned by QIT to: _____          Signed _____

                                                             Date _____

Corrective action taken to resolve problem

_____          Date - - - - - - - -

Completion

_____          Date _____

I am now satisfied that this error is no longer occurring, and that systems are in place to
ensure a permanent fix.

Signed _____          Date _____

lighting to design problems and in theory no subject is taboo. The report is filed with the HR director (as co-ordinator), and he approaches either the supervisor or the QIT. The report stays in existence until the problem has been dealt with, whereupon the document is signed off by the employee who originated the enquiry. A list of outstanding EIFs is displayed on the noticeboards, which provides some peer pressure on those responsible for dealing with the problem. There have been over 200 EIFs in the first two years, the vast majority of which have been resolved (for example, late delivery, part shortages).

According to managers, the main benefits of TQM are flatter structures and improved teamworking, particularly with the development of project teams and a common understanding throughout the organization of the value placed on quality. Prior to TQM, while design and production were organized around product families, support functions were not, and as departments grew this led to greater complexity with departmental goals being seen as superior to project goals. Under TQM half the site's workforce and equipment was moved to facilitate a greater cross-fertilization of ideas. In addition TQM is seen as having led to an increase in productivity (with less need for service engineers and quality staff), a significant percentage decrease in return of products during the warranty period, the maintenance of market share in a poor economic climate, and the assurance of a worldwide delivery guarantee for any configuration of oscilloscope. Electron has also achieved ISO 9001 registration and moved to a just in time system. The latter has enabled the company to maintain its build-to-order policy with a ten-day manufacturing lead time.

The HR department is central to TQM. It plays a central co-ordinating role, and is also responsible for conducting all awareness training seminars, with all staff having attended a two-day quality seminar – after some help from a consultant in the initial stages. During the introduction of TQM – when it was important to demonstrate good faith through visible actions and when a high proportion of the EIFs related to the working environment – the HR department was responsible for several actions including the installation of new floors, ceilings and air conditioning, improved lighting and new vending machines. All staff have attended a two-day quality seminar, with full union co-operation. Continuous improvement, personal responsibility, involvement and self-development are all part of the TQM approach. Staff are now less likely to 'go on living with problems' and the EIF provides a vehicle to address this. However, there has been some middle management concern that this undermines their authority. Communications have also been improved with a regular TQ newsletter and TQ noticeboards (updated every two weeks) to go alongside team briefing and publicity schemes such as TQ charity week. EIFs in particular appear to have reduced collective activity through the union, as issues such as health and safety and the working environment are increasingly dealt with through the EIF system rather than at the employee council. Finally, performance appraisal now gives greater emphasis to quality and employees' willingness to change, and the recognition team is responsible for a variety of prizes, badges and certificates.

## SOFTWARE LTD

Software Ltd is a software engineering consultancy founded in the early 1980s on a greenfield site in the south of England. It is a well-respected supplier of computer-based systems, products and services. It provides bespoke software, turn-key systems and consultancy to all areas of industry, commerce and central government. It specializes in data management systems, critical systems such as security and air traffic control, and infrastructure software. The company has faced the twin pressures of the recession and the contraction of the defence industry in recent years. Due to the former, customers have been inclined to defer investment in new computer systems, while the latter has led to increased competition for civil contracts as defence suppliers have sought alternative work.

Software Ltd employs just under 200 staff spread over three sites and numbers have risen steadily since its foundation. Indeed, the company actually recruited sales staff when the recession started as it believed an increase in market share could compensate for contraction in the overall market. Staff are largely made up of professional software engineers and unions are not recognized. The company operates a number of share option schemes and 70 per cent of staff are shareholders.

From its early days the concept of quality has been embedded in company culture and influenced the approach to systems design and development. When there were only 25 staff employed by the company, a full-time quality manager was appointed, and in 1986 the company became the first independent software house to achieve

ISO 9001 registration. The quality system was part of the marketing edge at Software Ltd over this period, but a feeling developed that the approach was too static and introspective because of the focus on procedures, and TQM began to be examined as the next step. In 1989 the company became a co-founder of the European Foundation for Quality Management and the company formally adopted the TQM label. Greater emphasis was placed on customer satisfaction, quality improvement processes and employee contribution. According to company literature, quality is not an abstract or introspective issue: 'We believe that it must be the central obsession of any successful business. Quality to us means providing the best possible service to the client at the best possible price – this time, next time, every time.'

The quality improvement process at Software Ltd does not have a separate infrastructure, but is seen as being integrated into the overall management process. However, there are quality improvement teams which comprise the owners, customers and participants of processes which have improvement potential. Once the process has been improved, written procedures are updated and the QIT disbanded. The quality manual is central to this system.

It is difficult to evaluate the benefits of TQM at Software Ltd because it is seen as implicit in everything the company does. Nevertheless, it is associated with good communication, flat structures, clear reporting systems and a performance-based reward system. The company stresses that the operating achievement can be gauged only by the satisfaction of clients, and client surveys report a high degree of satisfaction with the service provided. There was some concern that the company needs to be careful about being too systems oriented. When the company first started it was felt that people drove systems, but with the burgeoning of systems, and in particular the quality manual, there was a perception among some staff that systems now drove people. The company is now taking a broader approach to quality. For example, reviews undertaken with clients at the end of projects now go beyond technical issues and while the quality system had provided the means to control and standardize the processes, TQM is seen as a vehicle to improve them.

The HR function at Software Ltd is small and not represented at board level. To a large extent, HR issues have always been important because of the nature of the industry and of the company in particular. According to the Annual Report, 'all staff are given the opportunity to question management and to contribute to the making of significant decisions', but this has been given greater emphasis in recent years as a wider approach to quality has been taken. This has also given the HR function a more prominent role.

New developments in HR linked to QM have been the development of objective setting, a staff satisfaction survey and the extension of quality improvement teams. While the overall results of the survey were positive, some areas were identified which needed improvement, in particular career development, and these are being addressed through the development of performance and development reviews and the training of career reviewers. The HR function has responsibility for training, and quality is embedded within this at induction through a day spent explaining the company's quality philosophy and training on the use of the quality manual. Recently, workshops have been run for middle managers with the aim of getting them to empower staff. The training emphasizes the need for staff involvement and agreement in both objective setting and professional development.

The HR function has also applied TQM principles to its own work and has a document listing the main products and levels of services it provides. These products and services include recruitment, employment advice, salaries and grades; the customers might be staff or managers, and level of service specifies when it can be provided in terms of days, weeks or months (see Table 12.1). This list was drawn up following discussions with a selection of its customers. HR produced its own 'simple quality targets of Personnel Products and Services' after discussions with a 'selection of customers'. The overall objective of the personnel function at Software Ltd is to 'provide services for obtaining and maintaining a productive workforce for the group, through the provision of employment policies, services and information for directors, managers and staff, and by liaising, on employment matters, with outside training, recruitment and statutory bodies'. Examples of the products and services provided are shown in Table 12.1, which are related to the customer(s) and the time by which the service will be provided. In all, these cover ten areas ranging from recruitment through to pay and performance review.

The contribution of HR tends to be at a functional/operational rather than strategic level, and HR does not have a place on the board, nor is it given any particular primacy in the quality process. Indeed, in its earlier years, QM was heavily oriented towards a harder systems perspective, and HR is only just beginning to enhance its contribution at higher levels of the company.

**Table 12.1** Personnel products and services at Software Ltd

| Item | Customer | Level of service |
| --- | --- | --- |
| Offers and contracts | Managers | Within 24 hours |
| Administration of induction day and employment presentation | New staff | Every month (if sufficient new staff) |
| Advisory service on all aspects of employment terms and conditions | All staff | Advice given within five working days |
| Advice on dismissal, disciplinary procedures, low performance, etc. | Managers | Within 48 hours of request |
| Recording all personal training carried out | Quality | All supplied records on personal files |
| Provision of statistics reports and list | Directors, managers, outside bodies | As agreed with each request |

## Questions

1 Discuss the different routes to TQM which were taken by the three companies.

2 Analyse the links between TQM and HRM.

3 How can TQM principles be applied to the personnel function?

4 What contribution can HR professionals make to the development of TQM?

## References

Aubrey, C. A. and Felkins, P. K. 1988: *Teamwork: Involving People in Quality and Productivity Improvement*. ASQC Milwaukee, WI: Quality Press.

Bank, J. 1992: *The Essence of Total Quality Management*, Hemel Hempstead: Prentice-Hall.

Crosby, P. 1979: *Quality is Free*, New York: McGraw-Hill.

Cruise O'Brien, R. and Voss, C. 1992: In Search of Quality. London Business School Working Paper, London.

Dale, B. and Cooper, C. 1992: *Total Quality and Human Resources: An Executive Guide*, Oxford: Blackwell.

Dawson, P. 1994: Total quality management. In Storey, J. (ed.), *New Wave Manufacturing Strategies*, London: Paul Chapman.

Deming, W. 1982: *Quality, Productivity and Competitive Position*, Cambridge, MA.: MIT Press.

Deming, W. 1986: *Out of the Crisis*, Cambridge, MA.: MIT Centre for Advanced Engineering Study.

Drummond, H. 1992: *The Quality Movement: What Total Quality Management is Really All About!* London: Kogan Page.

*The Economist* 1992: The cracks in quality. 18 April.

Economist Intelligence Unit 1992: Making quality work: Lessons from European Leading Companies. London: Economist Intelligence Unit.

Giles, E. and Williams, R. 1991: Can the personnel department survive quality management? *Personnel Management*, April, 28–33.

Gill, J. and Whittle, S. 1993: Management by panacea: accounting for transience. *Journal of Management Studies*, 30(2), 281–96.

Grant, R., Shani, R. and Krishnan, R. 1994: TQM's challenge to management theory and practice. *Sloan Management Review*, Winter, 25–35.

Guest, D. 1992: Employee commitment and control. In F. J. Hartley and G. M. Stephenson (eds) *Employee Relations*, Oxford: Blackwell.

Hill, S. 1991a: How to manage a Flexible Firm, the total quality model. *Work Employment and Society*, December, 397–415.

Hill, S. 1991b: Why quality circles failed but total quality might succeed. *British Journal of Industrial Relations*, 29(4), 541–68.

Hunter, L. and Beaumont, P. 1994: Implementing TQM: top down or bottom up? *Industrial Relations Journal*, 12(4), 318–27.

Ishikawa, K. 1985: *What is Total Quality Control?* Englewood Cliffs, NJ: Prentice-Hall.

Juran, J. 1988: *Quality Control Handbook*, New York: McGraw-Hill.

Juran, J. 1991: Strategies for World Class Quality. *Quality Progress*, March, 81.

Kearney, A. T. 1992: Total quality: time to take off the rose tinted spectacles. A report in association with the TQM Magazine, Kempston: IFS Publications.

Lillrank, P. and Kano, N. 1989: *Continuous Improvement: Quality Control Circles in Japanese Industry*. Michigan, MI: Ann Arbor, MI Centre for Japanese Studies: The University of Michigan.

Oakland, J. 1993: *Total Quality Management*. 2nd ed., London: Heinemann.

Piore, M. and Sable, C. 1985: *The Second Industrial Divide*, New York: Basic Books.

Porter, M. 1980: *Competitive Strategy*, New York, Free Press.

Waldman, D. 1994: The contribution of total quality management to a theory of work performance. *Academy of Management Review*, 19(3), 510–36.

Wilkinson, A. 1994: Managing human resources for quality. In Dale, B. G. (ed.), *Managing Quality*, 2nd edn., Hemel Hempstead: Prentice-Hall, 273–91.

Wilkinson, A. 1992: The other side of quality: soft issues and the human resource dimension. *Total Quality Management*, **3**(3), 323–9.

Wilkinson, A., Allen, P. and Snape, E. 1991: TQM and the management of labour. *Employee Relations*, **13**(1), 24–31.

Wilkinson, A., Marchington, M., Ackers, P. and Goodman, J. 1994: ESOPS Fables? A tale of a machine tool company. *International Journal of Human Resource Management*, **5**(1), 121–43.

Wilkinson, A., Marchington, M., Goodman, J. and Ackers, P. 1992: Total quality management and employee involvement. *Human Resource Management Journal*, **2**(4), 1–20.

Wilkinson, A., Redman, T. and Snape, E. 1993: *Quality and the Manager: An IM Report*, Corby: Institute of Management.

Womack, J., Jones, D. and Roos, D. 1990: *The Machine that Changed the World*, New York, NY: Rawson Associates.

# 13

# Next Patient Please

*The operating theatres problem at
Leicester General Hospital NHS Trust*

DAVID BUCHANAN AND
BOB WILSON

## The Complaints

The surgeons and anaesthetists are complaining. There are too many delays in delivering patients to the hospital's operating theatres. This means that sometimes a patient's operation has to be cancelled, and this can be stressful for ward staff and for patients. Delays also leave highly paid and highly qualified clinicians and other theatre staff standing around doing nothing until the next patient arrives. On numerous occasions frustrated theatre staff find that they have to work beyond the end of their scheduled shift because the list of patients for that morning or afternoon theatre session is not finished. According to one surgeon, 'delays in operating theatres are a *bête noir* for surgeons and nurses alike'. The theatre services manager has been logging deviations from session plans for the past six months. This shows regular total monthly under-runs of 120 hours and monthly over-runs of about 130 hours. An under-run means that theatre staff may be idle, or carrying out routine maintenance instead of treating patients. An over-run may mean overtime payments, and staff are frustrated because they cannot leave their shift. The problem is thus affecting hospital costs, staff morale and quality of patient care. The typical cost of staffing a theatre for one hour is between £50 and £60, depending on numbers and grades but excluding surgeon and anaesthetist.

These complaints are being taken seriously. A steering group has been set up. The members of this group include two consultant surgeons, a senior anaesthetist, the business manager and senior nurse manager from the surgical directorate which manages the theatres department, and two senior members of the hospital's human resources department. One of the surgeons is the clinical director of the surgical directorate. You have been asked to join steering group as an independent adviser and consultant.

## The Surgical Directorate

Leicester General Hospital is a 740-bed acute care hospital with around 2,500 staff. The day-to-day running of the hospital is the responsibility of a chief executive. Reporting to the chief executive are 11 directors of the hospital's main functions. These include the directors of contracts, finance, estates, nursing and quality assurance, and human resources. There are six clinical directors, responsible for the directorates of obstetrics and gynaecology, medicine, renal medicine, clinical support services (radiology, pathology, physiotherapy, phlebotomy, pharmacy), anaesthesia, and surgery. There is no casualty facility; another nearby hospital has the district accident and emergency service, and all local hospitals share emergency admissions on a rotation system.

The surgical directorate is responsible for a suite of six main operating theatres and two orthopaedic theatres. These are where the complaints arise. The directorate is also responsible for two day-case operating theatres and for eight other wards and a total of 220 beds. The annual budget of the directorate is around £9 million, representing over 25 per cent of the hospital's annual budget. The directorate is managed by a three-person team including the clinical director (a consultant surgeon), a business manager and a senior nurse manager. In addition each clinical specialty has a head of service who represents colleagues at management meetings, co-ordinates clinical activity and acts as a communication channel between the clinical director and the specialty. The directorate organization structure is shown in Figure 13.1. Reporting to the senior nurse manager is a newly appointed theatre services manager responsible for the effective running of the ten theatres.

There are about 90 surgeons, anaesthetists, senior registrars, registrars, senior house officers and house officers associated with the directorate. They are organized into specialties, each led by a senior

**Figure 13.1**   Surgical directorate organization structure

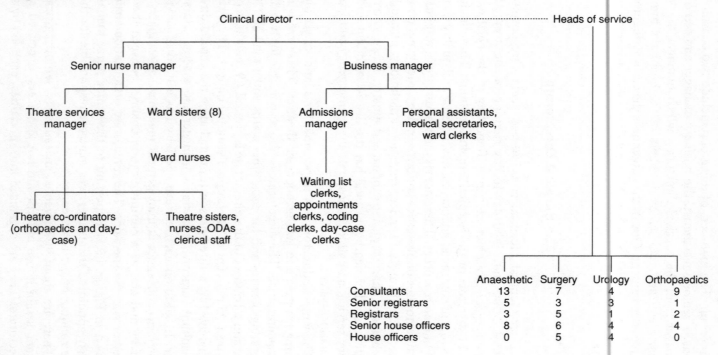

| | Anaesthetic | Surgery | Urology | Orthopaedics |
|---|---|---|---|---|
| Consultants | 13 | 7 | 4 | 9 |
| Senior registrars | 5 | 3 | 3 | 1 |
| Registrars | 3 | 5 | 1 | 2 |
| Senior house officers | 8 | 6 | 4 | 4 |
| House officers | 0 | 5 | 4 | 0 |

consultant or head of service. The specialties include orthopaedics, urology, anaesthetics and surgery. The total number of elective, non-elective and day-case procedures contracted by the local health authority for 1994–5 in general surgery, urology and orthopaedics was over 14,500. The contract also included over 28,000 outpatient episodes in those specialisms from which most elective admissions are taken.

Reporting to the senior nurse manager are 160 full-time equivalent staff including the theatre services manager, seven theatre sisters, 65 operating department nurses and 16 operating department assistants (ODAs) who carry out a dual nursing and anaesthetic support function in theatre. Reporting to the business manager are 56 staff including an admissions manager, 20 waiting list, appointments, coding, day-case and endoscopy clerks, and 35 personal assistants, medical secretaries, ward clerks and theatre secretaries. In total there are approximately 400 (full-time equivalent) people employed in and associated with the directorate. This is over 16 per cent of the hospital's total employment. Figure 13.2 shows an outline map of the main theatre suite which has its own reception, service, preparation and recovery areas. The two orthopaedic theatres and the day-case units are located separately from the main suite.

Each theatre is scheduled for two sessions each weekday – one morning and one afternoon session. Table 13.1 shows the weekly schedule for the the main theatres. Session start times depend on the surgeon's preference which explains the variations in Table 13.1 from day to day. The blank sessions are protected for emergency cases and for priority requests from general practitioners and other doctors in other hospitals. Consultants, and their respective firms, are allocated permanent outpatient clinic and theatre sessions. This allows consultants effectively to schedule their other work, such as teaching, ward rounds and private practice. When a consultant is absent (conference, holiday), his firm can continue to use that slot and handle the scheduled list. Session start and finish times, naturally, have implications for shift staffing patterns and for the load on the theatre porters who deliver patients to and from the wards.

In this kind of setting, is it possible to predict in advance how long a surgical team will take to operate on a list of patients? Each patient is unique, and the time they are likely to need to spend on an operating table must always be an estimate. If the consultant is demonstrating a procedure to junior colleagues, then it may take longer, as it may when the consultant is on holiday and a senior registrar is

**Figure 13.2**  The main theatre suite

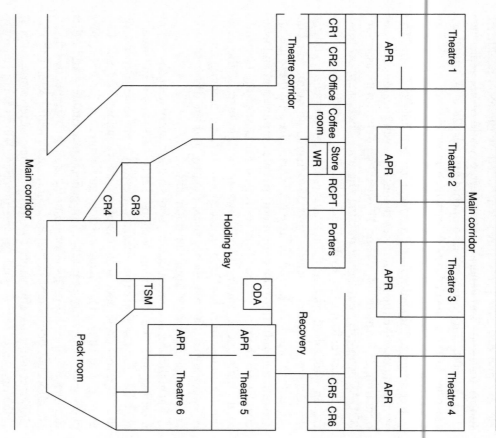

Key

APR   anaesthetic preparation room
CR    changing room
ODA   operating department assistants room
RCPT  theatres suite reception
TSM   theatres services manager's office
WR    waiting room

**Table 13.1**  Weekly schedule for the main theatres

| | | Theatre | | | | | |
|---|---|---|---|---|---|---|---|
| | | 1 | 2 | 3 | 4 | 5 | 6 |
| Monday | a.m. | Mr Stone 1,3,5 Mr North 2,4 8.30–12.30 | | Mr O'Brien 8.30–12.30 | Mr O'Brien 8.30–12.30 | Mr Ash 9.15–12.30 | Mr Vine 8.30–12.30 |
| | p.m. | Mr Iris 2,4 13.30–17.00 | | Mr Fish 13.30–17.00 | Mr Fish 13.30–17.00 | Mr Neale 13.30–17.00 | |
| Tuesday | a.m. | Mr King 9.00–12.30 | Mr Davies 8.30–12.30 | Mr Kirkup 8.30–12.30 | Mr Taylor 8.30–12.30 | Mr Neale 8.30–12.30 | Mr Moore 8.30–12.30 |
| | p.m. | | Mr Davies 13.30–17.00 | Mr Saker 14.00–17.00 | Mr Taylor 13.30–17.00 | Mr Dart 13.30–17.00 | Mr Blake 13.30–17.00 |
| Wednesday | a.m. | | Mr Marples 9.00–12.30 | | Mr Neale 8.30–12.20 | Mr Vine all day list 8.30 | Mr Moore 8.30–12.30 |
| | p.m. | | Mr Marples 13.30–17.00 | | Mr Neale 13.30–17.00 | Mr Vine 16.30/17.00 | Mr Moore 13.30–17.00 |
| Thursday | a.m. | Mr Storey 8.30–12.30 | | Mr Fish 8.30–12.30 | Mr O'Brien 8.30–12.30 | Mr Davies 8.30–12.30 | Mr Dart 8.30–12.30 |
| | p.m. | Mr Stone 13.30–17.00 | | Mr Fish 13.30–17.00 | Mr Neale 13.30–17.00 | Mr Neale 13.30–17.00 | Mr Dart 13.30–17.00 |
| Friday | a.m. | Mr King 9.00–12.30 | Mr Good 8.30–12.30 | Mr Saker all day list 8.30 | Mr Taylor 8.30–12.30 | | Mr Blake 8.30–12.30 |
| | p.m. | Mr King 14.00–17.00 | Mr Good 13.30–17.00 | Mr Saker 16.30/17.00 | Urology DS 14.00–17.00 TT 13.30–17.00 | | |

covering the list with an unfamiliar anaesthetist. Some teams just seem to work faster or more slowly together. It may be that the operating theatre is destined always to experience wide variations from schedule because of the inherent difficulty in making accurate scheduling predictions.

Is operating theatre work so unpredictable that it cannot effectively be planned and scheduled in advance? The data suggest that the problem may not be so intractable. Data collected over eight weeks in the first quarter of 1995 showed that 36 per cent of surgical procedures and over 75 per cent of urological procedures were carried out more than 25 times in that period. The consultant urologists carried out 369 endoscopic bladder examinations and 103 endoscopic prostate re-sections in that period. The consultant surgeons performed 59 varicose vein operations and 47 each of common vein and abdominal cavity procedures respectively. Over those weeks, 11.6 per cent of orthopaedic procedures, 9 per cent of surgical procedures and 4.5 per cent of urological operations were 'one-offs'. In other words, there is a lot of 'repeat business'. The full two-month pattern for surgery, orthopaedics and urology is shown in Table 13.2.

**Table 13.2**   Operations performed February and March 1995

| | No. of operations | Theatre time[a] (hours) | Average operation time (minutes) | % 'one-off' |
|---|---|---|---|---|
| Surgery | 894 | 731 | 49 | 9 |
| Urology | 967 | 308 | 19 | 4.5 |
| Orthopaedics | 646 | 381 | 59 | 11.6 |

[a] from start of anaesthesia to end of operation

On average, around 450 operations are carried out each week in the directorate's ten theatres. That average conceals a wide variation, in both number of procedures carried out and in the variety of the work. These theatres perform a range of procedures such as thyroidectomy, mastectomy, perforated ulcer closure, removal of appendix, colostomy, rectal examination, abscess drainage, pancreatic cyst removal, circumcision, foot ganglionectomy, amputations, various biopsies, and joint repairs and replacements (to cite only a few examples). Some procedures are common, while some are extremely rare, with the bulk of the 'repeat business' lying somewhere in between these two extremes. Table 13.3 illustrates this variability more clearly.

The first six items in Table 13.3 concern relatively common procedures. The first two are urological, the third and fourth are general surgical, and the fifth and sixth are orthopaedic. The last four items in Table 13.3 are less common general surgical procedures. The 'Surgeons' column lists the number of consultants who carried out that procedure during those two months. The 'Operations' column lists the total number of procedures carried out over that period. The 'Theatre times' columns record operation times, including anaesthetic preparation in the theatres department. The 'Fastest average' column identifies the average procedure time taken by the quickest surgeon; the 'Slowest average' column then identifies the average time taken by the slowest surgeon. A hip replacement will thus take one hour and a quarter in one surgeon's hands, and just under two hours with another. An operation on the ileum appears to be similarly unpredictable, with one surgeon taking almost two and a half hours compared with the fastest taking under one hour.

It is important to note the detailed data from which this summary draws. The two-and-a-half-hour ileum operation, for example, appears to be unusual. This was the only such procedure carried out by that surgeon in this two-month period, and this could have been a particularly difficult case or the surgeon may have been unfamiliar with the procedure. In addition, two related operations may in this instance appear under one operation code for the purposes of computer data input. The labels 'fast' and 'slow' in this context thus cannot be taken to imply competence and cannot be used as indicators of quality of treatment received by the patient. A similarly variable pattern is evident with respect to varicose vein procedures. Two surgeons between them carried out 42 of the 59 operations recorded; a third surgeon with the slowest average time – 48 minutes – carried out only two such operations over those two months. Of the two surgeons carrying out most of the varicose vein work, one's average operating time was 15 minutes and the other's was almost double that at 29 minutes. Clearly there is no 'one best way' to perform even relatively straightforward operating theatre procedures, and time differences reflect differences in training, in technique and in professional judgement. There are, therefore, systematic variations *between* surgeons. However, one particular surgeon, or surgical team, is unlikely to vary in pace much from operation to operation, particularly with more commonly performed operations. Because of this, theatre staff – sisters and ODAs in particular – believe they can estimate fairly accurately, most of the time, how long a particular

**Table 13.3**  Times for common and less common operations

| Procedure | Surgeons | Operations | Fastest average | Theatre times (minutes) Slowest average | Overall average |
|---|---|---|---|---|---|
| Endoscopic prostatic resection | 4 | 103 | 31 | 40 | 36 |
| Endoscopic bladder resection | 4 | 61 | 20 | 25 | 23 |
| Varicose vein evulsion | 6 | 59 | 15 | 48 | 20 |
| Total cholecystectomy | 8 | 40 | 45 | 83 | 56 |
| Total hip replacement | 7 | 45 | 74 | 115 | 87 |
| Total knee replacement | 7 | 43 | 55 | 117 | 84 |
| Haemorrhoidectomy | 4 | 5 | 15 | 30 | 19 |
| Excision of ileum | 5 | 9 | 50 | 145 | 83 |
| Excision of breast lesion | 4 | 11 | 17 | 27 | 21 |
| Inguinal hernia repair | 7 | 18 | 32 | 58 | 46 |

*Note*: Figures taken from procedures recorded over two months in 1995

team is going to take with a particular patient with a particular condition.

## The Patient Trail: What Goes Wrong in Theatre?

The steering group has generated a series of process flow diagrams for the various stages of the 'patient trail' – which begins with an outpatient department referral and consultation and ends (it is hoped) with the cured patient's discharge. Members of the steering group have also been speaking with staff, at all levels, involved in theatre work.

Figure 13.3 shows the segment of the trail which takes the patient through the operating theatre. Let us assume that you are the third patient on the morning list for theatre 4 on Wednesday, and that your operation concerns a hernia repair; this should take around 45 minutes 'at the table'. The list for this theatre session will have been drawn up some days ago, but will only have been finalized on Tuesday afternoon or evening. For many different reasons patients 'drop out' from, and are added on to, the list up to the last moment. When the second patient's operation is drawing to a close – say, with about ten minutes to go – the theatre sister fills out a 'patient request ticket'. She takes this out to the holding area and either gives it to a porter or puts it on a board for the next available porter to collect. The porter then walks to the ward to collect you and brings you down to the theatre suite with your ward nurse as escort. All patients must be escorted by a porter and a qualified nurse. When you get to the theatre holding area the ward nurse transfers you to an operating department assistant and they check your details to make sure that you are indeed expected. You are then transferred on to a special theatre trolley and wheeled into the anaesthetic preparation room outside the operating theatre. This is where you wait until the previous operation is over and the theatre has been made ready (fresh cutlery!) for you. If something goes wrong with the previous operation, you could be here for some time. If the nurse on the ward has given you any pre-medication, you should be relaxed and free from anxiety. Here also you meet again your anaesthetist, who visited you on the ward yesterday or this morning to check that you were fit to anaesthetize. When the theatre and surgeon are ready, your anaesthetist will induce anaesthesia, give you a breathing tube, and wheel you into the theatre where the team will lift you on to the table.

**Figure 13.3** The operating theatre trail

| Staff involved | Functions performed |
|---|---|
| Theatre sister or ODA | Puts patient request ticket on board |
| Porter and ward nurse (escort) | Collect patient from ward and deliver to theatre on bed or trolley |
| ODA and ward nurse | Check patient details; move patient on to theatre trolley (if on bed) |
| ODA | Wheels patient into anaesthetic room adjacent to theatre |
| Anaesthetist and ODA | Induce anaesthesia and intubate patient |
| Anaesthetist, ODA and theatre nurse | Wheel patient into theatre and lift on to operating table, with help of team |
| Surgical team: typically includes surgeon, junior doctor, anaesthetist, scrub nurse, ODA, one or two theatre nurses | Surgeon performs operation, assisted by junior doctor if present |
| Anaesthetist and ODA | Reverse anaesthesia, extubate patient; wheel patient to recovery area |
| ODA, theatre nurses and recovery nurses | Complete operation record forms after each procedure and complete session record form at end of session |
| Coding clerk | Codes operations on Theatreman forms at end of each session |
| Theatre clerk | Keys coded data from record forms into Theatreman computer system weekly |

The surgeon is now ready to start your hernia operation. A typical surgical team includes the surgeon, anaesthetist, a senior registrar, a scrub nurse (who looks after the instruments), an operating department assistant (who supports the anaesthetist) and one or more theatre nurses to assist too. When the surgeon has finished, the anaesthetist reverses your anaesthesia and removes your now redundant breathing tube. Seeing that all is going well, one of the nurses or the operating department assistant wheels you into the recovery area where the anaesthetist leaves you, if all is still well, to return to the theatre and to attend to the next patient. You are now in the temporary care of the recovery nurses, who phone your ward when you are fit to travel back with a porter and your escort nurse.

Conversations with staff show that this part of the patient trail does not always run smoothly. A porter may not be available at the moment requested to deliver you to the theatre. The theatres department does not have its 'own' porters, who all belong to a centrally allocated pool. As all the theatres start within the same hour, morning and afternoon, this places a heavy peak load on the porters. Even if a porter is available, the ward nurse may be preoccupied with some other activity or another patient. So, the surgeon may be ready, the theatre may be ready, you may be ready – but the operation cannot begin because transport cannot be arranged. Your operation may have been scheduled for 10.00 a.m., on the surgeon's estimate of how long the two previous cases would take. Suppose the previous cases run much faster than planned. Your ward is taken by surprise when you are called early. You are not ready. You are not in your theatre gown. You have not been given the pre-medication. The test results that are to accompany you and your patient notes to theatre have not been collected. The ward nurse who is to escort you is dealing with another problem and plans to be back just before 10.00 a.m.

On the other hand, you could be in the anaesthetic preparation room in the theatre suite at 09.50 a.m. – and find yourself waiting as the two previous operations have both over-run. A study in the main theatres in 1993 showed that in one month there were 137 instances when a patient waited for 20 minutes or longer in the anaesthetic room, the longest wait that month being over one hour. There is no direct communication between the wards and theatres to alert each location to problems and events in the other. It will often be a ward nurse who first realizes that there will be a problem with a particular patient (who has not arrived, or who is not going to be ready in time). The porters are the only staff who travel regularly between wards and theatres, but their relatively low status seems to inhibit nursing and medical staff from using them as a communications link. The theatres suite reception desk is not permanently staffed, so there is no single main point of contact between ward and theatre staff. As you are on a morning list your delay should not be serious. The single main cause of delay in the afternoon is a morning list that runs over. When the afternoon session is due to start, porters, nurses and operating department assistants may still be out to lunch. So some delays cause later delays.

Delays in theatre can also be caused by problems at the next step in the trail, in recovery. If a lot of patients are moved into the recovery area at around the same time, the nursing staff there may find it difficult to cope. When that happens, the theatre staff have to remain with their patients until they have recovered and can be moved back to their wards. This then means that subsequent patients on that theatre's operating list cannot proceed. Problems like this can become acute at the end of the afternoon session. Recovery nurses may go off shift while there are patients still in theatre. Theatre staff thus suffer the twin delays to their shift time, once because theatre is running late and second because they have to staff the recovery area.

## The Patient Trail: What Goes Wrong 'Upstream'?

Delays in the operating theatre schedules can also be caused by 'upstream' factors, at earlier steps in the patient trail. The most signifant factors in this repect are those surrounding the way in which a session list gets drawn up in the first place. You are on that Wednesday list for theatre 4 because your GP referred you to a hospital consultant who confirmed your diagnosis, gave your case an urgency rating and subsequently decided when to operate on you. The surgical waiting-list clerk who records patient details and doctors' decision sent you a letter with your admission date, which would either be the day before your operation or that morning. Sometimes, of course, it is not the consultant you see in the outpatient clinic but a more junior doctor. Whichever doctor you see completes a surgical waiting-list form, with your details and details of the procedure that you require. These forms are passed to the surgical waiting-list office. The consultants, senior registrars and registrars visit this office regularly to review the waiting-list forms and to make up session lists for the weeks ahead. Your case will have been rated 'priority' (operate immediately), 'urgent' (operate soon) or 'ordinary' (you can wait a while).

The first and most significant factor which determines your allocation to a theatre session list is thus the urgency of your case. However, other factors also apply. Patients undergoing major surgery typically go immediately to an intensive care bed. These are in limited supply, and operations are often moved to later lists for this reason alone. In drawing up a list of patients for a particular theatre session the surgeon may also consider the training needs and interests of the junior doctors on his firm. Operations may thus be scheduled at times when juniors can attend. Surgeons have personal preferences with regard to types of procedures, running order, the number and variety of the particular kinds of operation they will do in one session, and so on.

Once determined, typed and circulated to the theatres and to the wards where patients will be admitted, a theatre session list is not sacred. It is constantly subject to change. A patient may cancel because they now feel better. Another patient may be scheduled in their place, if there is time to arrange this, otherwise the session may just under-run. A patient may be found unfit to anaesthetize or unfit to operate on following admission, so once again another patient may be scheduled. GPs and doctors from other sections in the hospital may put surgeons under pressure to raise the priority on their patients and to operate earlier. When this happens, surgeons may try to 'stuff' lists: patients can simply be added to a list that was already considered full, and that list is liable to over-run.

There is one final issue concerning the surgeons themselves. The technique used to decide which and how many patients to put on a morning or an afternoon theatre list is known simply as guesswork. It is widely acknowledged, even by surgeons themselves, that the guesswork of surgeons in this context is highly ambitious. One reason for this is the ethos which surrounds the consultant surgeon's work, strengthened by a degree of professional competitiveness. A second reason concerns the fact that the surgeon tends to see only the patient on the operating table, and does not always see the clerical, anaesthetic and nursing preparation that brings the patient to the table. This is one reason why there is no common agreement on when a theatre session starts. For the ODA and scrub nurse, it starts about 45 minutes before the patient is on the table, as equipment is obtained, sterilized, counted and positioned. For the anaesthetist, it starts up to half an hour before the patient is on the table, depending on the complexity of the anaesthesia required. (Some anaesthetists will not induce anaesthesia until their surgeon arrives; some surgeons avoid arriving too early so they do not have to wait while the anaesthetist does his part.) But for the surgeon, the start of the operation is the 'knife to skin' time. Surgeons are thus not necessarily good estimators when compiling theatre lists.

## What Are We Going To Do About It?

The senior nurse manager in the surgical directorate has seen some recent publications on business process re-engineering. She sees a review of the theatres as a major opportunity to introduce new working practices. Re-engineering, she notes, can involve multiskilling, process teams, flatter organization hierarchies, case managers, and more employee empowerment. The business manager in the directorate is sympathetic to this view, but feels that it is the administrative staff who assemble patient documentation, who arrange appointments and who draw up the theatre lists, who are isolated and not effectively involved in the patient trail. The hospital's computerized Theatreman system captures a lot of information about the patient flow, including operation times, outcomes and delays. This information, however, is not used systematically to monitor what is happening and to trigger improvements. The theatre sisters and operating department assistants claim that the theatre lists would run to time more often if they did the scheduling themselves — once the surgeons have determined each patient's priority. The consultants, however, who can claim the highest status and expertise in this context, argue that the problem lies simply with the lack of adequate numbers of ward staff and porters, and with the way these staff are used and controlled. The problem could be solved, in their view, with more nurses, more porters, more effectively managed. The relevant data in the Theatreman computer, they feel, is inaccurate and unreliable, as information is recorded by operating department assistants and nurses under pressure, and keyed up by clerical staff who sometimes need to rely on 'informed judgement' when coding the information. They would like to see some straightforward remedial action taken immediately, to help them, to help their staff and to help patients. A major organizational review would take time, and is not really necessary.

## Questions

1 From the solutions offered so far, which would you support and why? What would your recommendations be?

2 What barriers are there to implementing change in this setting? Draw up a force-field analysis, identifying and weighting the driving and resisting factors with respect to your recommended solution(s), and assess the balance of forces in this setting.

3 With potentially large numbers of people involved in any significant changes, what approach to implementing change would you recommend in this context?

4 What are the main differences between this and a manufacturing setting with regard to the application of job and organizational design methods?

5 What conflict – if any – is revealed in this case between a customer care orientation which legitimates change in the interest of the patient, and the traditional autonomy of highly trained and qualified clinical professionals?

## Further Reading

Davenport, T. H. 1993: *Process Innovation: Reengineering Work Through Information Technology*, Boston, Mass.: Harvard Business School Press.

Grey, C. and Miter, N. 1995: 'Reengineering organizations: a critical approach', *Personnel Review*, 24(1), 6–18.

Hall, G., Rosenthal, J. and Wade, J. 1993: 'How to make reengineering really work', *Harvard Business Review*, November–December, 119–131.

Hammer, M. and Champy, J. 1993: *Reengineering the Corporation*, London: Brearly.

Hammer, M. 'Reengineering work – don't automate, obliterate' *Harvard Business Review*, July–August, 104–112.

# 14

# The Ministry of Education

*Action learning based management development*

## HENRIK HOLT LARSEN

This case describes a management development programme in the Danish Ministry of Education (Larsen, 1993; Head et al., 1993). In the late 1980s this organization initiated an action learning based management development programme which was in the following year supplemented by a series of other development processes (information technology, communication, corporate image, etc.). The most recent progress is a comprehensive human resource development programme established as a result of – and co-ordinated with – a vision management process, providing clear objectives for each organizational unit as well as the organization as a whole. The emphasis is put on the managerial role of the participants and the learning methodology as well as the outcome of the programme.

## Background

The ministry has the overall responsibility for the educational activities taking place in primary and secondary schools, vocational schools, universities and other related institutions. This sector employs in total approximately 150,000 people. Munipical institutions (primary and secondary education) count for a staff of approximately 80,000 employees. The remaining 70,000 people are employed by universities, vocational schools, etc. At the time of this programme the administrative core of the ministry – from which the national educational policy is determined and monitored – had about 800 employees.

It was organized into nine divisions, each headed by a division head (deputy permanent secretary).

The programme had three central objectives. The first was to enable the organization to cope with an ever-increasing workload at the same time as there was a cut in staff. Thus, there was a planned annual reduction in staff of at least 2–3 per cent over the coming years. The second objective was to improve the ministry's ability to adapt quickly to rapidly changing external demands. The third was to stimulate (an understanding of) professional management. Managerial staff had mainly been playing the role of specialists, monitoring the technical quality of the work of others, rather than focusing on managerial tasks. Also, the human resource responsibility of line managers for the subordinates was poorly developed.

The ministry had a fairly bureaucratic culture with a high emphasis on the written word, coupled with a strong belief in harmony. Unlike most other bureaucratic organizations the ministry was characterized by informal interpersonal behaviour, low power distance and a humanistic atmosphere. An ambitious information technology project had just been launched in the ministry.

## The Initial Phases of the Programme

Once it had been decided to initiate the programme, a major decision was the definition of the target group. The ministry and the consultants agreed on selecting all those persons who had a real, genuine impact on managerial processes, rather than looking solely at whether people possessed a formal leadership position in the organization. However, this organic selection criterion turned out to be so difficult to apply that the actual group of participants became the top 54 managers of the organization. It was never stated explicitly that the programme was compulsory, but the common understanding was that all managers had to participate, and nobody seemed to object to this.

Strong emphasis was put on informing (managerial and non-managerial) staff about the programme prior to the actual start. Considering that the management development programme took up about half the financial resources for training over a two-year period, it was feared (expected) that non-managerial staff would show signs of jealousy. This was not the case, primarily for two reasons. First, there was a general feeling among staff that something had to be done to professionalize management in the organization. Second, there was a positive reaction by non-managerial staff to the fact that the programme was not a *manager* development programme, aimed at developing 54 individuals, but rather a comprehensive management development programme.

Strong emphasis was also placed on a maximum 'custom tailoring' of the programme to the explicated need and interests of the participants and the organization. To establish this data material, three things were done. First, the consultants conducted individual or group interviews with approximately 150 persons in the organization. All 54 management participants were interviewed individually, and some 100 non-managerial staff (selected by and among the non-managerial staff as representatives of the various professions, levels and divisions) were interviewed individually or in groups. In addition, the consultants attended and observed a number of regular staff meetings in the organization, including the weekly management briefing with the Minister of Education. Third, a reference group was established as a central forum for contact between the consultants and the participants. The members of the reference group were eight representatives of the participants, the permanent secretary and the team of consultants. Also, the principal spokesperson of the non-managerial staff was a member of the group even though she did not participate in the programme as such.

The interview phase yielded unique data about management and personnel problems of the organization and served as raw material for a working paper, giving an 'X-ray' of the organization. This paper, which was written by the consultants, did not interpret or evaluate the situation, but described and summarized the situation as it had been expressed through the interviews. In this way it would be up to the organization to decide what to do about the problems expressed in the paper. The minister, and the ministry, tried in no way to alter or censor the paper, and it was distributed to all staff. Obviously the paper was intensively discussed in the organization – informally and formally. Thus it was discussed at seminars with representatives of all staff groups. Also, the top management team had a 24-hour workshop during which the team defined ten areas which would be given high priority in the future. These ten areas of action were communicated to and discussed with the organization, revised and reconfirmed by the top management team. One of these areas of priority was the human resource responsibility of line managers.

Among the conclusions in the working paper were three key points:

- The top management team was not perceived to be a decision-making and policy-formulating body. Too much time was spent on exchanging information rather than discussing strategic issues and developing general guidelines for the organization.
- The culture of the organization was perceived to be friendly and polite, but conflicts were suppressed.
- There was a strong desire among non-managerial staff that managers at all levels should focus more on general managerial problems and delegate functional/specialist problem solving and case handling to subordinate staff.

The activities described so far (the information phase, the interview procedure and the diagnostic working paper) were not just an initial start or diagnosis of the change process. On the contrary, they were believed to be an important first step of the change process itself. It had a great impact that a very large part of the entire organization was *de facto* involved in diagnosing the actual situation and/or discussing potential strategies for implementing change in the organization.

## Training Courses and Project Work

The systematic learning activities of the programme consisted of two main streams: management courses and individual projects. The courses covered issues with strong emphasis on the problems discovered during the initial interview study. It is important to note that the content of the courses was not developed until after the diagnosis. Emphasis was placed on down-to-earth subjects and experiential exercises rather than abstract conceptualization of general management problems.

Immediately after the first course module each participant was asked to define a personal management project theme, which:

1 contained important, complex management problems of a specific, realistic nature;
2 was of personal interest to the participant;
3 was of importance to the organization;
4 involved some degree of risk taking;
5 necessitated joint effort by the participant and his or her subordinates (to be solved);
6 had a clear formulation of targeted end result; and
7 could be documented and evaluated.

This design reflected an experiential learning model, according to which learning is facilitated if people are placed in an experience-loaded environment, involving a certain degree of risk taking and with a high level of commitment to the task performed. Also, as with the general programme, it was believed that management was not (solely) the behaviour, style or attitude of a specific group of individuals (managers). Management was rather viewed as an interpersonal process of influence and power. Therefore it was important to include the subordinates in the project work, although they did not take part in the courses. It was not a requirement that the projects should be successful from a functional or content (factual) point of view. As long as the project work involved experimentation and facilitated an intensive and positive learning process, the actual outcome of the project was of less importance.

The participants could choose a task (project theme) which was known or new to them. They could solve this problem by a known or a new method, and do it in co-operation with well-known or new persons/organizations. However, it was not allowed to play safe on all three dimensions, as this would restrict the learning potential of the project. Neither was it recommended to throw oneself at the deep end, as the risk taking on all three dimensions would be too demanding. Thus it was recommended to experiment on one or two dimensions.

The project proposals had to be presented in writing and accepted by the top management team and the consultants. In the course of the project work progress reports had to be produced at regular intervals. The consultants played the role of being process consultants, in that a consultant was linked to each project. The projects had to be finished in eight months which was coinciding with the official termination of the programme as a whole. At that time a residential two-day seminar was held to present the results of the project work, evaluate the programme as a whole and decide on follow-up activities of the programme.

## Evaluation of the Programme

The evaluation of the management development programme is divided into separate process, result and design evaluations.

The process evaluation shows that the initial reception of the programme was quite positive. The organization was quite excited by the diagnostic interviews, and the working paper was received with a fair amount of curiosity and excitement. The training courses were considered to be worthwhile.

The individual projects were generally considered to be interesting, necessary and important, but also time consuming. An attempt by the consultants to form small groups of participants who could support each other with the project work was rejected by the organization due to the workload already involved in the programme. The motivation and energy with which the programme participants dealt with their projects varied a lot. Put in popular terms, some participants were flying first class: exciting topics, lots of work done, experimentation and an openness to new experiences. Some projects were like business class: a considerable amount of motivation but the workload was in a pragmatic way kept at a realistic level. Finally, some of the managers were flying economy class with a minimum of effort to bring them from one place to another.

An overall evaluation of the results of the programme and its consequences was carried out at an evaluation seminar four months after the formal end of the programme. About 50 persons participated in this seminar, including the top management team, representatives of participants and their subordinate staff, the reference group and the consultants. The seminar report indicates that the top management team had enhanced its consciousness of and ability to carry out its strategic management role. The team had become more visible and significant in the organization. At the same time the meetings of the team had become more frank and involved more fruitful discussions. The management group as a whole (the 54 participants) had for the first time been together and participated in a common, long-lasting process. The programme had clearly led to an increased consciousness of the manager's roles, tasks and possibilities.

In the area of human resources management both managers and their staff had become much more aware of the content and importance of the staff development role of the line managers. Despite this, only few specific improvements were achieved in this area.

In general, there was a great variation of opinion as to whether management functions were better executed than before, dependent on the persons and subject areas concerned. The individual development projects clearly carried a central part of the effect of the project. Roughly estimated, a third of the projects had a rather significant effect; another third had a positive effect, although not overwhelming. The last third of the projects either did not find new paths or never started. However, it should be kept in mind that in total more than 50 projects were running at the same time. This contributed to developing a climate of development and renewal, even though some projects were very poor.

Despite these positive results there were limits to the impact of the project. The bureaucratic culture with its intellectual and analytic approach lingered on and acted as a curb on the more action-oriented approach which struggled to emerge. Also, the traditional culture counteracted a more extrovert orientation towards the 'customers' of the ministry.

## The Significance of National Culture

When the management development programme was designed and carried through, it was not considered whether the programme reflected specific Danish national culture characteristics. However, a subsequent *ex post facto* analysis (in co-operation with US researchers) has detected that the programme does actually have a 'Danish design' flavour. This will be illustrated by referring to the cultural mapping of Hofstede (1980; 1991), based on the four variables:

1 femininity versus masculinity;
2 individualism versus collectivism;
3 power distance;
4 uncertainty avoidance.

The Danish national culture is, in Hofstede's (1980) study, *feminine* in nature. This is reflected in the management development programme in a number of ways. Great emphasis was placed on interpersonal processes, social skills, consensus and suppression of conflict. Also, the selection criteria for the participants initially did not include hierarchical level, and various attempts were made to include people who informally participated in managerial processes. As mentioned above, these criteria eventually had to be abandoned.

Moderate *individualism* is another characteristic feature of the Danish national culture. Rather than putting high fliers of the organization on the fast track, this management development process made the distinction between individual development, management development and organization development disappear. The project work reinforced the link between the participant and his or her subordinates, but was also seen as a catalyst for organizational change. Great emphasis was placed on strengthening the competence of the group of particants as a whole, rather than explicating the progress of the individual members.

In Hofstede's study, the Danish national score for *power distance* is very low. The fact that non-managerial staff were not only interviewed as part of the diagnosis procedure but also received the resulting working paper and were involved in determining appropriate courses of action as a consequence of the working paper, shows how the distance between organizational levels is modest.

The fourth cultural dimension is *uncertainty avoidance*. Although the programme as a whole was fairly structured, a lot of ambiguity and uncertainty was deliberately built into the programme. Hence, the content of the course modules were not determined in advance. Participants were encouraged to experiment in their project work and go for the good learning experience rather than the 'right solution' to the task in question, if unable to achieve both objectives. The heavy process (rather than outcome) orientation of the programme as such put focus on 'how we are moving', rather than 'where we are going'.

Interestingly enough, Jaeger (1986) has put forward the hypothesis that Danish culture is very compatible with the underlying values of organization development (OD), despite the fact that OD as a discipline was invented in the US, which cultural profile (according to Jaeger) deviates from the ideal OD culture characteristics.

## Conclusion

Although we have focused exclusively on the management development programme, it should be mentioned that a large number of other development processes took place at the same time or in the following years. The ministry underwent an information technology revolution, a design programme, an effectiveness programme and a change in organizational structure. A development dialogue programme (that is, annual performance talks) was introduced, and this was later hooked on to a vision management programme. The idea of this programme was to discuss the overall visions and objectives of the organization and relate these to the 'psychological contract' of each individual.

The vision reports were written by a central planning function of the organization but based on close interaction with all layers of the organization. The middle managers were attributed a vital role as 'ambassadors' for this strategic plan, as well as that of collectors of input from non-managerial staff, and they pass this information on to the top management.

In order to match the human resources with the strategic plans, a comprehensive employee development programme was initiated in 1993. All staff were given an almost-free choice of a series of courses as well as on-the-job learning activities. The idea was that all development activities should facilitate the synergy between individual and organizational development. Thus, the range of development activities was designed in such a way that it stimulated the development of skills needed for the implementation of the vision reports. Also, the annual performance dialogues were extended so as to include a couple of questions which dealt with the individual consequences of the organizational vision and objectives.

The case illustrates how the very precise perception of the crucial role of the middle managers makes the organization run a management development programme. Delimiting the target population for this programme shows how difficult it is to define managerial roles and behaviours in an organization. The middle managers were clearly given the role of strategic ambassador, change agent and cultural catalyst. The subsequent vision management programme – supported by the staff development programme and the revision of the performance talks – reinforced the role of the middle manager as a strategic link between top management and the non-managerial staff.

Finally, the case shows that – although it was unintended – the design and implementation of the programme reflects the values of the national culture within which it was created.

---

## Questions

1  Discuss the advantages and disadvantages of running a *management* development programme rather than a *manager* development programme.

2  Discuss the effectiveness of training courses versus experiential learning situations (in this case project work).

3  Which fundamental national culture characteristics in your own culture should be taken into consideration, if one were running a management development programme similar to the one described in this case?

## References

Head, T. C., Larsen, H. H., Nielsen, P. L. and Sørenseń, P. F. Jr. 1993: The impact of national culture on organizational change: A Danish case study. *International Journal of Public Administration*, **16**(11).

Hofstede, G. 1980: *Culture's Consequences*. Newbury Park, CA: Sage.

Hofstede, G. 1991: *Culture and Organizations: Software of the Mind*. London: McGraw-Hill.

Jaeger, A. M. (1986): Organization development and national culture: Where is the fit? *Academy of Management Review*, **11**(1), 178–90.

Larsen, H. H. 1993: *Experiential learning in management development – a Danish case study*. Papers in Organization, No. 10, Institute of Organization and Industrial Sociology.

# 15
# British Rail

*Lessons in absence control*
PAUL EDWARDS AND
COLIN WHITSTON

This case concerns the control of attendance and related questions of the role of disciplinary systems in the process. These matters are placed in the wider context of discipline in the sense of morale, rather than limiting them to technical questions of how to design and operate a dismissal and discipline procedure. In this wider remit the case also touches on efforts to change organizational cultures. The case of British Rail (BR) is in many ways special, but the organization shares many features with the rest of the public sector (notably commercialization) while other developments (such as budgetary devolution and a growing focus on controlling absence costs) are common across much of industry.

One issue in considering the case is the identification of just which aspects are specific to BR and which are more general. This is important in making sense of any case study: many case books imply that there is such a thing as decontextualized 'best practice', whereas what is required is understanding of how broad ideas have to be adapted or even abandoned in particular circumstances.

This case draws on a research project funded by the Economic and Social Research Council. In the interests of sharpening the presentation, some details have been changed, quotes have been attributed to occupants of certain roles which their real counterparts would not necessarily endorse, and in some cases a composite portrait based on the views of several individuals has been painted. Personal names are pseudonyms.

## Background

The case relates to the early 1990s, when BR was in public ownership. Between 1979 and 1990/1, employment fell from about 180,000 to 130,000 while labour productivity improved by about a third. Government subsidy was also being cut, and in 1988 InterCity operations were required to operate on fully commercial principles. As an area manager interviewed by Ferner (1988, p. 120) put it, 'the budget is king'. Major changes in working practices were introduced throughout the 1980s, notably increasing use of driver-only trains and flexible rostering (Pendleton, 1993). These changes were often opposed by the unions, which maintained an important presence in the industry: in 1982 there was a strike by drivers against new working practices, and in 1989 came a national strike which, though ostensibly about wages, was also underlain by concerns about work organization and what was perceived as a 'hard line' management (*Financial Times*, 1989). Alongside efforts to change long-established patterns of industrial relations, BR nationally was introducing newer forms of human resource management, notably efforts to communicate directly with staff and to involve them in customer care initiatives.

The case concerns one of BR's Areas, which employed about 2,000 staff in a largely urban area. Beneath the area manager there were managers responsible for the main operations of train management, stations and carriage-cleaning depots. There was a single professional personnel manager. Traditionally, the personnel function had been little developed, with most duties being handled by the functional managers.

Despite efforts by BR nationally to reduce the influence of the unions, in practice change was much more limited (Pendleton, 1991). The Area followed this pattern: union representatives retained many of their traditional roles such as involvement in drawing up staff rosters. They were much more influential among train crew than among station or depot staff.

Rail work is a round-the-clock operation. Train crew worked variable shifts with a wide range of times for booking on and off work; an individual might start work at 4 a.m. one day and 7.30 a.m. the next. Other staff worked more standard eight-hour shifts. By the nature of their duties, train crew worked away from direct supervision; other workers were based at a fixed location and were subject to more normal monitoring by supervisors. The train crew were exclusively male; there were a few women among platform staff and rather more among workers in the cleaning depots. Train drivers were almost exclusively white, but among other grades there were substantial proportions of employees of Asian origin; there were some workers of West Indian origin in the cleaning depots. The workforce was highly stable: two-thirds of staff had been employed for at least ten years.

## Attendance and Discipline: Policy Initiatives

The disciplinary system is described in Table 15.1. Its formality marks it out from the approach in many organizations, but its essentials were similar to those of most large organizations. Rules identified actions such as lateness and absence from the place of work which were punishable. In addition, a wide range of work-related actions such as the failure to observe proper procedures in driving a train were liable to disciplinary action.

**Table 15.1** The disciplinary structure

Discipline in BR is more militaristic than in most large organizations. In effect, workers are 'put on a charge' for some specific offence such as driving a train incorrectly or being rude to a passenger. At the time of the study, management nationally was aiming to cut down the number of levels through which an appeal could go, but otherwise the disciplinary machinery was as it had been since it was formalized in 1956 and indeed for many years before that. Workers have the right to be informed in writing of a charge, which is done on a Form 1. They may respond in writing or reserve their defence until the hearing; may be accompanied by a spokesperson; and may call witnesses. The charge is heard by a manager, who can apply a range of penalties from a 'suitable serious conversation' through a formal reprimand which is recorded on the worker's file, to demotion or even dismissal. Form 2 states the punishment. Workers then have the right of appeal to higher levels.

The formal procedure is not used for absence, on the grounds that absence is not necessarily a culpable act and that the formal procedure is too rigid to deal with the issue. This means that the approach is more corrective than punitive, but also that workers do not have the rights attached to the procedure. Most absence cases are handled initially without the presence of a spokesperson. If further action is taken, union representatives may be involved.

Local managers were highly conscious of the need to control labour costs. For example, the area manager had ended the long-standing practice of allowing virtually unlimited overtime (which had been a traditional part of the informal bargain with workers: low basic wages, but reasonably secure jobs and plenty of overtime). There was now a standard limit for each operation. There was also a focus on absence rates, which ran through all levels and functions of management. Personnel managers at the level above the Area, the Region, saw it as important, as did many operating managers. The area personnel manager saw absence control as his main priority, signalled by the area manager's giving him a target of reducing absence rates below 10 per cent.

The approach was for the personnel manager to examine absence records and identify staff who appeared to warrant action, either because of an overall level of absence or because of a pattern such as absence during a weekend shift. There was no set trigger of so many spells of absence before the procedure was instituted. It was the responsibility of a section manager (not the first-line supervisor) to interview staff. This was carried out separately from the formal discipline procedure. The required approach was to raise the issue and point out that absence interfered with the running of the business, and not in the first instance to question the genuineness of a spell of absence. If necessary, further action could be taken. The procedure was a managerial initiative about which the unions had not been consulted or informed.

## Views of Life in the Organization

A team of researchers is investigating the organization. They obtain the following information from interviews.

They start by speaking with George Halford, the personnel manager, asking him first how he maintains consistency across 2,000 employees. He explains that there are only about 30 cases which are serious and it is possible to monitor them all. Asked whether the policy is working, he says he believes that it is, and in particular that the hard core of absentees is being reduced. Generally speaking the functional managers take their duties seriously. The researchers put it to him that in most organizations detailed control is exercised by first-line supervisors in BR are part of the problem: they are of 'poor quality', and are 'set in their ways', and they have never really exercised any normal supervision, being instead mere allocators of work and progress chasers, in many cases being more one of the work group than a manager.

Some functional managers share some of these views but are more robust in expressing them. Typical is Harry Preston, an operations manager responsible for station staff, who argues that management had only just learned to manage. 'In the past, no one in BR got the sack. Unions were powerful and managers were scared to act.' Then a manager in another area of BR dismissed a worker and this 'opened everyone's eyes' to what could be done. Now, there was a willingness to take control of issues like attendance and time keeping, which are real problems. But on other issues, too, notably when workers slip away from the workplace, he is willing to use the formal disciplinary procedure. A typical case, he says, is a member of the platform staff at the main station in a city centre. When work is slack it is easy to slip away for an hour or so. This comfortable 'fiddle' used to be tolerated by supervisors, but managers will now crack down if they come across examples. He admits that the practice still goes on and that some supervisors turn a blind eye to it, but claims that the practice is less common than it was. As for the formal absence procedure, this is too soft because it is hard to deal with someone who is talked to and who then improves behaviour for a time before going absent again. Senior management should be tougher, and the recent concession of paying sick pay from the first day of absence for the majority of staff should be ended. Workers' attitudes also needed changing. 'They will take a day off because of some domestic problem, and they expect us to accept that; we have to be clearer about our expectations that they will work unless they are genuinely sick.' Like most managers he believes that better sick pay and generally slacker attitudes have led to rising absence rates.

Others are more cautious. Train crew manager Mike Clifford, for example, stresses 'the sheer love of the job' among train drivers and the strong 'sense of duty' and commitment to safety among his staff. He is not sure about a hard line: 'we depend on them, for example to do overtime at short notice and they deserve some consideration in return'. He also argues that 'we used to be really militaristic in the style of discipline; and a lot of changes have made work easier'. Absence levels are 'not that high' especially when the hours of work and demands of the job are taken into consideration.

Train crew supervisor Jack Butler echoes these thoughts. On the one hand 'there is a good working relationship' with the men, and being tough for no reason is pointless. For example, 'why penalize someone who slips out for a few minutes when all he would be doing is sitting in the canteen?' On the other hand, it is impossible to deal with absence: 'if someone phones in sick, I can't query this. I am not a doctor'. Absence is a 'real headache' because, if someone does not turn up, his duty simply has to be covered. Staff shortages make his life particularly difficult. The researchers observe work in the supervisors' office, and describe it as 'managed chaos'; there is a constant stream of workers through the office and supervisors have to juggle staff availability with work schedules. It is not just a matter of having, say, a driver available, but one who knows a given route and who can cover a job without exceeding limits on hours of work.

Trade union representatives present a highly distrustful view of management in general. 'There is no attempt to negotiate any more', says one. 'Since the [drivers'] strike of 1982, management has had the whip hand', says another. There is a catalogue of complaints, symbolized by an intense personal dislike of the area manager. A man like Mike Clifford, though, is 'OK'. 'We can deal with him and get sensible agreements on immediate issues.' As for discipline, this has 'got a lot tougher'. Some celebrated cases are cited where workers have been warned for not wearing their uniform correctly. One particular event stands out in their minds: some drivers were disciplined for drinking on duty but managers, they claim, regularly do the same without penalty. The general image of management is of a distant group which is distrusted. But there is disagreement about the place of absence control here. Some argue that managers now unfairly sack long-serving workers whereas others stress the duty of attendance and feel that absence is controlled 'but not in an extreme way'. They all confirm that they were not informed about the control system and are very unclear about it; it seems to be some way down their list of priorities.

## Absence, Discipline Data and Opinion Surveys

The researchers then collect data on absence and the use of discipline, and conduct an interview programme with a cross-section of staff. They write a report which includes the following points.

BR has a distinctive absence profile compared with other organizations which they have studied. A relatively high proportion of workers never takes time off, but there is also a high proportion with six or more spells of absence in a year. The great majority of absences last only one or two days. The overall number of days absent per worker per year on their figures is 17, compared with 13 in a manufacturing company and 28 in a hospital. BR's own figures may look higher than this because people absent for 12 months or longer are still recorded as absent, and because shift rosters typically work on a pattern of six days a week; this means that there are more days 'at risk' than in a normal five-day-a-week environment. The researchers could find no official data on trends, but they discovered on top of a dusty cupboard some old staff records. From these, they calculate that absence levels over the previous five years have stayed roughly constant and for some groups have declined.

Data on discipline are more plentiful. They point to a sharp rise in the use of sanctions over the previous two years, particularly over absence but also on a range of work performance issues. There has been no trend for the more severe sanctions to be used, and most cases are resolved with 'suitable serious conversations'. Examination of disciplinary records reveals the continuation of a traditional low-key approach. In one case a guard admitted leaving the workplace for more than three hours in order to do some shopping. He received only a verbal warning, together with the loss of pay for the relevant period. There are no good data on whether there have been more dismissals, though evidence for one year finds 19 cases – 11 of these for absence-related offences. These cases involve both new and long-serving staff. The overall number is higher than is common in organizations of similar size in the country generally. The researchers concluded that discipline was being tightened, but that important elements of continuity remained.

Their study of worker opinions reflected this mixed situation. The general level of morale was very low, particularly among train crew. For example, asked how much trust they felt there was between managers and workers, 41 per cent of the sample said that there was little or none; and more than half felt that the quality of relations had worsened. Among train drivers, these figures rose to 75 per cent. Discontent was higher than those in other organizations, although quite similar to another public sector case. There was also widespread scepticism about what managers actually did. When given a list of three standard functions performed by management, including routine administration, a third of the BR sample denied that managers carried out any of them. Typical comments were that there were 'too many graduates' and that managers knew about budgets but not about the practical job of running a railway. Follow-up questions revealed a deep-seated suspicion of managerial motives in implementing change, combined with scepticism about managerial competence. Workers spoke at length about flexible rostering, arguing that it increased rather than reduced costs while at the same time putting more pressure on workers. There was also widespread scepticism about BR's efforts to improve customer care and to increase workers' sense of interest in the job. As one platform worker argued, customer care meant nothing when staffing levels were being cut and he was supposed to cover a dozen busy platforms at once.

However, this picture was balanced by two other sets of results. First, workers did not feel that they personally were directly under pressure from management. Asked about their awareness of pressures from management concerning work attendance, 40 per cent of BR workers (a proportion similar to that in other organizations studied) said that they were aware of none, BR's policy of tightening up notwithstanding. And 60 per cent had had no personal experience of being disciplined, with a similar proportion feeling that the rules were in general fair. Those who did have experience of discipline shared union representatives' complaints. As one argued, managers set train crew impossible targets in terms of punctuality but then disciplined drivers if they were found breaking a speed limit.

Second, generalized beliefs about the duty to attend and to perform adequately remained strong. Asked whether they had ever thought about not going in to work when there was nothing actually preventing them from attending, just over half of BR workers said that they had sometimes thought of this; this was much lower than the proportions in other organizations. Most notably, a group of white-collar office workers, who might be expected to be much more 'loyal', returned a figure of 79 per cent. The main reason which BR workers gave for attending work was loss of money if they stayed away; only 7 per cent cited fear of discipline. Asked why loss of money was important, given that sick pay was available for all absences, workers explained that this covered only basic earnings and that they would lose overtime and other bonuses. There were, however, some suggestions that the boundary between acceptable and unacceptable reasons for absence was drawn by employees at a point where managers may not want it to be. Thus some workers felt that 'being unable to attend' embraced pressing domestic tasks. The researchers attributed this to the long hours worked in BR (which meant that leisure was unavailable to deal with these matters) and to the previous relaxed approach to absence control which had allowed the relevant assumptions to grow up unchecked.

In presenting these findings in a report to management and unions, the researchers highlighted several issues for consideration.

First, was BR's absence problem real in the sense that workers generally were going absent too often, or was it a reflection of the fact that financial pressures were making the current levels of absence more of an issue for management than they had previously been? They also warned about simplistic use of data. Thus when they started the study they were told that the cleaning depot was a black spot for absence and poor work standards. Yet they discovered that the depot was used as what its manager called a 'dumping ground' where problem cases and misfits were sent; and people recruited directly to work in the depot were, as he put it, the 'dregs of the labour market'.

Second, there were clear problems of consistency in the application of discipline. Standards were highly informal and people with similar records appeared to have been treated differently. There could also be problems of racial discrimination, given that all the managers were white and that cultural stereotypes about black workers' work attitudes are commonplace.

Third, a disciplinary crack-down occurred a couple of years ago, when absence and work conduct issues were suddenly attacked. The researchers had the impression that after this purge managers were settling into former ways and that policing attendance had become a mere routine.

Fourth, there was an atmosphere of mistrust but also a reservoir of commitment to the service which could be drawn on.

Fifth, the gulf was particularly wide between managers and union representatives.

Sixth, although worker discontent was widespread there was little organized, collective, opposition towards management. Workers felt disgruntled but they lacked the tradition and organization to engage in overt disputes with management. In the cleaning depot, in particular, workers felt distant from management but they also had little belief in the effectiveness of trade union activity and they did not have much confidence in each other. Thus some spoke of a climate of suspicion: 'you don't know who your mates are'. Train crew had a more common sense of discontent, but the researchers saw this as 'permissive rather than consciously organized': a worker who was disciplined would be supported because workers shared his situation but there was little will to organize collective action, while in cases of absence from the place of work train crew acknowledged why someone was taking time off but saw it as a matter of individual conscience.

Finally, the researchers argued, the duties and position of supervisors needed consideration.

## Managerial Choices

In discussing this report, managers like Harry Preston argue for tighter control. 'We have only just started down the right road. A lot of them still think it is OK to stay at home to get the washing machine fixed. And we have still got people like Smith who should have been sacked years ago.' (Smith is something of a local notoriety who has poor work discipline and absence records but who has escaped dismissal.) Preston admits that overall absence is not that bad, but 'we have still got the hard core to deal with'. More generally, the report 'shows that there is still a lot of slackness on day-to-day issues. Our performance targets are getting tighter and tighter. We have got to get everyone aware of our intentions.'

'But', says Mike Clifford, 'it may be OK for you to crack the whip over your station people. I have skilled train drivers to deal with, and I need their co-operation. And they are a lot more organized as a group than your people. I can't afford to antagonize them.' He admits that worker opposition has slowed the introduction of new work practices but points to several recent instances of success. 'We can work round the unions and gradually change attitudes. We only need to crack the whip with the real hard cases.'

George Halford is mostly concerned about his absence targets. 'It is all very well for researchers to say that the problem is not that bad', but there are tight labour cost goals to meet. 'And you line managers tend to let things slide. We have got to keep on top of this problem.' He does, however, consult regional personnel staff, who make two points. First, there have been serious strikes in 1982 and 1989; BR cannot afford any more; and local managers adopting a hard line would 'take the consequences' if this provoked further militancy. Second, with growing commercialization it was crucial that the quality of the service be strengthened. The idea of building on the 'reservoir of commitment' is stressed, perhaps finding some ways to involve unions in disciplinary policy and in change more generally.

Halford is not sure that he fully understands this. When he mentions it to Preston, the reaction is clear: 'The report says that there is no organized opposition, so we can forget the unions as a threat. As for the idea of working with them, we have spent the past ten years putting them in their place. They have nothing to offer.'

The researchers are called back to discuss these issues. But when they arrive they find that a series of immediate crises – a bomb alert, a broken down train, a shortage of drivers – means that the meeting is cancelled. From what they have seen of the day-to-day pressures in the Area, this is a fairly average day. The meeting is never rearranged.

## Tasks and Questions

In the following, various roles can be taken. Tasks and questions also vary in difficulty and complexity, as indicated in each.

### Managerial and union roles

1 (Introductory) Advise Halford on the development of consistent procedures and the avoidance of race bias. How should workers and unions be consulted about the procedures?

2 (Introductory) Adopt the roles of a manager and a union representative faced with a case of 'absence from the place of work'. Play out the case, giving attention to the customary norms around this type of behaviour.

3 (Intermediate) How might the role of supervisors be strengthened? Consider in particular the day-to-day pressures faced by supervisors.

4 (Intermediate) How might local union officials aim to increase workforce unity? What tactics might be adopted in dealing with perceived managerial injustice?

5 (Complex) What does the existence of informal rules say about the relevance of standard ideas of good practice? Should workplace informality be implicitly tolerated or is there a way in which it can be recognized more formally?

6 (Complex) Adopting the role of a consultant to local management, develop a policy for the management of attendance. Pay particular attention to: the 'reservoir of commitment'; the links between absence control and wider issues of employee commitment; and the costs of any proposals in the light of financial constraints.

*Student/analyst/observer roles*

1 (Introductory)   Does BR have an absence problem? What are the best ways to measure absence patterns?

2 (Intermediate)   Why are relatively few workers aware of new policies on discipline and absence? Why do different groups think so differently?

3 (Advanced)   In what ways is the disciplinary framework in BR distinctive, and why does it have this character?

4 (Advanced)   What does this case tell us about the effects of commercialization in the public sector on traditional forms of management–worker relations?

## References

Ferner, A. 1988: *Governments, Managers and Industrial Relations*. Oxford: Blackwell.

*Financial Times* 1989: news item, 29 June.

Pendleton, A. 1991: The barriers to flexibility: flexible rostering on the railways. *Work, Employment and Society*, **5**(2), 241–57.

Pendleton, A. 1993: Railways. In Pendleton, A. and Winterton, J. (eds), *Public Enterprise in Transition*, London: Routledge.

## Further reading

Edwards, P. K. 1994: Discipline and the creation of order. In Sisson, K. (ed.), *Personnel Management*. Oxford: Blackwell.

Edwards, P. K. and Whitston, C. 1993: *Attending to Work*, Oxford: Blackwell.

Industrial Relations Service 1991: Discipline at work: 1, The practice; 2, Procedures. *Employment Trends*, 493; 494, Industrial Relations Service, August.

Industrial Relations Service 1994: Sickness absence monitoring and control: a survey of practice. *Employment Trends*, 568, Industrial Relations Service, September.

# 16

# LeisureCo

*Customer service, employee involvement and the Flexible Firm*

PETER ACKERS

## LeisureCo, HRM and the Flexible Firm Debate

The human resources problem at LeisureCo is how to deliver a high-quality service to customers through a highly casualized workforce. The seasonal character of the theme park product market, and the traditional characteristics of service and leisure employment, throw into question the human resources management (HRM) formula for 'mainstream' (Storey, 1992) businesses of long-term investment in training and employee involvement *for all the workforce*. From a purely business point of view, a more likely scenario is the flexible firm model (Atkinson, 1984), whereby the employer deliberately divides employees into an indispensable 'core' and a disposable 'periphery'. However, the situation is quite unlike some other private services, such as office cleaning, where casual employees operate behind the scenes, out of sight. At LeisureCo, these peripheral workers are the public face of the business to the customer, charged not just with fulfilling routine tasks but also with establishing empathy and creating a fun, happy atmosphere. This is the dilemma of HRM at LeisureCo.

The notion of HRM is a vague and ambiguous one; however, one of its core claims is that valuing and investing in the human resource is central to business competitiveness. This runs against the treatment of workers as disposable commodities who are freely bought and sold at the lowest price possible on the labour market. Rather, HRM claims to regard the workforce as a long-term investment, suggesting stability, commitment and a substantial investment in training. For manufacturing employees the logic of the HRM approach is found in efficient working and a high-quality product leading, indirectly, to customer satisfaction. In the service sector, however, the relationship with the customer is much more direct since the service is the product that is delivered on a face-to-face basis. Thus HRM, total quality management (TQM) and customer service sketch a virtuous triangle of business effectiveness.

In reality, there are grounds for questioning these desired and prescribed remedies. For instance, recent surveys have found limited evidence of the HRM approach sweeping British industry, and rather more of a 'Bleak House', tough, hire-and-fire, low pay, and discipline regime. Atkinson's (1984) theory of the flexible firm offers one explanation for these trends. Many employers are looking for more flexible employment alternatives to the standard model of the employee working to a narrow job description, engaged on an eight-to-five, five-day-week, full-time basis, and paid a regular going rate for the job (negotiated by trade unions and linked to the cost of living). In Atkinson's view, five environmental factors explain this reorientation. First, there is market stagnation, particularly in Britain, with firms looking for permanent reductions in unit labour costs. Second, there is a concern not to repeat the expensive and demoralizing process of job loss and redundancies. Third, and related, there is uncertainty about the pace and sustainability of economic recovery, making businesses reluctant to overcommit themselves by taking on large numbers of full-time employees. Fourth, there is the increasing pace and declining cost of technological change which make it unlikely that as in the past, any one set of skills will last the worker a lifetime. Finally, reductions in working time, in many cases to a 37-hour week, have caused employers to concentrate on how they can get the most out of the time worked.

According to Atkinson (1984), employers have sought four types of flexibility.

1 Functional flexibility – enables employees to be redeployed between tasks, through multiskilling and teamworking, in response to changes in production methods and product demand. This enables a standard, full-time workforce to respond flexibly to the new environment.

2 Financial flexibility – attacks the 'rate for the job' aspect of the standard employment relationship by attempting to link pay more directly to local labour market conditions, business performance or individual effort.

However, the biggest challenge to the standard employment relationship comes from the final two forms of flexibility, and these are the focus of the case below.

3  Numerical flexibility – allows the employee headcount to be increased or decreased in line with changes in the level of demand for labour, so that the number of employees at any one time exactly matches the number required. The most obvious method of achieving this is by increased use of part-time and temporary employees who can be hired and fired more easily.

4  Distancing, or subcontracting – takes this process a stage further by replacing the employment contract (and the restrictions of employment legislation) with a short-term commercial contract which can be terminated or cheapened easily.

In the most controversial part of his analysis, Atkinson links the four dimensions of his analysis into a new core and periphery model of the firm which, he suggests, will supplant the older workforce division between skilled and unskilled, and manual and white-collar categories of employees.

The Flexible Firm model (see Figure 16.1) has clear implications for the HRM debate. The core workers will remain full time and enjoy employment stability and good levels of pay. In exchange, they will be trained to be functionally flexible and have their remuneration linked to business and personal performance. Atkinson (1984) suggests that they will be managed in a participative style of employee involvement. This, in short, is the home of HRM in mainstream organizations. The peripheral workers, by contrast, will be casualized, insecure and low paid. They will be flexible, like a tap that can be turned on and off, according to the variable labour requirement of the employer, through numerical and distancing arrangements. Moreover, as in the Japanese subcontracting relationship (on which the Atkinson (1984) model draws heavily) the insecurity of the periphery is the price for the security of the core. In bad economic times businesses will, like plants in winter, shrink back to their essential labour core. Finally, the style of management here will be directive in the 'macho' management and 'Bleak House' mode of hire and fire. In short, labour will be regarded as an expendable commodity rather than a valuable human resource.

The Flexible Firm raises a number of questions for HRM. First, how far is it a global trend in capitalism and how far is it an aberration of the stop–go 1980s British economy? Of the five conditioning

**Figure 16.1**   The flexible firm

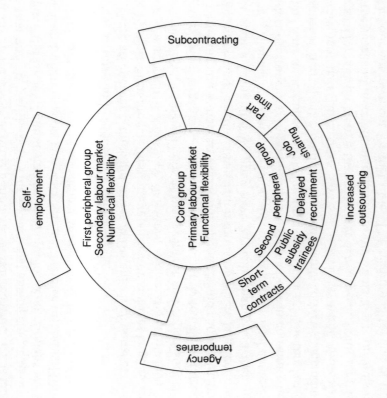

Subcontracting

Self-employment

First peripheral group
Secondary labour market
Numerical flexibility

Core group
Primary labour market
Functional flexibility

Part time

Job sharing

Delayed recruitment

Second peripheral group

Public subsidy trainees

Short-term contracts

Increased outsourcing

Agency temporaries

factors discussed above, only two, technological change and working time, appear general to advanced industrial economies. On the other hand, the uncertain British economic conditions of the early 1980s have repeated themselves in the early 1990s. Second, even if examples of the four types of flexibility can be found, is there any evidence of a strategic connection between them at the level of individual organizations? Many manufacturing firms have gone for functional flexibility while service-sector organizations have always employed substantial numbers of women on a part-time and temporary basis. Critics (Pollert, 1988; McInnes, 1989) argue that few organizations have deliberately brought together the various forms of flexibility in the configuration which Atkinson suggests, and that, instead, we have witnessed changes in the sexual and sectoral composition of the workforce, with the growth of female, service employment. Third, how far are organizations consciously differentiating in their management style between core and peripheral workers and, indeed, how far is this possible? For instance, in many service organizations, like the one discussed below, it is the peripheral workforce which deals face-to-face with the customer. This means that management have to square the circle of employing an insecure, low-commitment workforce and offering good customer service. Neither orthodox HRM, with its emphasis on the investment in the stable human resource, nor the Flexible Firm, with its twin-track employment policies, suggest how this can be done, if it can be done.

There are, perhaps, three industries in Britain which come close to the Flexible Firm model. First, the retail sector includes large super-store chains such as Sainsbury, Safeways, Asda and Tesco which, at the store level, employ a core of management and supervisory employees and a large, high-turnover, predominantly female workforce of part-time and temporary check-out operators and shop assistants. A second example is the construction industry, where large contractors such a Laing and Wimpey have virtually abandoned their in-house, manual workforce in favour of striking commercial contracts with subcontractors. In both instances fluctuations in consumer demand have undermined stable full-time employment. The third case, discussed here, is the outdoor entertainments industry, including amusement parks like Alton Towers, as well as theme and safari parks. Here the problem is that customer demand exists only for part of the year, and therefore management only wants to pay the bulk of its labour complement for that time. The traditional version of this problem is found at the seaside holiday resort, like Blackpool Pleasure Beach, and other, lesser-known, resorts such as Skegness or Southend, which effectively close down for more than two-thirds of the year. Unlike fireworks or photographic film manufacturers, management cannot employ workers to stockpile product for the peak season since the product concerned is a perishable service. This is the story of LeisureCo.

## THE CASE-STUDY: LEISURECO

LeisureCo is a themed, largely open-air, entertainments complex which is less then ten years old. Shortly after its foundation the business was acquired by a large leisure public limited company which manages hotels, bowling alleys and other theme parks. However, at LeisureCo on-site management have continued to run it as a separate business with its own working culture. Many of the employment characteristics of the firm are characteristic of the fixed-site, open-air rides and entertainment centre, whether these are located at the seaside or on some inland site. The LeisureCo complex has high year-round fixed overheads and a short season. The overheads are composed of a large site, several acres in size, expensive rides machinery and other entertainments provision, all of which require maintenance throughout the year. On the other hand, the open-air site only operates at anything near full capacity during the summer season from June to September. Even during this period attendances fluctuate greatly, and it peaks at weekends and during the holiday months. Before and after the main summer time, on the shoulders of the season, the park opens only at weekends and for special events designed to attract target niche markets such as youth groups. In recent years the depressing effect of the recent consumer downturn on turnover has been partly compensated by more people taking their holidays at home and in shorter breaks.

Work is organized around a series of themed rides and retail outlets. Employees are expected to operate these and to entertain and help the customers. This involves dressing up in themed outfits as well as undertaking more technical tasks such as running the numerous local variations on the big dipper, the log-flume and the rapids rides. Other workers fulfil shop and catering assistant roles in the various souvenir shops and fast-food outlets. Economics dictate a large seasonal, mainly student, workforce of up to 500 (allowing for turnover) through the season. Few of these stay for the entire season, even fewer return the following year, and many only remain for a few weeks. In addition, the park opens continuously, for seven days a week during the main season, which means that workers cannot be expected to occupy the same job every day, as in some factory settings. This combination of factors means that new workers must be recruited constantly, that they must be trained very rapidly and that they must be sufficiently flexible to do a wide variety of jobs according to the daily requirements of the park.

Since turnover of seasonal staff is very high, a major problem is how to deliver high-quality customer care with a transient workforce. This depends on a mixture of permanent staff experience and youthful fun and enthusiasm from the seasonal students. The seasonal staff are organized in teams under experienced leaders. Some of these are permanent employees but others are regular, older seasonal staff accustomed to the summer cycle of the industry. The former are part of a permanent management and administration complement of around 50, responsible for training and supporting seasonal staff, who

Copyright John Storey 1996, Blackwell Cases in Human Resource and Change Management

remain through the winter closing. This group also includes some non-management employees who, during the off-season, maintain the machinery, keep the park clean and do security work. Personnel at LeisureCo is a new function for this sales- and operations-driven firm, and its main role is recruitment and training.

The emergence of a deliberate policy which blends customer care with employee involvement (EI) has been part and parcel of the growing professionalization and formalization of general personnel policy. This fits into a broader pattern, that EI in the service sector is part and parcel of customer care. This is also true, for instance, of Tesco's communications groups. (By contrast, Marchington et al., 1992 found that manufacturing firms introduced EI techniques like quality circles and team briefing mainly to improve product quality or industrial relations.) There is no trade union or formal industrial relations structure, although pay rates were underpinned by Wages Council awards for the industry until their recent abolition. The interest in EI arose largely from the desire to maintain high standards of customer care, notwithstanding the dependence on a casual workforce. The objectives of the programme were to reduce labour turnover by holding staff through the season, and to create a more mature group among the seasonal workforce by recruiting local married women and encouraging returnees.

There were a number of rather experimental schemes, some of which have been abandoned. These include personal briefing of the different workgroups by the site manager; a suggestions scheme; a popular, photocopied newsletter; and a seasonal staff handbook, linked to the customer care orientated induction process. The induction programme has a particularly formative role given the short stay of many seasonal staff and the need to get them to adopt quickly good customer care habits. There are two small-scale incentive schemes for seasonal staff, rewarding merit and loyalty. The company's schemes, such as the employee report and the employee share scheme, have extended to LeisureCo employees. A change of site and personnel managers shifted the emphasis somewhat, away from specific add-on EI initiatives and towards strengthening the team-working system and improving training and recruitment procedures. The staff social committee has grown in importance, and noticeboards are more prominent. The initial succession of EI waves created an impression that many of the schemes were transient and with limited impact (see Figure 16.2).

Overall, LeisureCo, in a somewhat haphazard way, combines elements of the Flexible Firm, customer care and HRM. The workforce

**Figure 16.2** Wave diagram for LeisureCo

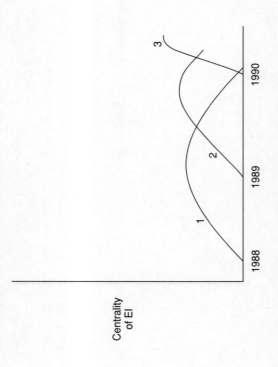

has clear core/periphery characteristics, with the core being composed largely of salaried management employees and the periphery of itinerant student workers. Moreover, it is imperative for the success of the park that visitors have a good time, spend lots of money and return again as soon as possible. Since the core workforce holds the administrative reins of the operation, it falls on the seasonal workers to entertain the guests, deal with the problems of families and children and generally to adopt a cheerful, 'the customer is always right' mentality. In this spirit the staff manual stresses a Disney-style, smiling workforce. However, personnel is a relatively low-status function in an organization driven by operations and marketing imperatives, and it is hard to justify great investment in the training and involvement of such a transient workforce.

## Questions

1  Which elements of the LeisureCo case conform to the model of the Flexible Firm?
2  Many service-sector organizations deal directly with the general public through their employees. How far does good customer service depend on effective human resource management?

3  Design an alternative approach to employment management for LeisureCo which is more consistent with HRM principles yet economically feasible.

4  Choose an organisation you are familiar with, perhaps the company you work for or the university you study at. Using the blank model of the Flexible Firm provided in Figure 16.3, write in some of the jobs of people in this organisation.

**Figure 16.3**  The flexible firm

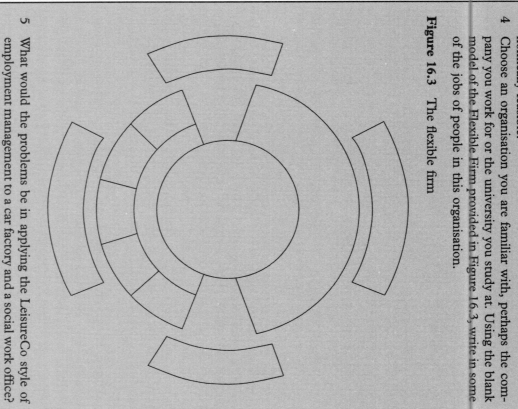

5  What would the problems be in applying the LeisureCo style of employment management to a car factory and a social work office?

## References

Atkinson, J. 1984: Manpower strategies for flexible organizations. *Personnel Management*, August, 28–31.

Marchington, M., Goodman, J., Wilkinson, A. and Ackers, P. 1992: *New Developments in Employee Involvement*. Research Series 2, Sheffield: Employment Department.

McInnes, J. 1987: *Thatcherism at Work: Industrial Relations and Economic Change*. Milton Keynes: Open University Press.

McInnes, J. 1989: The question of flexibility. Research Paper No. 5, Department of Social and Economic Research, University of Glasgow, reported in *Financial Times*, 29 September 1989.

Pollert, A. 1988: The 'Flexible Firm, fixation or fact? *Work Employment and Society*, **2**(3), 281–316.

Storey, J. (ed.) 1989: *New Perspectives on Human Resource Management*. London: Routledge.

Storey, J. 1992: *Developments in the Management of Human Resources*. Oxford: Blackwell.

## Further reading

Blyton, P. and Turnbull, P. (eds) 1992: *Reassessing Human Resource Management*. London: Sage.

Blyton, P. and Turnbull, P. 1992: *The Dynamics of Employee Relations*. London: Macmillan.

Burchill, F. 1992: *Labour Relations*. London: Macmillan.

Edwards, P. K. 1985: The myth of the macho manager. *Personnel Management*, April.

Guest, D. 1987: Human resource management and industrial relations. *Journal of Management Studies*, **24**(5), 503–21.

Harrison, R. (ed.) 1993: *Human Resource Management: Issues and Strategies*. Workingham: Addison-Wesley.

Keenoy, T. 1990: HRM: A case of the wolf in sheep's clothing. *Personnel Review*, **19**(2).

Marchington, M. and Parker, P. 1990: *Changing Patterns of Employee Relations*. London: Harvester.

Millward, N., Stevens, M., Smart, D. and Hawes, W. R. 1992: *Workplace Industrial Relations in Transition: The ED/ESRC/PSI/ACAS Surveys*. Aldershot: Dartmouth.

Nicholls, T. 1986: *The British Worker Question*. London: Routledge & Kegan Paul.

Storey, J. and Sisson, K. 1993: *Managing Human Resources and Industrial Relations*. Milton Keynes: Open University Press.

# 17
# Royal Mail

*A new industrial relations framework*

NICOLAS BACON AND
JOHN STOREY

In 1986 the Post Office split into divisions covering letters, parcels and counters. Of these the letters division, Royal Mail, employing 160,000 people, became the largest, accounting for three-quarters of the total turnover of the Post Office. In 1992 Royal Mail itself decentralized into nine regional divisions that operate as complete businesses. In each division the company separated the core functions of distribution, delivery and processing. The company has retained its market share and held off competition from other communication media to remain the most reliable postal service in Europe. Royal Mail consistently returns significant profit levels (£252 million in 1992–3). By 1994 the Government had failed to draw any firm conclusions about privatizing the service despite two reviews into its future.

The distinctive feature of developments at Royal Mail has been the importance attached by managers to industrial relations as a means of bringing about change. In the early 1990s the Advisory, Conciliation and Arbitration Service (ACAS) described the industrial relations climate in Royal Mail as one where 'to a large extent management, the Union of Communication Workers [UCW] and employees were seen to operate almost as three distinct parts'. A survey revealed that employees felt far removed from senior managers with authority exercised and decisions made at a distance. Furthermore employees felt that managers were not committed to change and continued to exercise a 'traditional' style of managing staff. Employees also criticized how the main trade union, UCW, communicated with its members, although they felt the union was necessary and it received strong support. Overall, employees felt uninformed by both management and unions. Consequently, in repeated attitude surveys, employees exhibited low morale, alienation and widespread frustration.

Royal Mail managers also shared this frustration as they had been largely unsuccessful in their attempts to introduce more part-time labour and new technology in the late 1980s. The unions blocked initial attempts to introduce team working when they failed to agree with management on the issues of grading, earnings and team leaders. Managers introduced some changes unilaterally including settled attendances (fixed shift-working patterns as opposed to rotating) and fixed duties. Senior managers also attempted to hold individuals responsible for quality improvements. At this time some managers considered marginalizing the union but strong support among union members deterred them from this. As an alternative, managers have sought a partnership approach towards employee relations by involving the union and promoting employee involvement. In 1992 managers and unions signed a New Industrial Relations Framework Agreement moving away from the conflictual relationship of the late 1980s towards a more constructive partnership. This agreement provided for a significant level of union involvement at all levels, a greater sharing of company information and a commitment to resolve grievances at the lowest possible level. The agreement suggests a new role for the unions with strategic involvement at all business levels and a voice in all business issues. Managers hoped that improved employee relations would enable them to change the organization of work and develop a customer-orientated culture. Involving the unions was also part of a wider package of changes including a new leadership style, a new organizational culture and the introduction of team working.

Despite real improvements, by the mid 1990s Royal Mail had not yet become consistently customer focused and employees continue to express low levels of satisfaction. The TQM programme, Customer First, launched in 1992 took some time to filter down and at the time of writing, front-line training was not complete. Even optimistic managers forecasted no more than 10–20 per cent of employees would be willing to participate in quality improvement groups. Despite future HR plans to improve leadership, develop managers and train employees, financial restrictions and a generally cautious approach to launching HR initiatives have inhibited the company. Managers have yet to see the strategic involvement of the unions result in employees displaying improved levels of trust and confidence in the company. The New Framework Agreement has been a partial success. In some regions managers and trade unions have developed a new partnership but in others the agreement has not worked.

## Questions

1 Why did Royal Mail find it necessary to focus on industrial relations issues?

2 Do you think the company was right to develop a partnership relationship with the unions? What other options might it have considered?

3 A centre-piece of the new framework agreement was the provision for the 'strategic involvement' of the unions. What do you think this might mean? Can you think of any examples outside Royal Mail where it may have occurred?

4 What challenges does 'strategic involvement' pose for managers and trade unions? What problems do you think occurred initially when it was implemented and how might they be overcome?

5 Do you think that such a strategy is likely to be successful in the long term?

## Further reading

Bacon, N. and Storey, J. 1995: Individualism and collectivism and the changing roles of trade unions. In Ackers, P., Smith, P. and Smith, C. (eds), *The New Workplace and Trade Unionism*, London: Routledge.

Involvement and Participation Association 1995: *Royal Mail in London: A Case Study of Employee Involvement in the Reorganisation of the Main Letter Offices, Towards Industrial Partnership: Putting it into Practice: No1.* London: Involvement and Participation Association.

Guest, D. 1995: Human resource management, trade unions and industrial relations. In Storey, J. (ed.), *Human Resource Management: A Critical Text*. London: Routledge.

Hyman, R. 1994: Changing trade union identities and strategies. In Hyman, R. and Ferner, A. (eds), *New Frontiers in European Industrial Relations*. Oxford: Blackwell.

# 18

# COCO, CECO and DECO

## Managing HR in the non-union firm
### IAN MCLOUGHLIN

The decline of trade unions in recent years has highlighted the management of human resources in non-union settings. In particular, government policy and practice in Britain since 1979 has been instrumental in placing non-unionism and the non-union enterprise firmly on the agenda. For example, a succession of new labour laws restricting trade unions has been passed, while policy statements have frequently espoused a view that unions and collective bargaining are an increasingly redundant feature in a 'modern' economy (see, for example, Department of Trade and Industry, 1990; Department of Employment, 1991; 1992). Combined with the effects of two major recessions, several major union defeats in set-piece industrial disputes, and the supposed widespread adoption of new USA-style management techniques of human resource management (HRM), credence has been given to the claim that a major transformation in British industrial relations and the management of human resources is taking place. Indeed, one commentator has gone as far as to claim that non-unionism is 'now dominant in Britain' (Bassett, 1988). On the other hand, much academic research has pointed to what is, at best, a transition rather than transformation (for example, MacInnes, 1988; Marchington and Parker, 1990; Kessler and Bayliss, 1992). Nevertheless, while in the past the non-union settings might have been safely regarded as 'outmoded relics' and as a 'vanishing species' (Newman, 1980) it is now quite clear that non-unionism and the non-union firm are an increasingly significant phenomenon.

However, our knowledge of how human resource and industrial relations matters are dealt with in the absence of trade unions is far from comprehensive or complete. In particular, the rather benign view of non-unionism as the locus of current best practice in the management of human resources is based rather more on assertion than hard evidence. Similarly, the non-union employee has been characterized as proto-typical of the 'new worker' for whom individual rather than collective values are paramount, while the non-union settings which they populate have been assumed to be inherently receptive to technical and other innovations and, as a result, to be highly productive. The cases presented in this chapter are intended to provide a test of aspects of this image of the non-union firm by providing an account of the management of human resources in the absence of unions in three contrasting settings. By the end of each case study, key human resource management problems and issues should be apparent which point to the rather more complex nature of the task when the decision is taken to manage without trade unions.

## COCO

### Background

COCO (UK) is one of 19 wholly-owned international subsidiary operations of a US manufacturer of specialist main-frame computers for complex data analysis. The US company has enjoyed phenomenal growth since its foundation in 1972 and has rapidly expanded into a multi-national *Fortune 500* organization. At the end of the 1980s, employment peaked at a worldwide total of over 5,200. The British company currently employs around 240 employees and is responsible for marketing and providing pre- and post-sales technical support. No hardware design or manufacturing is carried out in Britain, although some significant software development does take place, and the technical support activities are highly complex.

Hitherto, the competitive pressures faced by COCO have been relatively weak. The parent company dominates the world market for specialist computers with a 79 per cent share. Market entry into the specialized area in which COCO operates is also very difficult for new competitors. Indeed, such is the specialist nature of COCO's product that, when the US company had been founded, industry analysts estimated that the potential customer base was under 100 (in fact 265 COCO computer systems have been installed worldwide, 14 in the UK). The difficult trading conditions of the late 1980s and early 1990s in the computer industry have also acted as a further barrier to new entrants and two US competitors have in fact left the business, one a new entrant.

Recent years have also been more difficult for COCO. Little or no growth in revenue has occurred and new sources of uncertainty have become apparent. First, since COCO computers involve a major investment on the part of the customer, sales have proven vulnerable to cuts in public and corporate expenditure (government clients account for 30 per cent of the existing installed systems). In recent years growth in revenue has flattened out. Second, the founder of the US enterprise decided to leave, taking one-fifth of the assets and several key staff, to create a rival spin-off company to continue development of a new competitor product. Third, COCO's principal current rivals, the Japanese, now have products which are becoming more competitive. This is reflected by the fact that COCO's domination of the Japanese market is less strong than elsewhere. Fourth, customers are demanding greater connectivity and better post-sales service and, in common with most other computer suppliers, COCO's business is rapidly becoming more than just one of selling hardware to relatively unsophisticated corporate consumers. Products now have to be actively marketed, and sold as part of an overall service which embraces both pre- and post-sales. Finally, 400 redundancies in the US manufacturing operation, the first in the company's history, have been announced. Taken together, these developments have raised doubts throughout the enterprise about the company's future direction and created a climate in which competitive pressures are now perceived to be increasingly significant.

## The Management of Human Resources

The American parent has a well-defined corporate culture and an influential human resources function. Together with its typically high-tech origins and subsequent development around a single product strategy, the management of human resources in the US company bears many of the hallmarks of the HRM approach which is usually regarded as typical of non-union North American owned computing and electronics companies. An interesting question, therefore, is how far this approach has been transplanted and is evident in COCO's British operation. As one might expect, overall business strategy is defined by the US parent, although senior British managers are involved in this process. In general, however, high levels of control are not exercised by the US parent on either how business plans are implemented and, in particular, the approach taken to managing human resources.

For example, one potentially clear manifestation of American influence is a formal statement of the 'COCO style', reprinted in the British company's employee handbook (see Table 18.1). The importance of the role of this statement is set out by a senior US manager in the following terms: 'these values guide our behaviours, decisions and interactions with all our constituencies – customers, shareholders and communities. They are the values that ensure that COCO is the company we all want it to be'. However, in Britain at least, the COCO style and its underlying values have a more indirect influence on management policy and practice. Most managers in the British operation regard the 'style statement' as providing a broad backcloth or flavour rather than a detailed guide to management practice.

Rather, COCO is seen by British managers as providing an informal and 'fairly ambiguous environment' with very few written rules and, where these exist, they are not regarded as the sole basis of managerial authority. Moreover, senior British managers feel strongly that the company is, first and foremost, 'technologically led'. One consequence of this is that there is a predominance of technically qualified managers in senior positions reflecting a tendency for technical achievements to be rewarded by promotion into managerial roles, without the individuals concerned necessarily expected to be effective 'people managers' or 'team players'. Finally, previous managing directors have had, to varying degrees, an autocratic approach and little interest in the people aspects of the business.

Not surprisingly, therefore, there is considerable scepticism, if not fear, among some of the middle and more senior British managers concerning the role played by the human resources function in the US. In particular, there is a belief that US line management, with whom British managers have frequent contact, are constrained in their capacity to deal as they see fit with people issues. Indeed, it is widely held that line managers and some of the most senior executives in the parent company have similar reservations. Even the US vice-president is said once to have described the human resources function in private conversation as a 'bunch of fucking social workers'! In this context, the belief that in 'fast moving computer companies' like COCO there is no time to develop solid human resources policies is predominant. As such, to date at least, it has been regarded as inevitable that such considerations have dragged behind because the company has to run 'lean and tight'.

**Table 18.1** The 'COCO style'

At COCO, we take what we do very seriously, but we don't take ourselves too seriously.

There is a sense of pride at COCO, professionalism is important. People are treated like and act like professionals. But people are professional without being stuffy.

COCO people trust each other to do their jobs well and with the highest ethical standards. We take each other very seriously.

We have a strong sense of quality – quality in our products and services, of course; but also quality in our working environment, in the people we work with, in the tools that we use to do our work, and in the components we choose to make what we make.

Economy comes from high value, not from low cost. Aesthetics are part of the quality. The effort to create quality extends to the communities in which we work and live as well.

The COCO approach is informal and non-bureaucratic. Verbal communication is key, not memos. 'Call don't write' is the watchword. People are accessible at all levels.

People also have fun working at COCO. There is laughing in the halls, as well as serious discussion. More than anything else, the organisation is personable and approachable, but still dedicated to getting the job done.

With informality, however, there is also a sense of confidence. COCO people feel like they are on the winning side. They feel successful, and they are. It is this sense of confidence that generates the attitude to 'go ahead and try it, we'll make it work'.

COCO people like taking responsibility for what they do and thinking for themselves. At the same time, they are proud to share a single mission – making the world's best computers. Because the individual is key at COCO, there is a real diversity in the view of what COCO really is. In fact, COCO is many things to many people. This consistency comes in providing those diverse people with the opportunity to fulfil themselves and experience achievement.

The creativity, then, that emerges from the company comes from the many ideas of the individuals who are here. And that is the real strength of COCO.

The starkest manifestation of this is that there has never been a specialist human resource manager appointed in the British operation nor a human resource function established. Instead, responsibility for human resource matters has been the province of an administration manager in the finance department who has been required only to provide a basic advisory service to line managers on matters such as disciplinary procedures, areas covered by statute (for example, maternity leave, sick pay) and, most contentious of all, the company car policy.

In this context, line managers have largely been free to make decisions over human resource matters within the broadest of guidelines and, sometimes, if they felt it necessary, outside them. For example, departmental managers enjoy a wide degree of discretion with regard to matters such as recruitment, training, staff appraisal and pay determination. In consequence, procedures vary across and within departments, and no standard company-wide policies or formulas are systematically applied, even in key areas such as the setting of pay levels.

The 'COCO style' statement also places a great deal of stress on the individual nature of the employment relationship. This is amplified in the employee handbook which declares that 'respect for the individual is one of the Company's fundamental beliefs' and that employees should 'feel free to discuss any subject' with their manager and have 'the confidence that he will be sincere in his efforts to provide you with a correct and full answer'. Similarly, the grievance procedure encourages a 'prompt informal discussion' with the employee's immediate manager if a grievance arises. If this does not resolve the matter the immediate manager's superior is required to 'review all aspects . . . and decide on what action, if any, needs to be taken', the decision being 'final'.

A similar stress on direct individual relationships between managers and employees and a dislike for formal rules and lengthy procedures is evident with regard to informing, consulting and communicating with employees. On the one hand, a variety of fairly sophisticated communications techniques emanate from the US parent. The most notable of these is 'Link Up', a question/answer facility for employees to interrogate US managers and directors via the electronic mail system. However, as far as managers in Britain are concerned, the key means of communication is through the management chain. This is supplemented by quarterly employee meetings with the UK managing director, who provides information on performance and plans, and *ad hoc* briefings convened by project managers and departmental heads to discuss particular client contracts.

The absence of trade unions is partly a function of openly hostile management attitudes in some quarters. As one put it 'If anybody mentioned the word union here people would shudder'. However, it is also seen by more senior management as a reflection of the type of employee who is employed by the company. These are mainly highly qualified computer professionals and technicians for whom, it is felt, trade unions hold no attraction. Indeed, most managers have no reason to think deeply about and form views on the questions of why employees at the company do not seek to join trade unions and why the company has no recognition agreements. These issues are simply not salient and do not figure in the day-to-day management of employees. However, this has not always been the case. For example, a concerted attempt had initially been made to keep unions out when the British company was founded in the late 1970s. At this time there was an explicit attempt to establish a non-union operation. However, over time, unions have simply become a non-issue. As the managing director puts it, if the organization is run properly, employees are able to express their views, the management style is fairly open and employees are well paid, 'there shouldn't be any requirement for a trade union. What's the point of a trade union … We're hardly the sort of organization that's treating people badly.'

## Product Innovation and Organizational Change

One consequence of corporate perceptions of increased product market pressure is a parallel recognition among some, but by no means all, senior managers that their existing approach to managing human resources may be inadequate given the changes that are about to be set in train by the US parent which has announced a new business strategy. This is based around the introduction of a new range of 'entry level' computers with a high degree of connectivity to other manufacturers' machines. These products require no after-sales, on-site maintenance (the conventional highly complex COCO machines are normally sold with both hardware and software engineers permanently located at the customer location, although even here technical innovations are reducing the need for such on-site service to be provided).

These product innovations have spurned two major organizational changes. First, the marketing of COCO's products in Europe is to be given far greater emphasis by the creation of a new marketing and sales function at the British location. Second, a philosophy of centralized one-stop maintenance is to be developed. Here, engineers will gradually be relocated off-site in a new customer service department which will combine the previously separate hardware and software maintenance functions. At the same time, engineers are to be retrained with composite software and hardware skills. A further requirement here is to increase the number of COCO staff with industry software standard skills, required because of the greater connectivity built into the new products. This means both attracting and retaining labour whose skills are in wide demand in the computer industry as a whole whereas, in the past, the unique character and market domination of COCO's computer product has meant that employee skills to a large extent have been non-transferable.

It is against this background that a new managing director has been appointed to head the new European operation. He has worked in the computer industry for many years, much of the time for IBM. He sees as one of his major tasks that of addressing the hitherto neglected area of the management of human resources in the British operation. However, the large-scale and increasingly rapid changes in both products and, in particular, organizational structure are beginning to take their toll. Staff in general are increasingly dissatisfied with what they see as almost constant reorganization which is distracting them from their technical work. In part, this has been brought home to senior management by a sharp increase in labour turnover which has leapt to 30 per cent. At the same time, stresses and strains among the senior management group, consisting of five heads of department plus the MD, are beginning to show.

# CECO

## Background

CECO is a UK-owned consumer electronics firm whose main activity is the manufacturer of domestic loudspeakers. The present company was established following a management buy-out in the early 1980s. There are now about 400 employees, mostly unskilled and semi-skilled manual workers involved in assembly operations but also a small proportion of more highly qualified technical staff – mainly involved in product design and development – and a slightly larger contingent of office staff concerned with sales and marketing.

CECO has experienced a high level of competitive pressure in its recent past. Indeed, the management buy-out was a product of acute exposure to such pressures which resulted in the previous owners, a large UK-owned electronics group, deciding to withdraw from loud-speaker manufacture in the face of intense competition from the Far East. However, since the buy-out CECO has begun to enjoy a period of growth and relatively successful business. Indeed, in the past four years market share has increased and turnover quadrupled. To some extent at least the acute competitive pressures which had accompanied the buy-out in the early 1980s have now eased.

This period of successful growth has been achieved through the implementation of an innovative business strategy by the new management owners. One element of the strategy involved gaining a firm foothold as a supplier to automobile manufacturers. They had been identified as a new and fast-growing market since factory-fitted in-car entertainment systems were becoming part of the standard specification of vehicles across manufacturers' product ranges. 'Sole supplier' status has been won from one car manufacturer and additional contracts to supply another four manufacturers have been gained. Subsequently, further contracts and new orders to supply loudspeakers have been received from TV and audio firms (which include new UK–based Japanese manufacturers). The second element of the strategy is based around marketing a range of imported consumer electronics products (for example, televisions, telephones, satellite TV equipment, video recorders, microwave ovens). These products are 're-badged' and then marketed under the CECO brand name.

The beauty of this two-pronged approach is that each complements the other in ways which ease some of the product market pressures usually faced in the consumer electronics sector. For example, the seasonal nature of consumer demand means that most sales of consumer electronics products occur in the pre-Christmas period. Sales are also vulnerable to high interest rates and other factors which depress consumer spending. One benefit of the new business strategy has been to insulate the company from the worst effects of such pressures. Thus, when high interest rates choked off the consumer-led boom in the late 1980s, sales of loudspeakers to corporate clients remained stable since they were mainly tied to the six- to seven-year product life-cycle of the automobile industry. Conversely, when the company had been attempting to broaden its corporate customer base in the mid 1980s and to increase its manufacturing output, buoyant sales of its imported products had provided an important source of revenue. In addition, although corporate customers are in a strong position to demand competitive pricing, reliability and quality, supplier status also allows manufacture to be better planned and organized with longer production runs and a more efficient utilization of labour. This also serves to offset the seasonal nature of demand, which in many competitor companies normally results in short-time working at some points in the year.

## The Management of Human Resources

The management of human resources at CECO is conditioned by the decision, taken at the time of the buy-out, to de-recognize trade unions. Prior to this, several unions enjoyed full bargaining rights, the principal one being the AUEW. However, they had failed to prevent all but 50 of the then 1,000 strong workforce being made redundant as the previous owners wound down the factory for closure. The reasons for the de-recognition of the trade unions by the new management owners were: a perceived weakness in the position of the trade unions in general in the wake of the Thatcher Government's industrial relations reforms; a perception that there was a moderate tradition in the local labour market which meant employees would not react adversely to working in a non-union environment; the knowledge that the workforce felt let down by the unions' inability to prevent the redundancies and that employee support for the unions had collapsed; and a desire on management's part to 'make a new start, free of past history'.

In place of the trade unions the company has established a company council or committee (known as the staff association). The committee comprises 11 elected employee members and has monthly meetings chaired by the managing director. The meetings are also attended by the personnel manager. The committee has no formal negotiating role and is intended as a means through which employee views can be gauged, collective grievances dealt with, and information passed to the workforce.

These new arrangements notwithstanding, it is the case that the stance of management on the question of union recognition remains pragmatic. For example, while the reaction to a recent recognition claim by the EETPU (based on the unsubstantiated grounds that it had recruited sufficient members in the plant) was one of considerable scepticism, especially as no approach had been made by employees themselves, it was also agreed that, if the EETPU persisted in the claim (which in the event it did not do), then the company might have to decide to have an employee ballot. Privately, some managers concede that demands for union recognition from the workforce itself will inevitably arise in the future as memories of the way the unions failed the workforce in the past, and of how the new management saved and created new jobs, fade. In addition, there is also a feeling that newer employees, taken on as the company has grown, do not have the same loyalty or the commitment to the company.

Personnel policy has tended to evolve in a largely informal and *ad hoc* manner at CECO. For example, policy and procedures are fragmented and ill defined, described by the personnel officer as a 'very grey area' with little 'written down'. Responsibility for personnel matters is also unclear. While the personnel officer reports to the managing director, she is only responsible for routine administration, recruitment and welfare matters. *De facto* responsibility for policy making on personnel matters rests with the manufacturing manager to whom the personnel officer has an informal 'dotted-line' reporting link.

A recent attempt has been made to draft a formal written personnel policy. Significantly, it is the manufacturing manager who is the author. This document contains a general statement about employment philosophy, which declares 'the Directors' wish' that 'employees would be able look forward to full and rewarding long term employment with the Company'. The document goes on to explain elements of formal policies and procedures on matters such as consultation and grievances. A copy of the full policy has been provided to employee representatives on the staff association and it is intended that a short précis will be issued at some point to all employees in the form of a booklet. This will have an endorsement introducing the company, written by the managing director.

That such a document is regarded as relatively innovative is indicative of the fact that personnel matters are normally subordinated to line management concerns. In particular management are driven by the need to maintain the continuity of production and, above all, improve levels of output. These overriding objectives are emphasized in the organization and control of work on the shop-floor. This is accomplished along classic Taylorist lines. Assembly work is machine paced and consists of highly repetitive low-skilled tasks (cycle times range from 4.5 to 6 'seconds'). Work on the assembly line does not, in managements' view, 'require cleverness or a lot of thinking'. This is born out by the low level of training received by line workers, for example the vast majority receive no 'off-the-job' training at all. The monitoring and control of operator performance is also tight and involves both direct supervision and some rudimentary technical surveillance. For instance, once a production job is running, hourly output is recorded on a master board at the end of each assembly line. Along the lines are TV monitors which display production targets, the output achieved, and whether production is ahead (in green) or behind (in red) and by how many speakers. These devices are used by the production manager to motivate the staff by encouraging lines to compete with each other.

There is a marked degree of occupational segregation between assembly operatives, who are mainly female, and setters and maintenance staff, who are predominantly male. It is management's belief that males cannot cope with most of the assembly-line work which would 'just blow their minds' whereas, 'the girls' can work on 'auto-pilot' and have 'a natural skill to do highly repetitive work, at speed and talk to their colleagues'.

Attempts are made to 'humanize' the production environment in order to make the work more 'tolerable'. For example, supervisors try to keep the same operators on each line in order that friends can sit next to each other. To the same end, the assembly-line work stations are arranged so that operators are seated close enough to enable conversation. Radio music is played in the factory at certain times in the morning and afternoon. There is also recognition that the quality of direct supervision requires improvement and that there is a lack of people management skills among lower levels of line management. One important task facing the company that has been identified, therefore, is to improve the training of its first-line management.

## Managing Technical Change without Unions

It is against this backcloth that a number of serious employee relations issues have begun to emerge. These have been fuelled by a number of changes in production methods and related organizational changes. The most significant change in production methods followed from the introduction of new fast-curing glue.
Previously, every speaker had to be assembled and set aside at each

stage for the glue to dry. It therefore took three to four days to assemble a speaker. One disadvantage with this was that testing could be done only after a production run was complete. Thus, if a fault was identified the entire batch, sometimes of several thousand speakers, might have to be scrapped. The new instant-curing adhesive allowed 'straight-through manufacture'. This meant that gluing machines could be placed on the production lines and the layout of the shopfloor changed. Previously each line had been broken down into six segments spread around the factory. Now each line was run as a continuous sequence of tasks. This also allowed the testing of speakers during the production run. As a result, it now takes 15 minutes to assemble a speaker and scrap rates have been reduced from around 8 to 1.5 per cent.

In human and organizational terms the immediate implication of this change is in relation to the bonus system which forms one element of shopfloor pay. Longer-term considerations concerning the need for a greater stress on output quality are also beginning to emerge. A new quality manager has been appointed and privately he has challenged the prevailing production philosophy which requires a detailed division of labour and tight monitoring and supervision of production work. In his view the introduction of a quality culture and the empowerment of individual employees is what the company needs to move forwards in the long term. However, the current skill base on the shopfloor is such that few manual employees on the line are capable of taking on enlarged tasks, such as those that might follow from the adoption of quality circles and a move away from Taylorist methods.

# DECO

## Background

DECO is the main one of four operating divisions located in Britain owned by a highly diversified North American multinational founded in 1914. The British operation had been established in 1959 and its principal activity is now the design, on a contract basis, of offshore platforms for use in oil and gas exploration and exploitation. The customers are mainly corporate clients operating in the North Sea. The parent company employs over 52,000 employees worldwide, and 2,200 of these work in the main UK operating division. The core workforce consists of design engineers and technicians from across a range of engineering disciplines.

The company faces strong competitive and customer pressures. Although it has a technological lead over its UK competitors through the use of high-tech computer aided design (CAD) technology, the market for its design services is highly cyclical and is tied tightly to the fortunes of the oil and gas industry. In the 1970s and early 1980s the parent company was the market leader in offshore contracting. However, in the mid 1980s the collapse of oil prices resulted in a decline in offshore contracts. At the same time, the loss of a major law suit in the USA introduced considerable uncertainty at corporate level. The US parent restructured its operations and attempted to increase co-operation between the operating divisions which, hitherto, had tended to operate as separate companies. In addition, a programme of redundancies then occurred involving the closure of one of the US divisions, with some additional redundancies in Britain. Offshore work previously accounted for 90 per cent of workload but now diversification into other sectors, such as process plant design, means that the proportion has fallen to around 50 per cent. However, the highly unpredictable nature of contract-based business is reflected by the fact that, immediately following this period of retrenchment, the volume of new offshore contracts has started to grow once again, and the recruitment of additional staff is now seen as a priority.

It is, however, customer pressures which have the most direct influence over day-to-day operations. The company operates by gaining contracts to design major oil and gas installations. The large investment required on the part of the customer means that they can exert considerable pressure over the management of the project. This occurs most obviously through the provision of financial incentives and penalties as part of the terms of the contract. These require specified work to be completed on schedule at particular 'milestones'. In addition, the client can exert more subtle pressure by seeking to influence the selection of key personnel on the project and the length of their involvement.

## The Management of Human Resources

The way human resources are managed is not subject to direct influence by the US parent. Moreover, personnel matters and the personnel function play a marginal role in overall business decision making and planning. In practice, in the British company, personnel policy is largely dictated by the managing director and actioned by line management. The personnel specialist's role is thus one of providing administrative support to line managers. The company has an image as an autocratic and rather traditional employer and, although the hire-and-fire approach has softened in recent years, a strong machismo is still evident in the organization's culture and management style. In part, this reflects the physically hard and hostile nature of the environments in which the products being designed eventually operate. It is also supported by the particular demands and disciplines imposed by contract-driven project work and the unpredictable nature of demand itself which tends to promote a degree of mercenary behaviour as employees seek to secure continuity of employment.

Against this backcloth it should be no surprise that the regulation of the employment relationship is highly individualized. In the view of management, the organization of work reinforces, if not requires, a highly individualistic approach to the management of human resources. For example, the company is organized in a matrix structure with project management on one axis and engineering disciplines on the other. Individual projects are normally headed by a project manager with project engineers, in charge of staff and drawn from the discipline departments reporting to them. Within this framework there is a premium placed on employee commitment to the project. Getting the right person to fit in with the team, in terms of both technical experience and personal qualities, is given a high priority. In addition there is a need for employees to be able to work under pressure, be prepared and able to meet deadlines, and to be flexible in order to get the job done. On occasion this means long hours at short notice, spending periods away from home at the client's site or abroad and the delay or cancellation of domestic commitments such as family holidays. This is especially the case in the run-up to a project milestone. Recruitment and allocation of labour to a project is the responsibility of departmental managers in the various engineering disciplines. Departmental managers need to foster a close one-to-one relationship with their staff and to be able to strike an appropriate balance between the demands of individual projects, the business requirement and the career aspirations and domestic circumstances of individual employees.

Despite such demands on employees, the company regards itself as a 'people organization' and is keen to develop and promote the careers of those individuals prepared to show the appropriate level of commitment. Similarly, senior management see themselves as open and responsive. Employees are encouraged to speak-up and few are said to be afraid to make comments and criticisms about how the company works. Other examples of this people orientation are practices such as project managers sending flowers to team members' partners on special occasions or as compensation for when a spouse has been working particularly long hours. One often-repeated story tells of an occasion when a team member had been asked to cancel a family holiday during a three-month period in which the project team had been working 100-hour weeks. The company subsequently paid for the employee and his family to holiday at Disneyland in the USA.

The highly individualized nature of the employment relationship is demonstrated most clearly in the way pay is determined and by the extensive use of subcontract labour. Pay is dealt with on a strictly one-to-one basis between employees and their line manager. For example, company policy prohibits discussion between employees over individual rates of pay. Recommendations for pay increases are made on the basis of subjective judgements of individual performance by immediate supervisors or managers at 12-monthly reviews. These are then passed to the relevant discipline manager who, on advice from the personnel department, makes a decision. However, where pay rises are awarded, this still has to be sanctioned by project managers on whose budgets the cost actually falls. In practice, however, many individuals circumvent this formal process and engage in individual negotiations with project managers. These negotiations are described by project managers as typically a process of bluff and counter-bluff where employee demands are usually supported by claims regarding rates of pay being offered by competitors.

Sub-contract or agency staff are a widespread feature of employment at DECO and in some departments the majority of employees are employed on this basis. In large part this practice emerged as a result of labour market shortages in key skill areas (for example, as occurred with the introduction of CAD equipment – see below). However, subcontracting also allows management greater numerical flexibility in adjusting headcount to suit the overall pattern and volume of workloads on various projects. From the employee viewpoint, working through a subcontractor permits most individuals to command substantially higher remuneration which more than compensates for the loss of job security and other benefits of being a permanent employee.

It is in the context of the unpredictable nature of demand, contractual obligations to meet project milestones, strong client pressures and the need for a high degree of flexibility in the allocation, use and reward of labour that trade union presence is viewed by senior management as totally incompatible with DECO's business. Trade unions are seen as a handicap which would prevent the business operating with sufficient speed and fleet of foot to respond to changing market requirements. As such, any suggestion of union organization is seen as a threat and as an unacceptable constraint on the way the business currently operates.

## Technical Change without Unions

As already noted, a major contributory factor in DECO's competitive advantage is its use of high-tech computer-aided design equipment. In fact this new technology was introduced gradually over a number of years and is now beginning to highlight a number of human resource management issues. First, the implementation of the system has been accomplished in a top-down fashion with a minimum of information disclosure and communication with staff other than through the management chain and the office grape-vine. Second, pressures to demonstrate early pay-offs from the adoption of the system mean that mainly junior technical staff have been retrained to use the system for drafting (effectively substituting an electronic drawing board for the traditional pencil and T-square). It is also much easier to recruit and employ this kind of employee on a subcontract basis. Third, the focus on using the system for drawing means that its more advanced capabilities in assisting the design process (for example, it is possible to build a virtual model of an entire platform within the system's memory) are underutilized. It is now recognized that, in order to use the system fully, there is a need for drafting staff to gain a wider range of cross-disciplinary design skills and for project managers and senior design engineers to understand more about how CAD could aid basic design decision making. As a result, over the past two years an extensive training programme for these staff has been launched.

However, in the meantime, shortages of CAD-trained drafting staff has meant subcontract pay rates have been on the increase. This has eroded the differential with more senior staff employed on permanent contracts, and demands for more pay on the latter's part have arisen. In addition, the use of CAD on more and more projects tends to mean that meeting milestones increasingly requires extending the hours of the subcontract staff trained to use the system. This provides an opportunity for subcontract staff to make individual deals which further exacerbate the differential problem with permanent staff. As the labour market remaines highly competitive DECO faces a potentially damaging retention problem among the latter, especially as some are now electing to resign their positions and choosing instead to sell their services back to the company on more lucrative terms as subcontractors for an agency.

## Questions

1   To what extent do the three case studies provide examples of new human resource management techniques?

2   How, would you compare and contrast the management approach at the three companies in the light of the different product and labour-market conditions they face?

3   Make specific suggestions as to how each of the three companies might develop their human resource management policies and practice. In particular:

(a)   Should the COCO managing director seek to establish a human resource specialism in the British company? Why?

(b)   Given the CECO quality manager's desire to move towards a quality culture, what changes in the management of human resources at the firm would you say are necessary in the short and long terms?

(c)   How might DECO address the retention problem that has emerged as a result of the narrowing pay differential between permanent and subcontract staff?

4   Table 18.2 shows the results of an attitude survey conducted in the three companies (in the case of CECO both manual and non-manual employees were surveyed). What conclusions might be drawn from the information in the table regarding levels of current union membership in each company and the prospects for unionization of the four workforces in the survey?

**Table 18.2**   Propensity to join a union in the three cases study firms

| | DECO | CECO Manual | CECO Non-manual | COCO | ALL |
|---|---|---|---|---|---|
| | % | % | % | % | % |
| Current union member | 0 | 4 | 3 | 2 | 5 |
| Previously union member | 25 | 25 | 41 | 29 | 30 |
| No propensity to join a union | 62 | 26 | 69 | 58 | 50 |
| A propensity to join a union | 35 | 68 | 31 | 38 | 46 |

*Source:* McLoughlin and Gourlay (1994)

### References

Bassett, P. 1988: Non-unionism's growing ranks. *Personnel Management,* March, 44–7.

Department of Employment 1991: *Industrial Relations in the 1990s.* London: HMSO.

Department of Employment 1992: *People, Jobs and Opportunities.* London: HMSO.

Department of Trade and Industry 1990: *Britain: the Preferred Location.* London: Central Office of Information.

Kessler, S. and Bayliss, F. 1992: *Contemporary British Industrial Relations.* London: Macmillan.

MacInnes, J. 1988: *Thatcherism at Work.* Milton Keynes: Open University Press.

Marchington, M. and Parker, P. 1990: *Changing Patterns of Employee Relations.* London: Harvester Wheatsheaf.

Newman, N. 1980: Britain's non-union leaders. *Management Today,* July, 59–112.

### Further reading

McLoughlin, I. and Gourlay, S. 1994: *Enterprise Without Unions,* Buckingham: Open University Press.

# 19

# Metropol

*Devolving management and equal*
*opportunities in local government*
## NICOLAS BACON AND
## JOHN STOREY

During the 1980s and 1990s local government authorities experi-enced a turbulent environment. Successive Conservative governments reduced the powers of local authorities by introducing a series of initiatives including compulsory competitive tendering (CCT), self-governing status for schools and greater powers to housing tenants. The Conservatives gained control of a metropolitan district council in the north of England in 1988, which we shall here call Metropol. At that time Metropol covered a population of approximately 470,000 people (15–17 per cent of whom were from ethnic minorities) and employed the equivalent of 20,000 full-time staff.

The new ruling Conservative Group detected the breakdown of a clear consensus about the mission of local government and sought to effect a revolution in how the council delivered its services. The group introduced a new strategy to change the culture to create an 'enabling council' with the focus firmly placed on the service receiver as the customer. To achieve this turn-around it placed an emphasis on management autonomy with responsibilities devolved to those closer to the point of delivering council services. It introduced a structural overhaul creating separate service departments known as directorates. It also dissolved the existing personnel department of 140 posts and devolved powers to the directorates. A residual advi-sory group of 15 in 'strategic personnel' remained at the centre. Each directorate contained a director of personnel who could turn to the central group for advice. The Conservative Group gave managers within the directorates wide-ranging powers to drive through changes to make the organization more customer responsive. There was a shift in emphasis away from a set of rules common to all departments towards an established framework of standards to guide the activities of managers. Rather than bringing about change through collective bargaining with the trade unions, the new emphasis was on management development within the devolved culture. Radical plans to erase the council-wide grievance and disciplinary procedures had been drawn up. The role of the personnel directors had changed from 'making rules and checking that managers followed them', towards becoming 'the supporters, helpers and advisers' to the directorates. Within the directorates themselves managers responded with enthusiasm to their new-found freedoms. The council ran a high-profile series of seminars for managers aimed at developing a customer orientation. The works of management gurus flourished on the bookshelves in the offices of managers as they identified themselves as change agents and a new breed of local government managers.

Beneath this optimistic picture there were signs that things were not all going as planned. Employees brought 63 race discrimination cases against the council between 1988 and January 1993. The council had faced a hefty legal bill and had paid out over £100,000 in compensation. In one case alone, the tribunal had found the council's record so reprehensible that the settlement included an award of £2,000 in aggravated damages. (See Appendix 19.1.) Although the council had a formal equal opportunities policy since 1981, the Commission for Racial Equality (see Appendix 19.2) considered its record so poor it sought an injunction against further acts of discrimination under Section 62 of the Race Relations Act 1976, alleging that the council was a persistent discriminator.

After an industrial tribunal found the council had unlawfully discriminated on the grounds of race for the fifth time in six years the council commissioned a report by an independent consultant. In making the report, the consultant highlighted the absence of an adequate corporate framework and a failure to discipline employees responsible for discrimination despite the results from the industrial tribunals. Interviews with council employees revealed widespread dissatisfaction and, among ethnic minority staff, a lack of confidence in the internal systems to deal with complaints. An investigation into the operation of the equal opportunities policy revealed that the council had not approached the issue corporately. In the rush to devolve management responsibilities many managers were making decisions on staff recruitment, selection and promotion without having attended relevant training courses in managing a multiracial workforce. The consultant could find no accurate council-wide data on recruitment and selection according to ethnic origin. In the large social services department managers had not recorded the ethnic origin of all staff. In sum, the independent report called for sweeping changes.

---

## Questions

1  What do you think had gone wrong and why had it done so?
2  What equal opportunities issues are important to consider when organizations opt for devolving managerial responsibilities?
3  What basic information is needed to formulate and monitor an effective equal opportunities programme?
4  What should be the roles and responsibilities of the strategic personnel unit and the directorate personnel managers in the future to ensure a more effective equal opportunities policy?
5  What recommendations could the consultant have made to improve the council's equal opportunities policy?
6  It has been suggested that having the correct procedures may be insufficient to overcome discrimination. Do you think this is true? What opinion do you have of alternative methods used in other countries (for instance, positive discrimination and quota systems)?

---

## Further reading

Commission for Racial Equality 1984: *Code of Practice: Race Relations.* London: HMSO.

Dickens, L. 1994: Wasted resources? equal opportunities in employment. In Sisson, K. (ed.), *Personnel Management,* Oxford: Blackwell.

---

Appendix 19.1  Summaries of Two Industrial Tribunal Cases the Council Lost

In 1988 an industrial tribunal found that the council had discriminated against four employees of Afro-Caribbean origin on racial grounds. All four had been youth workers paid less than their white counterparts, in one case £6,000 less and in the others 50 per cent less. After failing to successfully resolve their problem internally they had resorted to the tribunal. The highest of the awards was £11,748 for loss of earnings while others received lower sums plus payments for injury to feelings.

In another case, two senior sports-centre managers had singled out Mr X, a black sports-centre duty manager, for harsher treatment and criticism than other employees. When the duty manager and a white colleague were both accused of sexually harassing a female colleague, only Mr X faced disciplinary proceedings and he was suspended before being cleared on appeal. The tribunal awarded £5,812 compensation, including £3,000 for injury to feelings and £2,000 aggravated damages as the council persisted in the attempt to 'defend the indefensible'.

## Appendix 19.2   A Summary of The Commission for Racial Equality Code of Practice

1. **Equal Opportunities Policy**: Should be adopted, implemented and monitored. It should be communicated to all and overall responsibility should be given to a member of senior management. The contents and implementation should be discussed with employee representatives. Relevant decision-makers should be trained and guided in the policy and the law. Existing procedures and criteria should be regularly reviewed and changed to meet the aims of the policy. Managers should make an initial analysis of the workforce and monitor the application of the policy by analysing the ethnic origins of the workforce and job applicants.

2. **Recruitment, Promotion, Transfer, Training, and Performance Appraisal:** Do not confine adverts to areas that would disproportionately reduce applicants from particular racial groups. Avoid prescribing requirements such as the length of residence in the UK. Comparable qualifications from overseas should be accepted. Job applicants should receive literature on the company's equal opportunities policy. Job and training vacancies should be made known to all eligible employees. Staff responsible should be trained and procedures assessed.

3. **Selection Criteria and Tests:** Selection criteria must be related to job requirements. Selection tests containing irrelevant questions should not be used. Any selection tests should be related to job requirements.

4. **Treatment of Applicants, Shortlisting, Interviewing and Selection:** Gatekeeping staff should not discourage applicants. Staff responsible for shortlisting should be clearly informed of selection criteria and consistency, given guidance and training on the effects of prejudice on selection decisions, and made culturally sensitive. Shortlisting and interviewing should be checked by several people.

5. **Genuine Occupational Qualifications (GOQ):** Selection on racial grounds is allowed in certain jobs where being of a particular racial group is a GOQ.

6. **Terms of Employment, Benefits, Facilities and Services:** Staff should be instructed and the criteria governing eligibility should be examined.

7. **Grievance, Disputes and Disciplinary Procedures:** In applying each of these consideration should be given to the possible effects of: racial abuse

and other racial provocation; communication and comprehension difficulties; and differences in cultural background and behaviour.

9. **Cultural and Religious Beliefs:** Employers should consider being adaptable, for example accounting for the needs of prayer times, religious holidays and dress.

10. **Training, Communications and Language:** Where possible employers should provide interpretation and translation facilities, training in English language and communication skills, managers should be trained in the background and culture of racial minority groups, and use additional methods of communication where appropriate, for example warning signs and symbols.

11. **Instructions and Pressure to Discriminate:** Employees should be given guidance in legal provisions, decision makers should be instructed not to give way to pressures to discriminate, and those applying pressure to discriminate should be disciplined.

12. **Victimisation:** Legal guidance should be given.

13. **Monitoring:** Employers should regularly monitor the effects of selection decisions, personnel practices and procedures. The CRE recommends analysing the ethnic composition of the workforce of each plant, department, section, shift, job category and the changes over time. In addition selection decisions for recruitment, promotion, transfer and training should be monitored.

14. **Positive Action:** Employers should encourage employees and prospective employees and provide training for under-represented racial groups. Policies to consider are: advertising in the ethnic minority press; recruiting in certain geographical areas; targeting school leaver recruitment; encouraging people to apply for promotion and transfer opportunities; and training people for promotion and in the necessary skills.

Commission for Racial Equality (1984)

Appendix 19.3   A Summary of the Race Relations Act 1976
(Not Applicable in Northern Ireland)

Prohibits direct and indirect discrimination in all areas of employment on grounds of race, colour, nationality, ethnic or national origins (includes some religious groups).

S.1 (1) (a) *Defines direct discrimination* as treating a person, on racial grounds, less favourably than others are or would be treated in the same or similar circumstances.

S.1 (1) (b) *Indirect discrimination* consists in applying in any circumstances covered by the Act a requirement or condition which, although applied equally to persons of all racial groups, is such that a considerably smaller proportion of a particular racial group can comply with it and it cannot be shown to be justified on other than racial grounds.

S.2 Discrimination by *victimisation* is unlawful.

S.4 and S.28 It is unlawful to discriminate, not only in *recruitment, promotion, transfer and training*, but also in arrangements made for recruitment and in the ways of affording access to opportunities for promotion, transfer or training. It is unlawful to discriminate on racial grounds in *dismissal, the operation of grievance, disputes and disciplinary procedures*. It is unlawful to discriminate on racial grounds in *appraising* employee performance or in affording *terms of employment* and providing benefits, facilities and services for employees.

S.5 and S.5 (2) (d) Selection on racial grounds is allowed in certain jobs where being of a particular racial group is a *genuine occupational qualification* for that job.

S.29 When advertising job vacancies it is unlawful for employers to publish an advert which indicates, or could reasonably be understood as indicating, an intention to discriminate against applicants from a particular racial group.

S.30 It is unlawful for employers to give *instructions to discriminate* (for example by indicating that certain groups will or will not be preferred) or to bring *pressure* on others to discriminate against members of a particular racial group.

S.38 Although they are not legally required, *positive measures* are allowed by the law to encourage employees and prospective employees and provide training for employees who are members of particular racial groups that have been under-represented in particular work.

# Richer Sounds

*Payment for customer service*
ADRIAN WILKINSON,
TOM REDMAN AND ED SNAPE

Service industries such as banking, retail, hospitality and public services are subject to increasing competition, deregulation, rising customer expectations and technological change. This has led them to become much more customer focused. Given the limits to the ability of many service institutions to differentiate their products or services, not least because of the ease with which competitors can match any innovation, individual organizations have attempted to differentiate themselves from their competitors by branding and advertising and improving the quality of customer service. Mission and vision statements and marketing and advertising policies proclaim the customer as the god to whom organizations must ritually genuflect. Just as zero defects is the goal of quality, zero defection is the sign of quality coming to services (Reichheld and Sasser, 1990). Organizations now have a whole host of mechanisms designed to elicit what customers want, including surveys and customer circles, for example. They have several methods of monitoring customer service quality such as mystery shoppers and the use of standard performance measures and procedures.

Hand in hand with these approaches have been attempts to change organizational values and culture, so as to encourage employees to identify with these ideals. The quality and performance of front-line staff has increasingly been seen as a key contributor to competitive advantage, especially when the service encounter, or 'moment of truth' (Carlzon, 1987) is seen as part of the act of 'consuming the product'.

Copyright John Storey 1996, Blackwell Cases in Human Resource and Change Management

A barrage of initiatives such as team briefing, videos and house journals have been introduced by management to communicate information direct to staff as part of attempts to educate them more fully about the business position and to stress the importance of the customer. Similarly, information is provided about the current state of the business or future plans, a process designed in part to convince staff of the logic of management actions and to engender commitment to organization goals (Marchington et al., 1992). Clearly, the assumption behind this is that workers who understand the context of their work will be more committed and these workers will also perform more effectively, reflecting an underlying assumption that employees will derive intrinsic satisfaction from doing a quality job.

However, the evidence about the impact of such schemes tends to be no more than mildly positive at best (Marchington et al., 1992). A number of writers have argued that exhortation and communication are, at best, weak vehicles of change (Schein, 1985; Hill, 1991; Wilkinson, 1994). Hill (1991) argues that writers understate the difficulties of getting staff at all levels to buy into the ideals of quality and to make such ideals and changes stick, and that managers need to use a broader range of reward and punishment policies to underpin this. Schuler and Harris (1992) claim that appraisals may contribute to quality improvement for customer satisfaction by ensuring that employees are aware of the behaviours which contribute to quality, and they endorse the use of financial incentives as part of a quality-enhancement strategy, for example by linking pay to customer feedback on service quality (p. 129). Similarly, Snape et al. (1995) have argued that while organizations should avoid attaching a price tag to customer service improvement, there may be a role for financial incentives in raising awareness and highlighting key areas for improvement.

The case study of Richer Sounds will enable us to examine some of these issues in the context of a retail company committed to achieving high-quality customer service through staff.

## The Company

Richer Sounds is the biggest hi-fi separates retailer in the UK with 15 branches, a warehouse and a head office, employing over 100 staff in total. The company is an unlisted plc, owned by a self-made entrepreneur, Julian Richer, who opened the first shop in 1978 on £20,000 borrowed from a photographic retailer. The company's success comes from high stock turnover combined with low overheads. It made its name selling discounted, often discontinued end-of-line products in small shops in cheap locations. Richer operates very much in a niche market, focusing on a closely related, narrow product range to a targeted customer group. Richer has overcome the unwillingness of some major companies to deal with them, with a profit of £1.8 million on a turnover of £18 million in 1991/2. Indeed, the company is in the *Guinness Book of Records* for having the highest sales per square foot of any retailer in the world. It also has the highest sales per employee.

## The Customer Service Philosophy

Customer service is seen as the driving philosophy behind the company. Officially, this is stated as 'providing second to none service and value for our customers'. More simply, the idea is that excellent customer service is not a sell-at-all-costs approach. The company say that employees are encouraged to 'help the customer buy' rather than go for the hard sell in order to develop longer-term customer loyalty. The company argues that its basic principles are quality products (branded names, and so on), value for money and customer service, and point out that while the first two can be controlled by head office, the latter is very much in the hands of the ordinary branch employee, and hence considerable attention needs to be devoted to this area. It is possible to trace a distinct American flavour of the type promulgated by Peters and Waterman's *In Search of Excellence* (1982). Indeed, the chairman claims that the book changed his life. Thus, staff are known as 'colleagues' and the organization chart is presented in inverted form, with the customer at the top, followed by sales colleagues and middle management and ending with the top management.

The emphasis is very much on fun for customers. Customers are invited to bring their pets to help them choose their purchase. Those buying a hi-fi when it is raining receive a free umbrella, and scratch cards with free gifts are distributed. Even the warnings to shoplifters are made with humour: 'Free ride in a police car for shoplifters only'. Humour also pervades the company's advertisements in such media as *Viz* and *Private Eye*. Goods are promoted in a positive and light-hearted way by mixing illustrations, technical detail and often (particularly in the *Viz* adverts) toilet humour.

The company has a freephone 24-hour-a-day customer problem line and a main board director is responsible for dealing with customer queries. A 'We're listening' suggestion card scheme provides the opportunity for those who do not purchase to make comments, and this is sent directly to the chairman. Sales assistants are expected to make a number of customer telephone calls each week, aimed at older age-group customers and first-time buyers, to ensure that they are satisfied with the items purchased.

## Management Style

Management style at the company has been described as 'fun but caring'. Influences include the American management gurus Peters and Waterman, and the UK retailer Marks & Spencer. The latter influence derives from the chairman's parents, who both worked there, and finds particular expression in paternalist attitudes. For example, 20 per cent of the profits are directed either to profit share (15 per cent), to charity (4 per cent) or to a staff hardship fund (1 per cent). Staff benefits include life insurance and a subsidized medical scheme. This paternalism is also reflected in the staff induction pack, which includes advice on health. In addition, there is an attempt to create a family feeling, with a bonus of £100 for staff introducing new employees to the company, and staff are provided with the chairman's home telephone number. The company provides subsidized outings for staff three times a year and training sessions take place twice yearly at the chairman's country home. Holiday homes are made available free to staff (a benefit which the Inland Revenue costs at £30 a day, on which the company pays tax).

Staff wear name badges to encourage greater individual accountability to the customer. Staff who perform above and beyond the call of duty (ABCD) receive gold aeroplanes as a recognition of their high achievement. Wooden spoons are given to staff for acts of amazing stupidity. On a more serious level, the company computes a customer service index (CSI) for each member of staff. Individuals are assessed monthly on a range of indicators with results related to payment (see below).

The array of incentives and innovations is quite wide and it is the management philosophy continually to develop these in a bid to maintain the sense of involvement and fun.

## Managing Staff for Customer Service

For a small firm the company has quite a sophisticated range of personnel policies and practices, yet has no personnel department or manager. This is reflected in the induction booklet which includes details of the company philosophy, the organizational chart, company history, contract, 100 blank suggestion slips, an A–Z of hi-fi terms, health booklet and a 50-page staff training manual.

Staff turnover is very low, although there is what management calls a 'high infant mortality rate', that is, people who leave in the early months of employment because they are unable to adapt to the 'peculiar' culture. The company has a policy of promoting internally, as a way of rewarding loyalty, except for expert specialists at head office such as in marketing. Pay is above average for the industry. Sales assistants earn a basic rate of around £10,000 but commission, profit share and the customer service bonus raises this to around £15,000 (in 1994). Profit share alone has worked out at around £1,300 for each sales colleague in recent years.

Communications are seen as vital. A weekly video is produced with details of company performance. The company has a highly successful suggestion scheme, which has won the UK Association of Suggestion Scheme prize for the highest number of suggestions per staff: 1,500 from 70 staff in 1991. Staff are rewarded with up to £180 for each suggestion, with the best two each quarter receiving a day trip on the Orient Express. To facilitate suggestions there is a monthly £5 drink allowance so employees can go out as a group to discuss possible ideas. Many of the ideas are hard to quantify in terms of bottom-line impact (for example, a bell provided for disabled shoppers), but the scheme is seen in the broader context of building morale. All suggestions are seen and replied to by the chairman.

Another part of the motivational approach is a competition held between all the branches and departments. This is the Richer Sounds Way League which is based on customer service and profit, rather than sales, and provides a prize of the use of a Bentley (first prize) or Rolls Royce (second prize) for a week. The company also achieves considerable free publicity in the regional press as a result of a local branch winning the league.

## Linking Pay and Customer Satisfaction

The company believes in making a direct link between individual pay and customer satisfaction. There is a customer service index (CSI) against which individuals are assessed on several indicators: how quickly they answer the phone, the number of customer complaints, quality of overall service, good and bad letters, positive and negative comments from questionnaires, and punctuality. Points are added and subtracted each month and reflected in a cash bonus paid with salary. Peer-group pressure is seen as critical, and CSI results are fed to managers on each individual's performance and then published and distributed internally.

The company believes in linking customer satisfaction and pay. Each customer receipt includes a freepost questionnaire mailed directly to the chairman, with the customer invited to assess the level of service provided by the salesperson, who is identified by payroll number on the form (see Table 20.1). Individual's bonuses are related to this feedback. Thus if a customer ticks 'excellent', the sales colleague receives an extra £3, if 'poor', a deduction of £3 takes place. These are totalled up at the end of each month and a bonus paid. The company is at pains to point out that any deductions are far outweighed by the bonuses. Indeed, it is unlikely that anyone with a stream of negative feedback would actually retain their job at Richer Sounds.

**Table 20.1** Pay and Customer Service

| Bonus to staff (£) | How would you describe the overall level of service you received? | Analysis June 1993 (%) |
|---|---|---|
| 3 | Excellent | 71 |
| 0 | Good | 28 |
| −1 | Mediocre | 0.75 |
| −3 | Poor | 0.5 |

An analysis of the overall CSI results is performed by a customer services group which meets on a fortnightly basis. The aggregate results for June 1993 are in Table 20.1.

## Conclusions

Richer Sounds provides a good example of how a wide range of HRM initiatives may be used to underpin the development of customer awareness and service quality. Much of the literature on TQM underplays the role reward strategies can play in developing a quality culture, but the Richer experience is that effective reward systems can supply a valuable change lever to focus employee attention on improving service quality.

Richer has achieved a considerable degree of success in matching its HRM practices to its business strategy with neither a personnel department nor a formal TQM programme. The success and relative sophistication (particularly for a SME) of Richer's people management strategy is indicative for the potential of general and line managers to devise and implement a strategic approach to HRM without the assistance of a specialized HR department, although the task may be made easier in Richer's case by the small size and youth of the organization.

The success of the Richer's quality initiative without a TQM programme also echoes recent studies that suggest that a formal programme is not necessary to deliver quality improvement and competitive advantage. Powell (1995) found that success derives more from such HRM intangibles as executive commitment, open organization culture and employee empowerment, all of which we find in abundance at Richer, and less on such TQM staples as process improvement, improved measurement and benchmarking.

Much of the quality management literature, particularly that deriving from the quality gurus, has a bias towards the practices of manufacturing, and it is often to this sector that the quality management literature turns for evidence of good practice. We thus know rather more about world-class quality management practices in manufacturing (see, for example, Oliver et al., 1994) than in services. We offer this case study as a contribution to the debate.

<hr/>

## Questions

1  Should organizations pay for quality?
2  Discuss how customer satisfaction is embedded in the corporate culture at Richer Sounds.

3  What developments in human resource strategy could be utilized to support an intended shift to a corporate culture based on customer service?

4  To what extent does Richer Sounds offer useful lessons for organizations in, for example, the public sector and other retail companies?

## References

Carlzon, S. 1987: *Moments of Truth*, London: Harper and Row.

Drummond, H. and Chell, E. 1992: Should organisations pay for quality? *Personnel Review*, **21**(4), 3–11.

Hill, S. 1991: Why quality circles failed but total quality might succeed. *British Journal of Industrial Relations*, **29**(4), 541–69.

Marchington, M., Goodman, J., Wilkinson, A. and Ackers, P. 1992: *New Developments in Employee Involvement*. Employment Department Research Paper Series No. 2.

Oliver, N., Delbridge, R., Jones, D. and Lowe, J. 1994: World Class Manufacturing: Further evidence in the Lean Production debate. *British Journal of Management*, **5**, June, 53–63.

Peters, T. and Waterman, R. 1982: *In Search of Excellence*, New York: Harper and Row.

Powell, T. C. 1995: Total quality management as competitive advantage: a review and empirical study. *Strategic Management Journal*, **16**(I), January, 15–37.

Reichheld, F. and Sasser, W. 1990: Zero Defections: Quality comes to services. *Harvard Business Review*, Sept–Oct, 105–11.

Schein, E. 1985: *Organisational Culture and Leadership*, New York: Jossey-Bass.

Schuler, R. and Harris, D. 1992: *Managing Quality: The Primer for Middle Managers*, Reading, MA: Addison Wesley.

Snape, E., Wilkinson, A. and Redman, T. 1995: Cashing in on Quality: Incentive pay and the Quality Culture. *Human Resource Management Journal* (forthcoming).

Wilkinson, A. 1994: Managing human resources for quality. In Dale, B. G. *Managing Quality*, 2nd ed., Hemel Hempstead: Prentice-Hall.

## Further reading

Cannell, M. and Wood, S. 1992: *Incentive Pay: Impact and Evolution*. London: IPM and NEDO.

Deming, W. 1986: *Out of the Crisis*, Cambridge, MA: MIT Centre for Advanced Engineering Study.

Goldsmith, W. and Clutterbuck, D. 1985: *The Winning Streak*, Harmondsworth: Penguin.

Kohn, A. 1993: *Punished by Rewards: The Trouble with Gold Stars, Incentive Plans, A's, Praise and other Bribes*, Boston, MA: Houghton Mifflin.

Lovelock, C. 1991: *Managing Services*, (2nd ed.), Englewood Cliffs, NJ: Prentice-Hall.

Moores, B. (ed.) 1986: *Are They Being Served?* Oxford: Phillip Allan.

Mumford, J. and Buley, T. 1988: Rewarding behavioural skills as part of performance. *Personnel Management*, December, 33–7.

Walker, T. 1992: Creating total quality improvement that lasts, *National Productivity Review*, Autumn, 473–8.

Williams, A., Dobson, P. and Walters, M. 1993: *Changing Cultures*, London: IPM.

# 21

# Unilever

*Flexible working: introducing annualized hours and 24-hour working*

NICOLAS BACON AND
JOHN STOREY

At Unilever the development of the single European market was the trigger for significant organizational restructuring. Traditionally the company had regarded Europe as a collection of national markets requiring specialized products suitable for different national tastes. Consequently, factories in each different country produced a wide range of products (foodstuffs, personal products, soaps and detergents). Senior managers decided that under the single European market the company could produce standard products for the whole of Europe from the most efficient factory site. This decision was to have important consequences for its factories and employees in the UK.

The soaps and detergents' division, Lever Brothers, had five factories in near proximity in the north of England. As a result of the change each factory manager suddenly faced direct competition with other factories in Europe rather than being the sole source site for the UK market. The company placed future investment decisions more firmly on a European-wide basis increasing the need to be the most competitive factory. For industrial relations purposes senior managers had traditionally regarded the five factories in Lever Brothers as one bargaining unit. To help improve productivity managers embarked on a new employment strategy negotiating with the trade unions one all-embracing package of changes, called 'New Horizons'. When signed in October 1991, New Horizons marked a continuation of the consensual approach to managing change through collective bargaining which distinguishes the company. Besides the introduction of

Copyright John Storey 1996, Blackwell Cases in Human Resource and Change Management

team working and multiskilling it introduced annualized hours contracts ending paid overtime. Managers introduced annualized hours (see Table 21.1) contracts based on payment for a 37.5 hour week. This allowed greater flexibility throughout the year and in hours of attendance around a nominated work pattern. If the working pattern did not exhaust the total number of contracted hours this resulted in the generation of banked hours. The company could call upon banked hours to cover absence, holidays, training, meetings, rectification work or extra production. In common with many companies in the 1990s, managers had come to regard overtime as too expensive and a reward for mistakes that sent the wrong cultural message about the organization.

The banked hours system harmonized the number of hours employees were contracted to work and it gave managers greater control over the work patterns of individuals. Most managers supported this scheme but many employees thought the move regressive despite having rostered periods away from work as long as three and four days. Before New Horizons, extra work had been voluntary overtime. When the company now called in its banked hours it compelled employees to attend. Consequently it restricted the individual freedom of employees, particularly in how they organized their private lives. Managers discerned the change had a negative impact on employee motivation. The new contracts had broken the relationship between hours worked in any week and reward. The pay packet did not immediately reflect effort and hours worked so many employees felt they were losing money. As an operations engineer explained: 'They are now paid a salary but people look at cash in the hand. There is less incentive as people see the same figures but have worked more hours. It is what's up-front that counts. We have lost the motivational bit. The banked hours are seen as extra hours and it is difficult to get them to accept they have already been paid for it. There is a lot of trouble when you ask people to come in.'

Another shift leader explained how a 'caravan culture' had replaced an 'overtime culture'. Employees had bought caravans believing the new system ensured them four-day holiday periods. When managers then asked them to work in this period not only did they feel they were working for nothing but it involved significant disruptions to their social plans. Even senior managers who firmly backed the changes could see problems ahead after the first year of operation. Employees were working fewer hours due to a downturn in the market. This had resulted in the generation of a large number of

**Table 21.1**  Example of the annualized hours system

Where four crews are working a three shift rotational system (6–2, 2–10, 10–6) each week contains 16 planned shifts from 6.00 a.m. on Monday to 2.00 p.m. on Saturday. Each employee will work 16 rostered shifts in each four-weekly cycle where attendance is mandatory. Rostered working will produce 1,500 hours worked each year. Besides this the company can call on approximately 400 'banked' hours of working to cover holidays, training, absences and, if necessary, extra work periods. To give an example from the possible working pattern detailed below: employees in crew one may have to work an extra shift on the first Sunday; they then work three rostered shifts Monday to Wednesday; this is followed by seven days rostered off, but with only the Sunday guaranteed; three rostered days are then worked (Thursday to Saturday); an extra 17th shift on the third Sunday may then be necessary; five working days are then rostered from Monday to Friday; Saturday is guaranteed off; a possible 18th shift may be required on Sunday; five working days are then rostered (Monday to Friday) with the final Saturday guaranteed off.

*Possible working pattern: 4 crews working 3 shifts*

|           | Crew 1 | Crew 2 | Crew 3 | Crew 4 |
| --------- | ------ | ------ | ------ | ------ |
| *Week 1*  |        |        |        |        |
| Sunday    | (6–2)  | *      | (10–6) | (2–10) |
| Monday    | 6–2    | —      | 10–6   | 2–10   |
| Tuesday   | 6–2    | —      | 10–6   | 2–10   |
| Wednesday | 6–2    | —      | 10–6   | 2–10   |
| Thursday  | —      | 6–2    | 10–6   | 2–10   |
| Friday    | —      | 6–2    | 10–6   | 2–10   |
| Saturday  | —      | 6–2    | *      | *      |
| *Week 2*  |        |        |        |        |
| Sunday    | *      | (10–6) | (2–10) | (6–2)  |
| Monday    | —      | 10–6   | 2–10   | 6–2    |
| Tuesday   | —      | 10–6   | 2–10   | 6–2    |
| Wednesday | —      | 10–6   | 2–10   | 6–2    |
| Thursday  | 6–2    | 10–6   | 2–10   | —      |
| Friday    | 6–2    | 10–6   | 2–10   | —      |
| Saturday  | 6–2    | *      | *      | —      |
| *Week 3*  |        |        |        |        |
| Sunday    | (10–6) | (2–10) | (6–2)  | —      |
| Monday    | 10–6   | 2–10   | 6–2    | —      |
| Tuesday   | 10–6   | 2–10   | 6–2    | —      |

**Table 21.1** (cont.)

*Possible working pattern: 4 crews working 3 shifts*

|  | Crew 1 | Crew 2 | Crew 3 | Crew 4 |
|---|---|---|---|---|
| Wednesday | 10–6 | 2–10 | 6–2 | — |
| Thursday | 10–6 | 2–10 | — | 6–2 |
| Friday | 10–6 | 2–10 | — | 6–2 |
| Saturday | * | * | — | 6–2 |
| *Week 4* |  |  |  |  |
| Sunday | (2–10) | (6–2) | * | (10–6) |
| Monday | 2–10 | 6–2 | — | 10–6 |
| Tuesday | 2–10 | 6–2 | — | 10–6 |
| Wednesday | 2–10 | 6–2 | — | 10–6 |
| Thursday | 2–10 | — | 6–2 | 10–6 |
| Friday | 2–10 | — | 6–2 | 10–6 |
| Saturday | * | — | 6–2 | * |

*employees will never need to work these shifts

Key
6–2, 2–10, 10–6 are rostered shifts
(10–6) is the possible 17th shift
(2–10) is the possible 18th shift
(6–2) is the possible 19th shift

To utilize these banked hours if cover is needed then shifts can be extended four hours before or after the normal roster. Possible extra shifts can be added to extend the length of the normal working week should demand warrant it (given in brackets in the above example). Planned time-off is guaranteed unless employees are to attend training courses, special meetings or in the exceptional circumstances of the three shifts rostered failing to provide cover themselves.

unworked banked hours that the company had not used but for which they had paid. In effect they had bound themselves to a system that appeared to give them flexibility, but it had resulted in their paying for unworked time. At the end of the first year, senior managers were nervous. How could they justify having paid for the unworked hours? In the new competitive market had they pushed up the labour costs in the UK factories, weakening their competitiveness vis-à-vis other European plants? All had not gone quite according to plan and managers debated changes in the annualized hours system.

Elida Gibbs, a large plant in the north of England, and part of the cosmetics division of Unilever, faced a different set of issues when managers introduced 24-hour working in 1992. The European-wide restructuring described earlier had led to greater technical investment at selected 'lead sites' as the company concentrated its production facilities. With this investment there was a greater need to increase asset utilization and hence managers introduced 24-hour working into the company to fully utilize the new production processes. Tradition-ally, packing lines had been run on a 15-hour day working pattern with three five-hour shifts. When the site was built in the 1970s relatively high employment had made recruitment difficult and five-hour fixed shifts had attracted a female workforce earning a second wage in the family.

One factory manager was resistant to the idea of forcing change on the workforce and (by agreement) he moved to manage another factory. He was replaced by a younger manager from The Nether-lands who was eager to make his mark and could appropriately be described as a 'change agent'. In changing to 24-hour working, managers rejected the notion of 'bolting on' a permanent night shift of new recruits for two reasons. First, they feared the physiological strain of working permanent nights would reduce product quality and output. Second, they felt it would create two cultures. Managers' working days would rarely see the night shift and they felt that the notion of first- and second-class citizens ran against a total quality culture. The desires among managers to create a unified culture led them to prefer a rotating work pattern. The new system involved employees working eight-hour shifts as managers were determined to break what they regarded as a 'part-timer mentality' in packing op-erations. Senior managers felt that the level of commitment displayed by part-time workers was incompatible with world-class production. Full-time workers, managers hoped, would be more compatible with the team-working concept.

Although employees welcomed the move to full-time status and pay and the unions accepted the changes, it did create serious problems for many. After extensive consultation, managers discovered that the major obstacle preventing the changes being readily welcomed was the social impact of the changes on the lives of employees. When the company built the plant, part-time working had suited the needs of many employees in the local labour market. However, by the early 1990s the social composition of the nearby estates had changed with high unemployment and a high number of single-parent families becoming prevalent features. For many of the women employed the potential doubling of pay was welcome and much needed, but it made their other social roles very difficult. Initially, the announcement had de-motivated the workforce and the company expected to lose many of their better-skilled workers who could find part-time work elsewhere. The company had traditionally adopted a paternalistic stance towards its workforce and tried to alleviate some of the hardships. With the help of the local council the company developed a child-minding scheme and a family-minding scheme to allow people who cared for relatives to work the new patterns. By 1994 these schemes were up and running but the company expected to lose staff in what it described as an 'HR planning nightmare'.

---

## Questions

1   What broader economic, political and company-wide considerations were being taken into account in changing working time?
2   What were the key HR strategy considerations?
3   What were the implications for employees?
4   What limits are there on managers who seek to change working time?
5   What labour market and social factors need to be considered when planning working-time systems?

---

### Further reading

Blyton, P. 1994: Working hours. In Sisson, K. (ed.), *Personnel Management*, Oxford: Blackwell.

Horrell, S. and Rubery, J. 1991: *Employers' Working Time Policies and Women's Employment*, London: HMSO.

# 22

# Superco

## Employee involvement in food retailing
### MICK MARCHINGTON

Over the last decade, employee involvement (EI) has been the focus of many employer initiatives and academic publications in the field of human resource management, not only in Britain (Marchington, 1992, 1995a), but also in the rest of Europe, the USA and Australia (Cotton, 1993; Gold and Hall, 1992; Lansbury and Davis, 1995). The British case is particularly interesting given the highly voluntarist and deregulatory approach which has characterized its recent development, and has led to a whole series of employer-led initiatives in all sectors of the economy (Millward et al., 1992). For the most part, the practice of EI is controlled by employers, and decisions about whether or not to 'involve' employees rest with management, who also define the grounds on which EI is to take place. EI needs to be distinguished from industrial democracy, as the latter rests on assumptions that employees have a right to be involved in the governance of the enterprises for which they work. Industrial democracy is likely to be extended during the latter part of the 1990s as large multinational employers establish works councils (Hall et al., 1995). However, the creation of works councils is unlikely to be at the expense of EI, even in well-organized union workplaces.

EI techniques can be categorized into five groups (Marchington, 1995a, pp. 283–6):

1 downward communications from managers to their staff, the principal purpose of which is to inform and 'educate' employees, and which is practised via written reports to employees, house journals, training videos and team briefing;

2 upward problem-solving, which is designed to tap into employee knowledge on an individual or collective basis through techniques such as suggestion schemes or quality circles;

3 task participation, which aims to encourage employees to extend the range and types of work undertaken or take greater responsibility for decision making;

4 representative participation, which seeks to involve employee representatives in consultative committees, for example; and

5 financial involvement, which links part or all of an employee's rewards to the success of the unit or enterprise as a whole, encompassing forms of EI such as profit sharing and employee share ownership.

It is common for a mix of these techniques to be employed in organizations, sometimes with competing and contradictory aims and often pursued with differing levels of managerial commitment and interest (Marchington et al., 1992).

It is sometimes assumed that EI is more extensive in and relevant to organizations which are competing at the 'quality' end of the market, aiming to satisfy customers on the basis of superior products and high standards of service (Schuler and Jackson, 1987). This should apply therefore to the leading food retailers – companies such as J Sainsbury, Tesco and Safeway, in particular – which have differentiated themselves from the low-cost, no-frills segment of the market. If excellent customer service is so important to companies such as these, it might be expected that they would have developed EI in order to communicate with, involve and motivate their front-line staff to promote customer satisfaction and loyalty.

It will be apparent from the case study below that this has indeed taken place, but the range of EI initiatives which has been introduced is rather limited and their impact has not been substantial. In addition, it is also clear that the operation of EI suffers from a number of tensions and contradictions which render its application in the industry problematic. While there are pressures on the one hand to treat customers as individuals, there are also expectations that staff conform to specification and follow routine instructions about how to interact with customers. Similarly, the front-line staff who represent the major point of contact with customers are among the lowest-paid and most-recently recruited employees in the industry, often with little interest in, or anticipation of, long-term employment and no great reason to demonstrate high levels of commitment to their company. Moreover, there are also aspects of the control and surveillance systems used to monitor employees (electronic point of sale technology and 'mystery' shoppers, for example) which have greater resonance with a 'low-trust' image of employees than with the 'high-trust' scenario theoretically associated with EI. (Fox, 1974; Marchington, 1995b).

Before moving on to present the case, which reviews the attempts by one of the leading food retailers to develop EI, some background information is needed about the industry as a whole in order to place the analysis in context.

## The Changing Context of Food Retailing

Food retailing is one of the major industries in Britain, and its market leaders rank among the largest in the country, both in financial and employment terms. Much of their success has been built on rapid advances in information technology, food hygiene, marketing, physical distribution and, of course, customer service. It is an extremely competitive sector of the British economy, comprising not just the well-known leading superstores but also a mass of small (often family-owned) shops across the country. The market share held by the latter has been declining for many years, and the large multiples now account for about 80 per cent of all grocery sales in Britain (Mintel, 1995, p. 89). Indeed, by the mid 1990s, the top four (J Sainsbury, Tesco, Asda and Safeway) held almost half the market between them, a share which had grown dramatically over the previous decade.

There has also been an enormous growth in the number and size of stores, with most of the newer units occupying more than 25,000 square feet and employing more than 100 staff. A high proportion of the staff employed work part time, the number of temporary staff increases dramatically at certain times of the year, and the workforce as a whole is relatively young (certainly compared with a well-established manufacturing or high technology company). A majority of the staff employed are women, the vast proportion of whom are on the lower grades, and the ratio of men to women increases the further one goes up the hierarchy – in common with most industries. Stores are typically open for 75 or 80 hours per week (including six hours on Sundays), and there has even been experimentation with 24-hour opening in some areas. Most of the leading companies also employ staff in the evening or at night (shelf-filling, warehousing, cleaning), and some occupations (for example, bakers) start work several hours before the shops are open to customers.

The mid 1990s brought new pressures to bear in the industry, stimulated by the entry into Britain of large European-owned companies such as Aldi and Netto, which compete on the basis of low prices and few frills. This has had some knock-on effect via the reintroduction of price wars (last visited in the 1970s) to follow the store wars of the 1980s (Wrigley, 1994), as well as attempts to reward customer loyalty. It still appears that the challenge has had little impact on the shopping habits of people using the leading 'quality' food retailers, especially among the higher-income groups, because the major assault has been on the recession-hit and value-conscious industrial areas of the north of England. The rate of increase in out-of-town new store development has slowed during the 1990s, and there has been a renewed interest in high street shops among the multiples as well as an increasing tendency to shift capital abroad. But saturation of the UK food retailing market has yet to arrive despite dire warnings since the 1980s. There is evidence of local saturation (Guy, 1994, p. 3), but the leading companies recognize that there are still parts of the country without a large superstore in the vicinity. Given that three of the most important factors influencing store choice are convenience, closeness and car-parking facilities, new developments are likely to continue throughout the remainder of the century. Moreover, the most profitable stores are those which have opened recently (Wrigley, 1994, p. 6).

## Superco: Employee Involvement in Context

*Organization structure and employee relations*

Superco employs 75,000 staff across Britain, both at the headquarters in the south-east and in about 300 stores which are located around the country. It has a national coverage, having expanded from its southern base, although there are still parts of the country where stores are less likely to be found. The company is organized into districts, each of which comprises approximately 15 stores. In addition, Superco has a number of warehouses, each of which is located in a strategic position to ensure maximum speed of response for deliveries to the stores. The vast bulk of products is held at these large warehouses and deliveries are made to every store several times each day.

Superco operates with a fairly traditional organization structure.

At head office there is a range of functions, including human resource management (HRM), the role of which is to implement the core policies and offer advice to the stores. A skeleton staff is employed at each district, again including an HR presence. The district managers are the main point of contact between the centre and the individual stores, visiting each store every two weeks on average. Each store is run by a store manager, who has a number of deputies working to him or her, and below this there is a series of departmental heads covering areas such as grocery, warehouse, bakery and customer service. Finally, there are a number of junior managers, often supervising no more than a handful of people, for sections such as fresh foods, the delicatessen and the staff restaurant. The departmental and section managers spend a large proportion of their time on the same duties as the staff they supervise.

Superco has a recognition agreement with the Union of Shop, Distributive and Allied Workers (USDAW) solely for individual grievance and disciplinary cases and joint consultation. The agreement allows representation by the union if there is a 'substantial' membership at the store involved – although no figure is quoted for this. Once it is agreed that the union should have these rights at a store, members are allowed to nominate a shop steward to represent them should the need arise. It is often difficult to find a willing recruit for the position of shop steward, and representing up to 100 members is no easy task. Less than 10 per cent of all staff are union members and union consciousness is low.

Pay rates are determined by management in line with a recently implemented job evaluation scheme. The previous system was felt to be too subjective and open to abuse by managers favouring specific individuals, a situation compounded by the growth of the company since the previous system was introduced. Senior management was also concerned that the previous system was potentially discriminatory, in that manual jobs (such as those typically undertaken by men in the warehouse) attracted higher rates of pay than those which involved contact with customers (such as those typically done by women on the checkouts). Pay levels are good for the industry, and top-grade butchers and bakers can earn a basic rate of nearly £10,000 p.a., while full-time checkout staff can earn about £7,500. This puts staff at Superco well within the top quartile for the industry as a whole, though not at the very top of the pay league.

Despite these high relative wages, labour turnover levels are also high, at about 35 per cent per annum across the company as a whole.

Copyright John Storey 1996, Blackwell Cases in Human Resource and Change Management

In some Superco stores, figures can be two or three times higher than this. Although these figures are high compared with those generally found in manufacturing, they are not untypical for the retail industry as a whole. These crude figures also mask the fact that some of the turnover is due to seasonal and temporary employment, as well as the fact that many of the leavers go within the first month of arriving.

## Management style and employee relations

In the past, Superco's management style has been referred to as almost militaristic in approach. In recent years, however, this has softened and there has been a drive to create a more open style which encourages managers and supervisors to seek ideas from staff and operate in a more informal manner. To some extent this shift in approach has been stimulated by the fact that managers are highly dependent on staff for consistently high-quality service to customers. The importance of customer care is continually stressed to employees, starting with their induction package and then being reinforced via training programmes and messages on notice-boards and in the company newspaper. One of the company's objectives is to 'offer our staff outstanding opportunities in terms of personal career development and in remuneration relative to other companies in the same market, practising always a concern for the welfare of every individual'.

A unitarist philosophy is evident in much of the audio-visual material which is produced by the company, with regular references to being 'vital members of the team', and to the ethos of all working together for the good of the company as a whole. For example, one of the company's induction videos encourages staff to 'buy into' the benefits offered by the company; if staff work hard, look smart and maintain strict hygiene and service standards, it is suggested, Superco will be able to ensure that customers receive quality products and treatment as well as value for money. This will then result, it is argued, in secure employment for staff, profit sharing, good promotion prospects and job satisfaction, something which is reinforced by the existence of relatively open lines of promotion, at least into departmental management.

This benign image of team working and co-operation masks to some extent the tight controls which are exerted within the company. There are strict formulae for the amount of labour which can be employed in any one period, and this leads to problems in achieving the company's commitment to minimize queue lengths. In addition, district managers make spot visits to each of the stores on a regular but unscheduled basis to check on overall performance. These visits are aimed at 'keeping staff on their toes', making them constantly aware of the need for high-quality service. This is also reinforced by the use of 'mystery shoppers'; individuals purporting to be customers who are paid to observe staff and record their experiences. This, it is argued, is a more effective method of gauging the quality of customer–employee interactions than is relying on the recollections of ordinary customers, whose perceptions are often clouded or confused. On the other hand, the fact that the identity of these mystery shoppers is not revealed to employees does conjure up an image of low-trust employment relations, in which customers are assumed to be the ultimate assessor of employee performance. No recognition is given to employee perceptions of customer behaviour or for the fact that employees may have to suffer abuse from customers or work to unrealistically high and unilaterally set standards (IRS Employment Trends, 1995, p. 10).

A poster in the training room emphasizes the more instrumental reasons why employees should wish to deliver high-quality service: 'Satisfied customers who keep coming back again and again strengthen sales and jobs; CUSTOMERS make pay days possible!' Furthermore, disciplinary standards are laid down precisely in the company rule book, and there are specific instructions about standards of cleanliness and dress. Video cameras are trained constantly on the sales area in an effort to deter pilferage by customers and ensure that there is a record of events if the need arises for prosecution. At the same time, although this is not its purpose, the video cameras also act as an instrument of surveillance over staff who are aware that these recordings could be used against them as well as customers.

## Employee involvement techniques at Superco

Superco has a number of mechanisms to develop EI, which can be analysed under each of the categories outlined earlier. Downward communications is the most extensive area, being formalized through a centrally administered house journal and set of videos, and locally organized informal briefings and notice-boards. The company prides itself on the quality of its house journal, a newspaper which has been published ten times a year since the late 1940s and has won a string of awards for its presentation and content. It is edited by a small team of public relations staff based at head office. The journal operates according to a set of written objectives which are broadly concerned with 'furthering good employee relations', 'improving the process of change' and 'conveying information accurately and effectively'. The journal has the glossy image of a Sunday newspaper colour supplement and contains the usual mix of information about business items and social activities, although there is rather less of the former than is typical in house journals. All new store openings are reported in the newspaper, along with information about important events; for example, there is an annual report focusing on the company results, there have been a number of feature articles on environmental affairs, and there was a profile of a company which had recently been acquired.

Superco also uses video campaigns and training sessions to highlight the importance of good customer service. The videos are shown by a staff trainer, with employees drawn from different parts of the store to minimize disruption to service levels. There is no attempt to use these sessions as a vehicle for team building, and it is rare for line managers to attend these meetings. The messages conveyed in these videos tend to be prescriptive about the 'one best way' to serve customers, with the latter being portrayed as all-powerful. For example:

Customer care is the Number One skill all Superco employees must have. Our future success will depend upon how well you apply this skill.

Make sure that you always say good morning, please and thankyou; use the customer's name if known; always apologise if something is wrong or there is a delay; take customers to a display.

Some of the more experienced staff in the stores found these customer care videos extremely simplistic and actually became annoyed by them. They resented the way in which the message was put across, the patronizing and condescending tone of the presentation and the image which was conveyed by the stores in which the films were made; in these, the actors who were playing staff worked at a very leisurely pace and had time to laugh and joke with the actors who were playing customers. The experienced staff also queried the value of making these expensive videos, although senior management saw them as necessary to maintain the emphasis on quality customer service.

Unlike many other large organizations Superco has not introduced a formal communications policy such as team briefing, preferring to rely on informal channels and face-to-face contact between managers and their staff on an *ad hoc* basis. Senior management justify this because of the nature of the product market in which the company competes; that is, continuous pressure from customers which requires immediate attention, allied to an employment policy which maintains strict controls on the total number of hours worked in any one store. Accordingly, management has been unwilling to provide extra payment/hours for the purpose of communicating information to staff. There are disagreements as to the effectiveness of the informal system, with some staff feeling it works well while others are unhappy at the lack of information about developments in the company. Much depends on the personal style of the store manager and the degree to which he or she is regarded as open or secretive; in the latter case, the grapevine may prove to be a more useful source of information. There are, however, notice-boards within each store which are located prominently, updated regularly and well managed. All employees walk past the board several times each day to and from the restaurant, and new items are highlighted either on the board itself or on the door into the restaurant.

Representative participation is practised through a system of joint consultative committees (JCCs), established in the early 1980s. These are formed at district level if union membership exceeds a certain threshold level – currently 250 members in the district. This is equivalent to about 10 per cent of all eligible employees. Management was keen to initiate the JCC machinery because a number of similar problems recurred in various stores at the same time, and it was felt that these were better resolved at district rather than unit level. The JCC structure provides union officials with the opportunity to meet with a senior personnel manager from headquarters as well as several line managers within the district. The committees meet up to three times a year at a neutral venue – usually a hotel – and the JCC is preceded by a meeting between the full-time officials and representatives from the stores in the district. The issues which are dealt with at the JCCs typically include health and safety, terms and conditions of employment, union reactions to company pay reviews, policies on time off for trade union affairs and various general items (such as security in stores or information about new openings). Since the JCCs meet at district level they have little meaning for most employees and do not have an explicit impact on their jobs or their perception of what USDAW does for its members.

Finally, there is a profit-sharing scheme for staff with more than two years consecutive service, irrespective of the number of hours worked. Approximately one-third of those employed are members of the share scheme, and payouts for these staff can represent up to an additional month's salary each year. People who leave employment prior to the qualifying date are not entitled to any profit-share payment. Staff can opt to take the profit payout either in cash or as shares, and a large proportion choose to take it in the form of shares; indeed, many see working for Superco in highly positive terms, and given the increase in share price over the last decade their loyalty has been rewarded by extra financial gains. As with wages, though, profit share allocations are determined by management alone.

Table 22.1 summarizes the range of employee involvement techniques which operate at Superco.

**Table 22.1**   Employee involvement techniques at Superco

| *Category of EI technique* | *Specific technique at Superco* |
| --- | --- |
| Downward communications | House journal |
| | Videos |
| | Notice-boards |
| | Informal briefings |
| Upward problem solving | No formal policy |
| Task participation | No formal policy |
| Representative participation | District-level JCCs |
| Financial involvement | Profit sharing |

### The attitude survey

An attitude survey has recently been undertaken among shopfloor staff at two stores within the company, and a number of the questions relate directly to EI. The samples in each store were quite small, so any conclusions need to be drawn with care, but the survey is at least representative of the mix of staff within the company. The results are presented below in Tables 22.2–22.10.

**Table 22.2**   Do you feel that you have enough say in decisions which are made at your place of work?

| | Yes (%) | No (%) |
| --- | --- | --- |
| About your own job/conditions? | 59 | 41 |
| About the operation of the department? | 47 | 53 |
| About the store as a whole? | 26 | 74 |

**Table 22.3** How would you describe relations between management and staff here?

| | % |
|---|---|
| Very co-operative | 44 |
| Sometimes co-operative | 51 |
| Uncooperative | 5 |

**Table 22.4** In what ways do you find out about things which are going on in the department/store/company?

| | Often (%) | Sometimes (%) | Never (%) |
|---|---|---|---|
| Department manager tells me | 26 | 67 | 7 |
| I hear from other members of staff | 65 | 35 | 0 |
| The trade union rep tells me | 3 | 7 | 90 |
| From the notice-boards | 55 | 41 | 4 |
| I read it in the house journal | 17 | 53 | 30 |
| From staff meetings/training | 14 | 57 | 29 |

**Table 22.5** Do you feel that you find out enough about what is going on in the department/store/company?

| | % |
|---|---|
| Usually | 36 |
| Sometimes | 34 |
| Not really | 30 |

**Table 22.6** What do you think about the house journal?

| | % |
|---|---|
| Never read it – does not interest me | 28 |
| It does not tell me enough about what is going on in the company | 19 |
| Enjoy the personal items but find the company news boring | 17 |
| Think its a good paper – well worth reading | 36 |

**Table 22.7** What has the house journal achieved for you?

|  | Yes (%) | No (%) |
|---|---|---|
| Improved your understanding of company decisions? | 31 | 69 |
| Increased your commitment to the company? | 21 | 79 |
| Encouraged you to work harder? | 2 | 98 |

**Table 22.8** What do you think about the Superco profit-sharing scheme?

|  | % |
|---|---|
| I see it as a useful cash windfall | 27 |
| I see it as a good way to invest and save money | 54 |
| I think it provides an incentive to work harder | 19 |

**Table 22.9** What, in your view, does the Superco profit-sharing scheme lead to?

|  | Yes (%) | No (%) |
|---|---|---|
| People working harder | 47 | 53 |
| The company doing better | 83 | 17 |
| Staff being more aware of company performance | 96 | 4 |

**Table 22.10** Taking a broad view of employee communications and involvement in the company, what would you say that the situation now is compared with the position three years ago?

|  | % |
|---|---|
| Much better | 14 |
| Slightly better | 35 |
| About the same | 38 |
| Slightly worse | 7 |
| Much worse | 6 |

## Summary

This case has focused on EI at one of the leading food retailers and has outlined a range of techniques which has been implemented with a view to increasing the involvement of employees at Superco. It is clear that the emphasis is on direct EI, especially downward communications (both written and verbal) and financial involvement. These techniques are designed to encourage a greater awareness of company activities and the part which all staff can play in gaining improvements in market share and profitability through excellent customer service. But EI can also be thwarted both by conflicting operational pressures (such as commitments to minimize queue lengths) and traditional management styles which do not place a premium on employee involvement. The recent employee attitude survey provides some feedback for management on this particular matter.

## Questions

1 Review the range of EI techniques which are employed at Superco and analyse why these particular techniques are used as opposed to any others. Further information can be gained about human resource management in food retailing from Freathy and Sparks (1994), Marchington and Harrison (1991), and Ogbonna and Wilkinson (1988; 1990).

2 Management at Superco has commissioned you to interpret the results of the attitude survey and produce a short report (verbal presentation and/or written summary) about the adequacy of existing EI techniques at the company. Using the results from the survey, make a number of recommendations for future action.

3 In your view, do the tensions and contradictions which surround EI in food retailing outweigh any benefits which may be derived from its use?

4 How well does the description of EI at Superco compare with your own experiences or knowledge of similar practices in:
   (a) the leading high-quality food retailers?;
   (b) supermarkets at the low cost end of the market?;
   (c) a manufacturing plant, financial services company, or public-sector organization?;
   (d) a pub, restaurant or hotel?

If you do not have direct experience of working in these, do your own research by asking others who do have this knowledge.

## References

Cotton, J. 1993: *Employee Involvement; Methods for Improving Performance and Work Attitudes*. Newbury Park, CA: Sage.

Fox, A. 1974: *Beyond Contract; Work, Trust and Power Relations*. London: Faber.

Freathy, P. and Sparks, L. 1994: Contemporary developments in employee relations in food retailing. *The Service Industries Journal*, **14**(4), 499–514.

Gold, M. and Hall, M. 1992: *European-level Information and Consultation in Multinational Companies; an Evaluation of Practice*. Dublin: European Foundation.

Guy, C. 1994: Grocery store saturation: has it arrived yet? *International Journal of Retail and Distribution Management*, **22**(1), 3–11.

Hall, M., Carley, M., Gold, M., Marginson, P. and Sisson, K. 1995: *European Works Councils, Planning for the Directive*. Warwick: University of Warwick.

Industrial Relations Review and Report 1995: The customer is boss; matching employee performance to customer needs. *IRS Employment Trends*, **585**, 7–13.

Lansbury, R. and Davis, E. (eds) 1995: *Managing Together: Consultation and Participation in the Workplace*. Melbourne: Longman Cheshire.

Marchington, M. 1992: *Managing the Team: A Guide to Successful Employee Involvement*. Oxford: Blackwell.

Marchington, M. 1995a: Employee Involvement. In Storey, J. (ed.), *Human Resource Management: a Critical Text*. London: Routledge.

Marchington, M. 1995b: Shopping down different aisles; a review of human resource management in retailing. *Journal of Retailing and Consumer Services*, **2**(3).

Marchington, M. and Harrison, E. 1991: Customers, competitors and choice: employee relations in food retailing. *Industrial Relations Journal*, **22**(4), 286–300.

Mintel Retail Intelligence 1995: *Food Retailing*. London: Mintel Intelligence Group.

Ogbonna, E. and Wilkinson, B. 1988: Corporate strategy and corporate culture: the management of change in the UK supermarket industry. *Personnel Review*, **17**(6), 10–14.

Ogbonna, E. and Wilkinson, B. 1990: Corporate strategy and corporate culture: the view from the checkout. *Personnel Review*, **19**(4), 9–15.

Schuler, R. and Jackson, S. 1987: Linking competitive strategies with human resource practices. *Academy of Management Executive*, **1**(3), 206–19.

Wrigley, N. 1994: After the store wars: towards a new era of competition in UK food retailing. *Journal of Retailing and Consumer Services*, **1**(1), 5–20.

## Further reading

Fuller, L. and Smith, V. 1991: 'Consumers' reports; management by customers in a changing economy. *Work Employment and Society*, **5**(1), 1–16.

Keenoy, T. and Anthony, P. 1992: HRM: metaphor, meaning and morality. In Blyton, P. and Turnbull, P. (eds), *Reassessing Human Resource Management*. London: Sage Publications.

Legge, K. 1995: HRM: rhetoric, reality and hidden agendas. In Storey, J. (ed.), *Human Resource Management: a Critical Text*. London: Routledge.

Marchington, M. 1995: Fairy Tales and Magic Wands; New Employment Practices in Perspective. *Employee Relations*, 17(1), 51–66.

Marchington, M., Goodman, J., Wilkinson, A. and Ackers, P. 1992: *New Developments in Employee Involvement*. Employment Department Research Series, No. 2, London: HMSO.

Marchington, M., Wilkinson, A., Ackers, P. and Goodman, J. 1994: Understanding the meaning of participation: views from the workplace. *Human Relations*, **47**(8), 867–94.

Millward, N., Stevens, M., Smart, D. and Hawes, W. 1992: *Workplace Industrial Relations in Transition*. Aldershot: Dartmouth.

Sparks, L. 1992: Restructuring retail employment. *International Journal of Retail and Distribution Management*, **20**(3), 12–19.

Storey, J. 1995: Human resource management; still marching on, or marching out? In Storey, J. (ed.), *Human Resource Management: a Critical Text*, London: Routledge.

# PART IV
# International Management

# 23

# FMS at Diesel Engines plc

*The flexible manufacturing system*
HARRY BOER

In June 1988 Diesel Engines plc conducted a manufacturing audit at its UK manufacturing plant. One of the conclusions was that the manufacturing of cylinder blocks and heads needed a closer look. First, it appeared that some of the present equipment had become technically obsolete. Second, the company's future plans included the development of a new generation of engines and it was expected that future market demands would require a much more flexible plant. This led the company to conduct a greenfield study aimed at finding a feasible technology for the manufacturing of the new generation of cylinder blocks and heads. The investigation took about a year and in November 1989 it was concluded that FMS technology would provide the most suitable solution.

## Diesel Engines plc

Diesel Engines plc is a manufacturer of diesel engines with plants in the United Kingdom, Belgium and The Netherlands. Basic facts about the company's size, its products and market situation are shown in Table 23.1. The company and its plants are highly departmentalized (see Figure 23.1). Marketing and Sales (M&S), Finance and Accounting (F&A), Research and Development (R&D) and also Corporate Capital Planning (CCP) are concentrated at the company's headquarters in The Netherlands. The board of directors consists of John Hunter (CEO), Hans van Drunen (VP M&S), Dr Victor Fisscher (VP R&D), Paul Hill (VP Operations) and Jan van Tongeren (VP Engineering). Operational functions such as manufacture, process

**Table 23.1**  Some characteristics of Diesel Engines, its products and its markets

| Size | Products and market | Market demands |
|---|---|---|
| UK plant: 400 employees | UK plant: medium duty, 6-, 8- and 11-litre diesel engines | 1987 order winners: price and quality qualifier: delivery speed |
| company (world wide): 1,900 employees | main customers:<br>• truck producers<br>• shipyards (medium-sized yachts and small fishing boats)<br><br>The other plants produce heavy duty diesel engines | 1992 order winners: delivery reliability, product range and modification qualifiers: price, quality and delivery speed |

planning, production planning, quality control and maintenance are performed at plant level and their managers report directly to the local plant manager.

### Capital planning at Diesel Engines

Corporate Capital Planning (CCP) is managed by Jan van Tongeren, the vice-president of Engineering, and there are small local groups, called Plant Capital Planning (PCP), in each of the plants. CCP is divided into three groups: a quality management group (which also comprises just in time (JIT) and TQM experts and has gradually obtained some experience with Kaizen – continuous improvement), an advanced manufacturing technology group (predominantly people with a technical background, mostly in manufacturing engineering) and a purchasing group (also mostly engineers who are involved in legal and contractual aspects of purchasing new equipment). The local PCP groups are mostly young manufacturing engineers who spend a couple of years at plant level in order to learn the job before they are transferred to CCP.

CCP plays a key role in the formulation and implementation of the company's manufacturing strategy. Although the department and

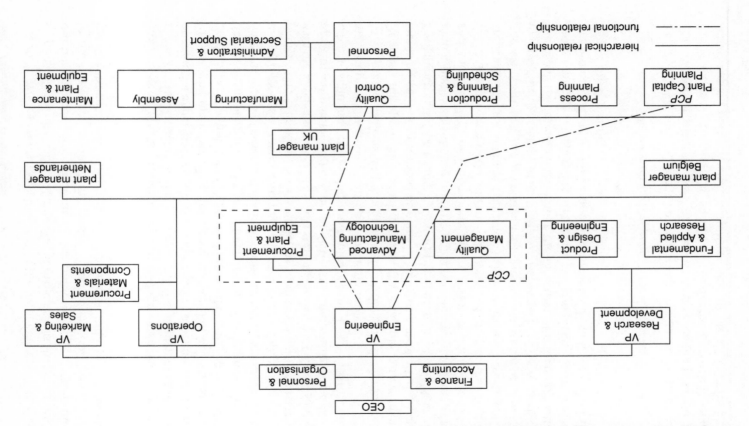

**Figure 23.1** Diesel Engines' organization structure

the PCP groups co-operate closely with the local plant staff, they are responsible for all the capital investment projects conducted throughout the company, from drawing up the request for approval through to the implementation of the project. Only after completion, when the investment is performing up to expectations, is the project handed over to the plant.

CCP tends to adopt a careful approach by always trying a new technology or system in just one plant or even one area. Only after it has proven beneficial, the concept and the implementation and operational experience obtained are migrated to other areas or plants. Just-in-time manufacturing, for example, had first been tried in the Dutch plant) and those requiring concerted action between a plant production of manifolds in the Dutch plant. Furthermore, several different forms of advanced manufacturing technology and also group technology-based manufacturing cells have been adopted in all three plants. The UK plant, for example, had obtained some experience with the application of CAD/CAM stations, which were directly linked up with corporate R&D. One or two cells comprising stand-alone CNC machining centres. However, most of this plant's manufacturing equipment were conventional machine tools.

All major projects require approval by the board of directors. Requests for approval of small projects (for example, a new manufacturing cell) are prepared at plant level, by the local PCP groups. Larger projects (for example, the implementation of TQM at the Dutch plant) and those requiring concerted action between a plant and another plant or a corporate function (for example, the CAD/CAM link between R&D and the UK plant) are prepared at corporate level. Investments are appraised using return on investment as one criterion and the investment's contribution to the company's manufacturing strategy as another. After approval has been obtained, the project is implemented under the direction of a then appointed project manager. Depending on the size and complexity of the project, the project manager will be one of central CCP staff, or one of the local capital planners.

*The manufacturing audit at the UK plant*

In June 1990 the CCP finished a manufacturing audit at its UK manufacturing plant as part of the company's ongoing manufacturing strategy process. The audit was conducted by Dick Peters, a senior capital planner, and Andy Voss, one of the PCP staff. They concluded that two areas needed a closer look. In particular the manufacturing of cylinder blocks and heads caused great concern.

This area consisted of four transfer lines, comprising over 100 conventional machines, dedicated to the production of cylinder blocks and heads for three main types of engines: a 6-litre engine, an 8-litre engine (in two variants) and an 11-litre engine (also in two variants). The first line produced 6-litre blocks, the second 6-litre heads. The third and fourth line produced 8- and 11-litre blocks, and 8- and 11-litre heads, respectively. Both six-litre lines were operated in day-shifts of 15 operators and one supervisor each, the 8- and 11-litre lines in two shifts of 20 operators and one supervisor each, respectively. All machine tools were over 15 years old and, installed in the late 1950s, half the equipment was even more than 25 years old. One or two boring machines had reached the end of their technical life and needed major repairs prior to each production run. And still, some of the boring operations were insufficiently accurate, resulting in some scrap and a lot of rework on, in particular, the 8-litre cylinder blocks and heads.

All four lines were rather inflexible. It took about half a day to change lines 3 and 4 over from the manufacture of one variant of the 8- (or 11-) litre engine to the other variant. Changeover from the 8-litre to the 11-litre engine, and vice versa took two full days. Consequently, batches were very large, on average 400 for the blocks and 800 for the heads (two heads per block). Lead times per batch were about two weeks. The batch size on the 6-litre lines was 'indefinite', as these lines were never changed over to another type or variant. Weekly output of these lines was about 100 blocks and 100 heads (one head per block).

According to the audit report there were two main problems:

R&D are developing a new engine generation. Job-one is planned to take place in August 1995. This will cause two problems. Firstly, M&S expect that future market demands will require us to become much more flexible than we are today, in terms of product range and modification and, as many of our customers are considering JIT delivery, lead time as well. And secondly, some of the present equipment has become technically obsolete. All of the line is 15 years or older, and half of the machine tools were implemented in the 1950s. According to Maintenance, some machines need virtually complete overhaul with every new batch.

Copyright John Storey 1996, Blackwell Cases in Human Resource and Change Management

The report concluded with the proposal to conduct a greenfield study aimed at finding a feasible technology for the manufacturing of the new generation of cylinder blocks and heads. Jan van Tongeren accepted the proposal and appointed a small team consisting of Dick Peters, Andy Voss and Chris Johnston, a blocks and heads process planner. The investigation took them about 15 months and in November 1989 it was concluded that FMS technology would provide the most suitable solution.

## The new engine generation

Previously, in January 1991, technological developments by Fundamental & Applied Research, had led the board of directors to ask M&S to find out how the market would respond to a new generation of engines. The present generation had been produced for some 13 years and, although many improvements had been made over the years, it was now nearing the end of its life-cycle. New technologies would enable a much better performance, not only in terms of fuel consumption but also as regards air pollution and noise. Furthermore, due to the use of new materials, the engines would be less heavy and, designed using Design for Manufacturing and Assembly techniques, they were also expected to be able to be produced more cost effectively.

A thorough survey, based on, among other things, discussions with the main customers, suggested that the market would be quite willing to adopt the new concept and it was forecast that annual sales would increase from about 24,000 now (6-litre: 4,800 and 8- and 11-litre: 9,600 each) to between 26,000 and 30,000 engines. The survey also suggested that market demands would change considerably over the next few years. Whereas previously price and quality had been the dominant market demands, many customers, in particular the truck manufacturers, had discovered the benefits of JIT delivery. Furthermore, many customers increasingly demanded products modified to their own particular needs. Based on this, the board of directors had given the go-ahead to the development of the new generation of diesel engines. This started by the end of 1991 and trial production of the first new engine was planned to start in August 1995.

## The greenfield study

CCP thought it highly unlikely that the present production facilities would be capable of cost-effectively producing the new engines. They also expected that it would take at least three years to phase out the present generation and phase in the new one. This meant that a new technology would need to be capable of producing both generations. So, the main objective of the greenfield study was to identify the technology and organization needed to produce the present and the new generation of engines both cost effectively and flexibly in response to the changed product envelope and market demands.

The greenfield study was conducted by Dick Peters, Andy Voss and Chris Johnston. At the outset, Jan van Tongeren formulated a range of objectives.

- the required capacity is 30,000 cylinder blocks and 54,000 cylinder heads per year;
- the product envelope will increase from 3 main types (5 variants) to, initially, 6 main types (at least 10, but possibly up to 15 variants; including both the present and the new generations) and back to 3 main types (5 to 10 variants) after phasing-out the present generation;
- the new system will need to allow for a much higher design flexibility so that new or modified designs can be phased in easily;
- batch sizes are very small, and ideally just one; lead time is less than an hour, to enable us to achieve shorter delivery times, the flexibility to respond to rush orders, and JIT delivery to our customers;
- justification as usual for this type of investment: payback within 5 years; note that the unions are not likely to accept redundancies!

The team talked to several departments, including M&S, R&D and F&A, visited other engine manufacturers, went to machine tool exhibitions and also visited several machine tool suppliers. It soon appeared that the real trade-off would be between a highly flexible FMS type of system or a more conventional but state-of-the-art production line. The trade-off between these two would be determined by volume and cost and some rough calculations showed that at volumes below 35,000 engines, a flexible system would be the most cost effective alternative. So Jan van Tongeren told the team to concentrate on this.

## Flexible Manufacturing Systems

FMS technology is based on a number of previous technological developments:

1    group technology (GT), which provides the basis for organizing facilities into cells containing all the equipment needed to produce a family of parts;

2    computer numerical control (CNC), the automated and re-programmable control of machine tool operations and parts and tools transport, handling and storage;

3    direct numerical control (DNC), the operation of a group or cell of CNC tools under the overall control of a host computer controlling the scheduling and routing of parts, monitoring status and feeding new programs;

4    machining centres (MC) in which CNC operations previously provided by different machines are combined into one machine comprising also a tool magazine to enable automatic tool change;

5    transport, handling and storage systems such as industrial robots, auto-mated storage and retrieval systems and wire- or rail-guided automated guided vehicles.

Based on these technologies, an FMS is a group of CNC machines or other workstations which are interconnected by an automated material handling system. The system operates under central computer control using DNC and is capable of processing a variety of different types of parts simultaneously under CNC control at various workstations.

## FMS characteristics

Typical characteristics of FMS compared to previous technologies are:

- *Integration* – FMSs are able to perform different types of operations, to change tools, to transfer and load workpieces and to down-load part programmes and production schedules from a central storage.
- *Mechanization and re-programmable automation* – FMSs perform opera-tions such as workpiece transfer, loading/unloading and fixturing, tool change, machine tool control, cutting tool control and quality control automatically, without human intervention.
- *Technical flexibility* – FMSs are able quickly to change mix, routing and sequence of operations within the parts envelope.
- *Complexity* – FMSs comprise a wide range of interrelated elements, such as CNC workstations and tool- and material-handling systems, a host computer providing DNC control of all the system's operations, and possibly also automated linkages with process planning, production planning and other software applications.

- *Regulation* – FMSs regulate to a great extent the work of operators, process planners, production planners, maintenance engineers and other personnel.
- *Expensiveness* – the costs incurred in the investment in, and the operation, maintenance and operational management of, FMSs are usually high compared with conventional equipment.

## *FMS benefits*

Designed to fill the gap between high-volume transfer lines and low-volume stand-alone conventional or (C)NC equipment, FMSs are supposed to provide adopters with the opportunity to produce a family of parts both flexibly and cost effectively. More precisely, the advantages of FMS technology can be classified as follows:

1  improved market performance – a more adequate response to market demands for higher product diversity and product innovation; lower sales prices; shorter delivery times and higher delivery reliability; and improved quality.

2  reduced costs/times of operations – reduced labour and overhead costs; reduced floor space; shorter processing, set-up and lead times; reduced batch sizes and work-in-progress; increased machine utilization.

3  Improved operations management – linking of production control and manufacture; increased scheduling flexibility; just-in-time manufacture; fewer human errors; and improved and consistent quality and productivity.

## *Organizational adaptation*

For many companies the implementation of FMS requires a range of organizational adaptations in order to achieve the benefits pursued. Exactly what adaptations are required depends on:

- the state of the organization as it is before the implementation of the system;
- the exact characteristics of the FMS involved;
- the benefits pursued.

Generally speaking, the trade-off is between a highly functionalized type of organization structure and an autonomous, self-managing team approach. However, the former lacks the flexibility most companies pursue when adopting FMS technology. The latter is usually considered too expensive. Furthermore, FMSs require a wide variety of tasks, ranging from rather low to very highly skilled, and this range is usually too high to combine within one team. The solution in many situations, therefore, is a semi-autonomous group which performs all the operational and most planning, control and maintenance tasks, and is supported by functional specialists for tasks that lie beyond the scope of the team. The exact design of this varies from company to company.

# The Decision to Implement an FMS at Diesel Engines' UK plant

After about a year, the greenfield study is completed and presented to the board of directors. The proposal comprises a four-stage investment programme which is aimed at eventually replacing most of the present equipment, that is, some 80 of about 100 machine tools. The first stage will be to install a six machine tool FMS to perform the grinding, boring and drilling operations on the 8- and 11-litre engines. In the second stage, a similar though smaller FMS will replace part of the 6-litre lines. The third stage will involve the replacement of the rest of the 8/11-litre lines by two more CNC machining centres and a washing station, and integration of those tools into the FMS. The fourth stage involves the same, for the 6-litre lines.

The first stage is justified on the basis of reductions in direct labour, work-in-progress, stocks of finished goods, floor space, and handling and transport. There are also a number of intangible benefits such as increased product and scheduling flexibility, which are difficult to assess financially. As it is expected that there will be enough vacancies elsewhere in the plant, the reduction in direct labour will not lead to redundancies. Furthermore, although product quality will not increase very much it is expected to become more consistent, so that the costs associated with the present quality problems (scrap, rework and excessive maintenance) will reduce quite considerably. It is also assumed that the FMS will not differ much from conventional manufacturing as far as tooling, maintenance, lubrication and other operational costs are concerned. The payback period will be five and a half years. This is slightly longer that the standard five years for this type of investment. Yet the board accept this as the new system will contribute considerably to Diesel Engines' market strategy.

After negotiations with the company on relocation of superfluous personnel, and training requirements and pay rates for the FMS operators, the unions agree with the intended investment. In November 1994 the board of directors formally approve the proposal.

## The design stage

The go-ahead given, Jan van Tongeren decides to establish a project organization. The core of this is the greenfield study team, Dick Peters, Andy Voss and Chris Johnston, who are now called the FMS project team. The brief of the team includes:

Your task is to plan and supervise the design and installation of the new facility, the reorganization of the plant, the selection of a supplier, to start up production in April 1997, and to hand over the project to the plant by July 1997. I expect you to inform me monthly of progress being made and will be available to discuss any major problems whenever they occur.

The team sets out drawing up a network schedule planning the specification of the system (eight months); the selection of a supplier (four months); the construction, production, test, acceptance, transport, installation and commissioning of the FMS (16 months); and, simultaneously, all the reorganization that is required (12 months). The first cylinder blocks and heads are to come off the FMS in April 1997. This leaves some slack as regards job-one of the new generation engines.

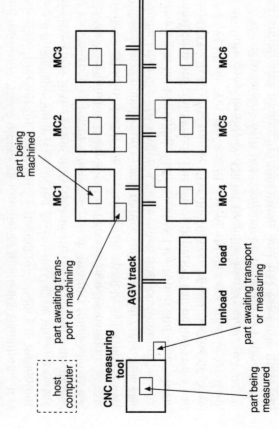

**Figure 23.2** Envisaged layout of the FMS (First stage)

**Table 23.2** FMS elements and capabilities

*Elements*

6 CNC MCs, 1 rail-guided AGV, 1 CNC co-ordinate measuring tool, 14 flexibly automated fixturing tools, 2 load/unload stations, 1 host computer

*Capabilities*

30,000 blocks and 54,000 heads blocks per year, initially the present two main type (four variants), growing to four main types (8–12 variants, including the present generation); to replace some 40 conventional machine tools

When the specifications are finished, four machine tool manufacturers are invited to send a quotation. Four months later the quotations are received and analysed, and one of them, Comatec of Italy, is selected to supply the new system. Included in the system are six CNC machining centres which are interconnected by a rail guided vehicle (see Figure 23.2). Each of the machining centres has a tool magazine with a maximum capacity of 72 tools. The system is laid out for the manufacture of 30,000 blocks and 54,000 heads per year. It will be operated in three shifts, with four operators per shift (see Table 23.2).

The pre-machined blocks and heads are manually loaded into and unloaded from flexibly automated fixturing tools. Once in the system they are transported between the CNC machines until they are finished. After that, the parts are transported to the CNC co-ordinate measuring machine and, if necessary, to a previous station for some rework, before they are unloaded. On average, each part will visit two machines and the measuring tool, in order to be finished and tested before it is despatched to the engine assembly area, via a washing station. The network schedule is shown in Figure 23.3.

In comparison with the supplier ranked second, Comatec's system is slightly more expensive, but the quality of the machine tools is considered much higher. A weak point may be that Comatec does not have much experience with FMSs, but its reputation in the field of stand-alone CNC equipment is excellent. It is agreed that Comatec will subcontract those elements of the system it lacks experience with, in particular the AGV, the measuring tool and the host computer

**Figure 23.3** Network schedule of the FMS project

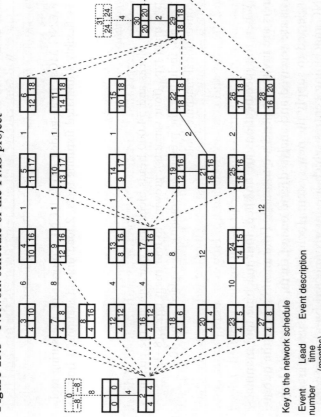
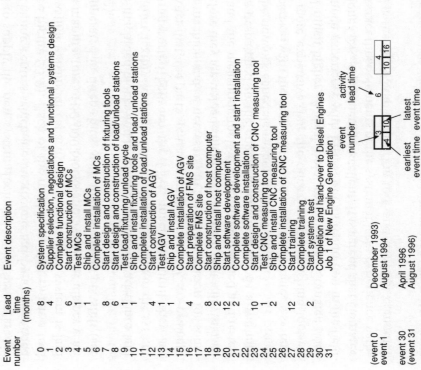

Key to the network schedule

| Event number | Lead time (months) | Event description |
|---|---|---|
| 0 | 8 | System specification |
| 1 | 4 | Supplier selection, negotiations and functional systems design |
| 2 | 6 | Complete functional design |
| 3 | 1 | Start construction of MCs |
| 4 | 1 | Test MCs |
| 5 | 1 | Ship and install MCs |
| 6 | 8 | Complete installation of MCs |
| 7 | 6 | Start design and construction of fixturing tools |
| 8 | 1 | Start design and construction of load/unload stations |
| 9 | 1 | Test load/fixturing/unload cycle |
| 10 | | Ship and install fixturing tools and load/unload stations |
| 11 | | Complete installation of load/unload stations |
| 12 | 4 | Start construction of AGV |
| 13 | 1 | Test AGV |
| 14 | 1 | Ship and install AGV |
| 15 | | Complete installation of AGV |
| 16 | 4 | Start preparation of FMS site |
| 17 | | Complete FMS site |
| 18 | 8 | Start construction of host computer |
| 19 | 2 | Ship and install host computer |
| 20 | 12 | Start software development |
| 21 | 2 | Complete software development and start installation |
| 22 | | Complete software installation |
| 23 | 10 | Start design and construction of CNC measuring tool |
| 24 | 1 | Test CNC measuring tool |
| 25 | 2 | Ship and install CNC measuring tool |
| 26 | | Complete installation of CNC measuring tool |
| 27 | 12 | Start training |
| 28 | | Complete training |
| 29 | 2 | Start systems test |
| 30 | | Completion and hand-over to Diesel Engines |
| 31 | | Job 1 of New Engine Generation |

| | |
|---|---|
| (event 0 | December 1993 |
| event 1 | August 1994 |
| event 30 | April 1996 |
| (event 31 | August 1996) |

*The construction and reorganization phase*

together with all the software controlling the operation of the system. Comatec will concentrate itself on the hardware of the machine tools and project management, by tying the contributions of its own suppliers together.

It soon emerges that Comatec is not too happy with the level of detail in the specifications. This especially regards the fixturing tools. It takes more than two months of discussion and negotiation between Diesel Engines, Comatec and the subcontractors involved to reach consensus about this. Then, a first design of the fixturing tool is made and the pros and cons are weighed up. However, both parties agree that the concept is too complex and needs to be simplified. Diesel Engines takes over and the AMT group designs a much simpler concept. However, this also means that the load/unload stations have to be reconstructed as well, which leads to a further delay. Consequently, this part of the project is four months behind schedule now. Although this was not on the critical path, it is now, and any further problems with the load/unload stations and/or the fixturing tools will delay the whole project.

Perhaps even more seriously, however, and certainly having impact on the lead time of the project, is the fact that the FMS project team not only gets the feeling but also proof of Comatec having trouble with managing the project. It is difficult, even with hindsight, to determine exactly when and where the problems started and how they affected the lead time of the project, but several of the elements were not duly delivered to Comatec. Halfway through the project it is agreed that the project team will visit Comatec and some of its subcontractors once a month or as often as is deemed necessary, in order to follow up the project and to discuss any problems. The first real proof of delay comes when the subcontractor of the fixturing tools has to admit that it will not be able to deliver its part of the project on time. Although Diesel Engines is now checking progress on a weekly basis, the deadline is not met and the whole project is delayed by three months. The company now realizes it will never make jobone to schedule. A delay of at least four months to the original network schedule is expected and now even the launch of the new engine generation is in danger.

In the meantime, preparations at Diesel Engines proceed according to plan. At Dick Peters' request, the future FMS operators are selected by the present line supervisor, Noah Cane, in consultation with his boss, Chris Morrison, the shopfloor manager. According to Noah, 'the main criterion we used to select the operators was that we were looking for a mixture of well-educated, young lads who would not be afraid of computers and some of our more experienced people who knew all about the manufacturing of engines and had operated all or most tools in the old lines. This was not easy. We needed just a crew of 12, but many more were eager to operate the FMS and we certainly had to disappoint one or two.'

Furthermore, training programmes for the process planners, the operators and also the maintenance engineers are agreed upon between Diesel Engines and Comatec. The operator training includes the theoretical and practical aspects of CNC control, programming and operating the FMS, as well as some preventive maintenance. The training will be given in Italy, during the build-up of the system, and continue in the UK, during the installation of the system. Furthermore, it is planned that, initially, for the first four months after final acceptance of the FMS, the system will be operated at some 50 per cent of capacity in order to allow for further training on the job. The training, which is given by the supplier's engineers and Chris Johnston, Noah Cane and Andy Voss, started in February 1995.

Preparations of the FMS site started in June 1995. Part of the existing production lines are relocated in order to enable production to be continued at its present level. Both lines now need to be operated in three shifts as, due to insufficient floor space, they can only produce at two-thirds of normal level. The foundations of the FMS are excavated and laid. Hook-ups for electrical, hydraulic and pneumatic utilities are installed and the host computer room, above the system, next to the supervisor's office is built. The work does not present any major problems and is finished by early October.

### Testing the FMS

The first two machining centres are finished in January 1996 and tested using 50 blocks and 100 heads. The results are satisfactory and an additional 200 blocks and 400 heads are used for pre-acceptance test. As these test results are satisfactory as well, all the machining centres are pre-accepted, including the four that had not been tested, shipped to the UK and installed. In the next four months the remainder of the system follows, including the load/unload stations, the AGV system, the fixturing tools and the CNC measuring tool. None of these had been tested to win back some of the time lost during earlier stages of the project.

The FMS operators, some maintenance engineers and the project team are assisting the suppliers' engineers in the installation, as part as their training programme.

In July 1996, five months late, trial production is started, meaning that part of the production flow is now led over the FMS. It appears that one of the machining centres is not operating properly and there are also problems with the measuring tool and the fixturing tools. It takes five months to bring about a number of adaptations and to prove the capability of the whole system using long run tests.

In December 1996 the FMS is formally conveyed to Diesel Engines, although it is only working at 40–50 per cent of capacity. It is therefore considered sensible that CCP will not hand over the system to the plant until it has proven to be capable of operating to full capacity for at least six months.

At this point in time, with the whole project delayed considerably and the total budget overrun by some 20 per cent, the board want to know how this could have happened and Jan van Tongeren is asked to commission an evaluation. He replies in a memorandum:

At your request, my staff have evaluated the FMS project. I am afraid that the results are not very favourable for both ourselves and Comatec. To start with the latter, the conclusions are:

- poor delivery reliability (the fixturing tools were developed late, causing the whole project to delay; my staff admit, though, that, initially, specifications were too complex and they should have realized that these were one-offs); poor project management and scheduling (also due to bad choice of subcontractors; too many subcontractors);

- insufficient acceptance testing, due to major previous delays and a, consequently, high time pressure; some tests were rushed and several even skipped; for example: only two MCs had been tested using 50 blocks and 100 heads; as these machines performed well, it was hoped that a long run test of 200 blocks and 400 heads on the same machines would be sufficient; this proved not to be the case: one other MC caused severe problems after installation, one or two others also took some time to get fully operational; my staff still do not quite understand why this happened as the MCs were relatively standard; the fixturing and measuring tools had not been tested at all;

- worst of all, the cycle time of the AGV, which is the capacity bottleneck in the system, is almost one minute longer than specified; in effect, this will reduce the capacity of the system to 90 per cent of specified capacity; there is no way that the cycle can be accelerated;

- from the installation of the FMS onwards, operators and senior staff alike have worked in three shifts to get the system operating on its present level, which is still unacceptably low: the system is working at 40–50 per cent of capacity; this should have been 100 per cent by now; of the four present engines types, only two are machined on the FMS, the other two are completed on the old lines.

On our side:

- we underestimated the training requirements of the operators, process planners and maintenance engineers;

- operator training has fallen behind schedule; part of the programme has been completed, but the remainder cannot be accelerated as the operators cannot be released for training, due to operational pressures (output);

- however, Dick, myself and also Jan DeWever have the feeling that our present organization and procedures are not optimal either, and I propose a thorough investigation into this matter.

Conclusion and action:

- with hindsight, we should have selected another supplier; our previous experience with them, albeit with a much simpler system (four stand-alone machining centres in Belgium) was quite good but FMS technology appears to be beyond their head; in future FMS projects, only experienced FMS suppliers should be invited for quotation;

- there are two solutions to resolve the capacity problem: (1) outsourcing part of our production or (2) keeping more of the old lines operational than expected, in particular some of the downstream operations; we opt for the second alternative; this will cause certain logistical problems: batches of at least 10 (rather than 1 or

2), considerable work-in-progress not only between the FMS and the upstream part (which was accepted pending phase 3) but also between the FMS and the downstream operations (which we had not expected to need in the first place); however, subcontracting has even more disadvantages in terms of cost, lead time and also we would not like external parties to get to know too much about our products;

- I asked Dick Peters to review our present procedures and to adjust them to the new situation;

- considering all the extra costs we made, I propose that we do not pay the last instalment (10 per cent of the total sum).

Confronted with the decision not to pay the last instalment, Comatec threatens that it will no longer supply service, spare parts and software updates if Diesel Engines is not going to pay quickly. It takes a visit by John Hunter to his Italian colleague to settle the argument.

An investigation by the FMS team, to which, for the occasion, one of the maintenance supervisors and one of the P&O staff are added, shows that Jan van Tongeren and Jan DeWever are right. The team reaches a couple of conclusions. First, the training needs of process planners, maintenance engineers, supervisors and operators had been grossly underestimated. The operators felt quite insecure when having to deal even with relatively simple problems. They had difficulties understanding some of the messages the system issued on screen. The maintenance people did not understand all the error messages the system issued either. It was found that this was also partly due to the fact that, in spite of contractual agreements, the supplier had not sent all of the information, including updated drawings and screen texts translated into English, and some of the spare parts had not arrived either. Furthermore, the operators and the maintenance engineers still stuck to their previous habit of firefighting problems rather than trying to identify the real causes and resolving those.

An in-depth analysis, based on so-called Ishikawa (or fishbone) diagrams, suggests several areas for improvement, including: the tool grinding quality, the timely availability of documentation, the speed of response by the maintenance department and the quality of the NC part programmes. More generally it is recognized, only at this stage, that the performance of the FMS, apart from technical performance, depends a great deal on the operators' routine, preventive maintenance (including relatively simple actions such as performing some status checks, and cleansing and lubricating the system, all of which are to be performed by the operators themselves) and taking care that cutting tools, ancillary equipment, operators, spare parts, NC part programmes, and raw materials are available to the right quality, quantity and at the right time. It is also concluded, however, that, whatever the result of those actions, the company has to accept that the system will never be able to produce to 100 per cent of capacity; the theoretical maximum is and will be 90 per cent.

After the identification of these factors, the team proposes to take more time than anticipated to resolve the teething problems and to get the system and its crew up to the expected level of performance. Plant management accepts this. The old lines still being available, production on the FMS is reduced to about one-third of maximum capacity, allowing the team to design and implement a wide range of operating, maintenance, inspection and scheduling procedures, in close collaboration with the operators and to take time really to resolve rather than firefight problems. This approach, which also involves that sufficient time is taken to teach the operators and also the maintenance engineers and the process planners involved about the ins and outs of the system, bears fruit and this time much sooner than expected. Now that they really have time to learn to understand the system, the way it has to be operated, how to respond to any messages, the operators and the maintenance engineers alike start to feel much more confident and they quickly lose their fear to take action. Whereas previously they tended to call the supplier (which usually took more than 48 hours, rather than the negotiated maximum of 24 hours), they are now able in most cases to resolve problems immediately. In the meantime, the screen texts, drawings, listings and other manuals are translated into English, and this further improves their confidence. Within two months, the system works at 80 per cent of its capacity.

## Epilogue

It is now two years after installation. Due to all the problems encountered, the project lasted 25 months instead of the anticipated 20 months. And after installation, it took another ten months to get the system operating to such a level that it was thought appropriate for CCP to hand it over to the plant. Most of the objectives set were achieved at least partially (see Table 23.3).

The development of all the new generation engine types has been finished and they prove to be quite a success in the marketplace, with

**Table 23.3**   FMS benefits achieved

| FMS benefits | achieved |
| --- | --- |
| Product innovation | Fully |
| Product modification | Fully |
| Product quality | Fully |
| Shorter delivery time | Partially |
| Reduced sales price | Partially |
| Reduced direct labour | Partially |
| Reduced handling/transport | Partially |
| Higher machining capacity | 90 per cent |
| Fewer machines | Partially |
| Shorter set-up times | Fully |
| Shorter lead times | Partially |
| Smaller batch sizes | Partially |
| Reduced work-in-progress | Partially |
| Reduced floor space | Partially |
| Linking of production control and manufacturing | Fully |
| Increased scheduling flexibility | Fully |
| Technical obsolescence of existing equipment | Fully |
| Payback period | Partially (7 years) |

sales going beyond the wildest expectations. In April 1996, considering its experience with the FMS project, Diesel Engines decided to postpone phases 2, 3 and 4, but now the immediate decision is whether to expand the FMS and take the opportunity to add two machining centres, an extra measuring tool and also a faster, state-of-the-art AGV to replace the present one. All this will need to be delivered by Comatec. The alternative is to make the instinctively more difficult decision to make a step back and build a whole new line dedicated to the present portfolio, and use the FMS for testing and phasing-in new designs and phasing-out the previous generation of engines.

## Questions

1  What were the major difficulties Diesel Engines encountered during the FMS project? Make a distinction between the *process* and the *content* of change.

2  What could the company have done in order to prevent these difficulties?

3  Which alternative would you choose as regards the decision either to expand the present FMS or to build a whole new line to produce the present portfolio of products while using the FMS for testing and phasing-in new designs and phasing-out the previous generation of engines? Explain.

### Further reading

Boer, H., *Organising Innovative Manufacturing Systems*, Aldershot: Gower/Avebury, 1991.

Storey, J. (ed.), *New Wave Manufacturing Systems*, London: Paul Chapman Publishing, 1994.

# 24

# ABB

*Local presence and cross-border learning within a multinational*

## CHRISTIAN BERGGREN

The international ABB corporation was formed in 1987 by a merger of two national electrotechnical companies, the Swedish ASEA and the Swiss Company Brown Bovery. This merger was the first step in a bold attempt to restructure a traditionally conservative, heavy engineering industry on European lines. The next step was taken in the US in 1989, when Combustion Engineering and the power transmission and distribution business of Westinghouse were acquired. From this Western base, the group has continued its growth by 'going east', investing in and acquiring new companies in former Eastern Europe as well as South-east Asia. ABB has been heralded as a new kind of international enterprise, neither centralized and ethnocentric nor multinational in the old sense of largely autonomous national subsidiaries. The group has reinvented the matrix organization in an attempt to achieve both global scale and decentralized multi-domestic presence. Central staffs have been dismantled and the merged companies divided into several thousand profit centres with a remarkably lean corporate management at the top. This case study relates the ABB structure to its strategy of growing by acquisitions, and analyses the fundamental dilemmas in its organizational form: how to combine scale and scope with speed and local presence. Two business areas,

This case study is based on an international study, initiated by Torsten Björkman, of the relationship between corporate strategies and national responses within ABB. A key part of the project is a systematic comparison of the transformer plants in Sweden, Germany, Spain, Canada and Switzerland. The analysis of Ludvika draws on a preliminary report by Lars Bengtsson. ABB Guelph was visited by the author, together with Nomura Masami from Okayama University.

*ABB* 321

Transformers and Process Automation, are discussed in more detail, paying particular attention to time-based management and cross-border organizational learning, which are key to the competitive success of the group.

## ABB – a Global Innovator in a Traditional Industry

ABB is a Swiss–Swedish multinational in the electrotechnical industry, employing more than 200,000 people. In 1993 total sales amounted to US $28,300 million. The group is organized in five business segments: power plants, power transmission and distribution, industry and building systems, and transportation and financial services. The segments are subdivided into 50 international business areas. Within power transmission and distribution, for example, there are business areas responsible for cables, transformers, high-voltage switchgear, network control, installation and low-voltage apparatus. The five core countries in terms of employment are located in Western Europe and North America (see Table 24.1).

**Table 24.1**   Core countries in the ABB group

| Country | Employment 1993 |
| --- | --- |
| Germany | 36,600 |
| Sweden | 25,700 |
| US | 22,300 |
| Switzerland | 13,700 |
| UK | 10,400 |

In total, Western Europe accounted for 63 per cent of the workforce. Since the early 1990s the group has been expanding rapidly in Eastern Europe. In 1993 it employed 5,100 workers in Poland and 6,200 in the Czech Republic. As a part of an extended 'Go East' programme ABB intends to build a major presence in China before the turn of the century.

### Brief History

The electrotechnical industry developed as a major part of the second industrial revolution in the late nineteenth century. In most countries one or two national champions rapidly gained pre-eminence, General

Electric and Westinghouse in the US, Siemens and Allgemeine Elektrizitätsgesellschaft in Germany, and GEC in Britain. Brown Bovery of Switzerland and ASEA of Sweden were also founded in this period, but remained marginal players until they unexpectedly joined forces in 1987. Percy Barnevik of ASEA was chosen as the chief executive officer (CEO) of the new group, the headquarters were located to Zurich and English was designated as the corporate language. ABB set out to restructure a traditional, conservative industry which for a century had been closely linked to national standards and public authorities. Sweeping financial decentralization was combined with corporate programmes emphasizing time-based management, rapid response time and customer focus. In a few years, the new group was heralded as 'the most successful cross-border merger in Europe since Royal Dutch Shell' – which was formed before the First World War (Rapoport, 1992).

Why do different MNEs choose different organizational models? National traditions could be part of the picture, but it does not explain the co-existence of different organizational models within one country. A favourite theme in the business press and with management consultants is the orientation and predilections of the chief executive officer. This case study takes a different view. In a line of thought inspired by Chandler (1969) it analyses ABB's structure from the perspective of its growth strategy. The second part of the study proceeds from the corporate level to a detailed discussion of two business areas, Power Transformers and Process Automation. These businesses are different in important respects, thus illustrating the diversity within the group. The Transformer business area deals with a mature technology, and research and development (R&D) spending is low at only 2–3 per cent of sales. Process Automation is a rapidly evolving technology and R&D spending here amounts to 10–12 per cent. In the market for power transformers, ABB is a global leader; in the elusive process automation business, competition is fierce and there is no clear market leader. BA Transformers enjoys a manufacturing presence in 17 countries. Process Automation has centralized the manufacture of vital components to one site but has a widely diffused network of local sales and engineering companies. In spite of all differences they face similar organizational challenges: in the short term, how to combine distributed local presence with effective cross-border learning; in the long term, how to substitute unified global products and processes for the amalgam of diverse technologies which ABB inherited as a result of its aggressive acquisition strategy.

*ABB* 323

## Back to Strategy and Structure

Since the publication of the pioneering study by Perlmutter and Heenan (1979) there has been a long discussion concerning how to classify the structure of internationals. Perlmutter et al. distinguished between globalized and decentralized companies. Two forms of global enterprises were identified: the 'ethnocentric', where policy is central-ized from the home country headquarters, and 'geocentric', where policies are developed on a world-wide basis. As a contrast to these centralized types there was the multi-domestic, 'polycentric' type. In the subsequent literature, the ethnocentric structure of Japanese MNEs have often been contrasted with the polycentric character of European multinationals, the Dutch Philips corporation being a prominent case in point (Bartlett and Ghoshal, 1990).

ABB has gone to great lengths to present itself as a new type of multi-domestic corporation, a company with many home countries ('being local world-wide' is an official slogan) while at the same time enjoying the advantage of global resources and co-ordination. Using Perlmutter's terminology, ABB could best be described as a hybrid between a polycentric and geocentric organization. It is a non-public company, 50/50 owned by the Swiss and Swedish partners. The CEO is a Swede, the corporate headquarters are located in Zürich, Switzerland and the company language is English. The head office is inconspicuous and the corporate staff small, approximately 150 people.

To structure its broad product scope and geographically dispersed presence, the group applies an elaborate matrix. One dimension is products and markets. Here the organizing principle is business areas, reporting to five business segments: Power Generation, Power Transmission and Distribution, Industrial and Building Systems, Traction, and Financial Services. The senior executives running the segments are positioned in Zürich and are members of the executive board, whereas the headquarters (sometimes called 'co-ordination offices') of the business areas are located in several different coun-tries, mainly Sweden, Finland, Norway, Germany, Switzerland and the US. Geography is the other organizational dimension. Local op-erations are federated into strong national or regional structures. After the reorganization in 1993 the national/regional organizations were consolidated in three continental groups, Europe, the Americas and Asia Pacific. In 1993 ABB had a total of 206,500 employees – down from 213,400 the previous year. In Germany, ABB employed

36,600 people, in Sweden 25,700, in the US, 22,300, in Switzerland 13,700 and in the UK 10,400.

The matrix organization gained wide popularity among multinational firms in the 1970s but was later criticized for considerable drawbacks such as ambiguity, increased costs of communication, slower decision making and lack of clear responsibility. At ABB the matrix principle is defended as the only one possible in a complex world. The basic argument is quite similar to Evans and Lorange's (1989) discussion of the two logics behind human resource management, the product-driven logic of business dynamics and the geographically based socio-cultural logic. According to the CEO of ABB, Percy Barnevik, the matrix 'is a fact of life. If you deny the formal matrix, you wind up with an informal one – and that's much harder to reckon with' (Taylor, 1991, pp. 95–6).

A basic management principle at ABB is to allocate financial responsibility to the lowest possible level. Local operations, reporting to international business area centres, are normally incorporated as separate legal entities. The introduction of this principle implied major break-ups of previously consolidated organizations. The German subsidiary of Brown Bovery Company, for example, was a single company before BBC's merger with ASEA in 1987. Four years later it consisted of 54 separate legal companies. The majority of these companies are further divided into several thousand profit centres/business units. Journalists and management consultants have explained the ABB structure by focusing on Percy Barnevik and his personal experience. He is presented as a man 'abhorring bureaucracy' – 'his abiding hatred of bureaucracy is critical to making the ABB structure work' (Peters, 1992, p. 47). Barnevik's father was the managing owner of a mid-sized printing shop. That is referred to as a formative experience for the CEO of the multinational ABB, shaping his determination to break up the corporation into a multitude of accountable small businesses in order to avoid the 'Big Company Sickness' (Kapstein, 1990). Biographical details of this kind may be interesting but hardly suffice as an explanation. It is time to go back to Chandler's (1969) insistence on the necessary relationship between strategy and structure.

Since the mid-1980s the basic strategy of the Swedish management at ASEA, now controlling ABB, has been a strategy of mergers and acquisitions in order to achieve market leadership and, in selected markets, global dominance. This strategic goal of gaining a dominant share in mature markets has characterized many other Swedish

*ABB* **325**

corporations in the engineering industry, for example Sandvik Coromant (hard materials), Volvo Trucks and Alfa Laval (separators), and Electrolux (household appliances). Here there certainly is a 'national tradition'. The expansionist drive of ASEA started in the Nordic region, where Finnish Strömberg and Norwegian Elektrisk Bureau were acquired, followed by the merger with Brown Bovery in 1987. Two years later this was followed by two major American acquisitions, of the transmission business of Westinghouse and the whole of Combustion Engineering. These grand deals have been supplemented by a multitude of acquisitions in other countries, such as Denmark, the UK, Italy, Spain, the former East Germany, Poland, the Czech Republic, Hungary and, lately, also the Ukraine and Russia.

The key organizational themes of ABB are closely related to this strategy of mergers and acquisitions. The emphasis on 'being local world-wide' and having 'many home countries' serves to reassure governments, public utilities and private customers who fear that service and technical support will deteriorate when ABB acquires local businesses. The breaking up of previously consolidated national companies is an important mechanism for creating transparency and accountability in order to discover excess costs and put pressure on low-performing units. The formal decentralization is accompanied by the introduction of the Abacus accounting system, which collects monthly performance data from every profit centre. Abacus is a very important element of uniformity within the group. ABB has a radical policy of slashing the corporate staffs of acquired companies. The German HQ of BBC used to have a staff of 1,600 people. ABB reduced it to 100. At the Finnish Strömberg company, the headquarters staff was trimmed from 800 to 60 employees; at Combustion Engineering the staff was reduced from 600 to 90 – and the fleet of corporate jets was disposed of. This policy is an important corollary to the mergers and acquisitions strategy in the way it eliminates national fiefdoms and increases the visibility and accountability of the operating businesses. ABB has also devoted considerable effort to international management training. In the two years 1990–1, 1,000 managers participated in three-day corporate seminars, attended by members of the executive board. An important goal was to build common values and a more cohesive management culture across borders. The training efforts are linked to the company's explicit policy of internal promotion to all important positions in the business area and business segment management. Another method to promote the development of global managers is the assignment of specialists and managers to international tasks. In 1992 international assignments had been awarded to more than 1,000 people in the company.

## Aggressive Rationalization . . .

Mergers tend to result in lost market share. The customer focus programme espoused by headquarters in Zürich is thus well adapted to its mergers and acquisitions (M&A) strategy. In the US, for example, Combustion Engineering was itself a conglomerate, which had been taking over numerous companies immediately before it was bought by ABB. These acquisitions included AccuRay, a specialist in paper machine control and Taylor Instruments, a supplier of the MOD Taylor industrial control systems. As a result of the merger between these two companies, AccuRay lost half its salesforce. When ABB took control, customers of the MOD Taylor system were further worried that ABB would not support and service that system any longer. One of the first items on the agenda of the new ABB management was to recruit and train sales engineers and to meet and assure customers of future deliveries. 'They did all the right things', as an American manager commented in an interview in 1993, but their success was limited. A strategic part of the corporate customer focus programme is the insistence on responsiveness and speed, short delivery times and rapid introduction of new products. This particular part is inspired by the concept of time-based management (TBM), as successfully marketed by the Boston Consulting Group. According to its major proponents, 'time is a more useful management tool than cost. Cost is by and large a lagging indicator, a symptom, a set of control accounts after the fact' (Stalk and Hout, 1990, p. 192). By contrast, a focus on time allows scrutiny down to the physical level and opens up companies for deeper analysis. ABB engaged Boston Consulting Group in several countries. Especially in the US, Motorola has also served as an important inspiration. TBM reinforces the emphasis on customer focus. At the same time it is a low-cost approach for improving performance and freeing working capital. This aspect is hardly lost on a company where the aggressive M&A strategy is resulting in high debts and restructuring costs. Further, the TBM concept has served the purpose of counteracting the risks of fragmentation and management myopia, which could result from the sweeping breaking up of cohesive organizations. As the American VP of Quality at

*ABB* 327

ABB Process Automation observed in an interview with the author in May, 1993: 'The Motorola Institute was really important to give impetus to this process. ABB tended to optimize organizational entities, but suboptimize the total process. The Motorola approach stressed process management and measurement.'

A traditional dilemma for multinational organizations is how to achieve scale without compromising scope and local presence. ABB has added the extra challenge of combining scale and scope with speed. This runs counter to much of the argument by the proponents of time-based management. Stalk and Hout repeatedly refer to geographical transfers as a major obstacle to rapid processes. In a case study of a 'slow innovator', they describe its development process as very complex: 'Typical programs involved 35 to 55 people. These people reported to 8 to 11 functional heads and were scattered over 5 locations and 12 buildings in 3 countries.' By contrast, they argue that a company with a rapid new product development cycle 'gathers all development resources for one product in one group – including marketing, design, manufacturing, and, in some situations, finance and sales. The participants in these functional areas work together on a full-time basis. Often, they are physically located at the site where the new product is to be manufactured' (Stalk and Hout, 1990, pp. 121, 124). ABB attempts to attain the goals of time-based management in a geographical and organizational structure very different from this vision of a compact, consolidated unit. As we will see, this is a daunting endeavour.

## . . . But Uninspiring Profitability

'If lean and mean could be personified, Percy Barnevik would walk through the door. . . . Barnevik is Europe's leading hatchet man. He is also the creator of what is fast becoming the most successful cross-border merger since Royal Dutch linked up with Britain's Shell in 1907' (Rapoport, 1992, p. 24).

Barnevik's aggressive, fast-moving style has earned him accolades in the business press. Unfortunately that is no guarantee for success. In the mid 1980s leading American consultants and business writers, such as Peters and Waterman (1982) perceived and presented IBM as the incarnation of excellence. The acid test for ABB is its long-term performance compared with the competition. In financial terms, however, ABB's record was uninspiring during its first years. In fiscal year 1992 the major American and European competitors – General Electric, Siemens and GEC Alsthom – booked increases in earnings, whereas ABB suffered a decline. In fiscal year 1993 ABB earnings were hurt by major restructuring costs. These were treated as non-recurring costs in the annual report, so the company was able to report stable operating earnings. The net profit, however was a negligible US $68 million (*Affärsvärlden*, 16 March, 5 May 1993). The performance is far behind American General Electric, the star in the industry. General Electric reports operating earnings in relation to revenues of 17 per cent, compared to ABB's 7–8 per cent. The financial costs of ABB's many acquisitions have been considerable. The solidity in fiscal year 1992 was 14 per cent, compared to General Electric's 50 per cent. Restructuring costs have been increasing from US $200 million in 1990 to US $600 in 1993. In the same period, stockholders' equity has declined from US $4,200 million to US $3,500. The market value of the founding companies, ASEA and BBC, has increased impressively, however, reflecting the strong confidence ABB and its CEO enjoys on the stock-markets. The argument is that ABB's global presence has made the group more robust than the competitors, all heavily dependent on their respective domestic markets. Further, the global spread will make it much easier for ABB to take advantage of changing exchange rates than for its contenders.

If strategy drives structure, if organizational arrangements are solutions to particular problems rather than being incarnations of management beliefs, then the structure of ABB should be changing as the competitive position evolves. That is exactly the case. The emphasis of multi-domesticity served important purposes in the wake of the M&A strategy, to ensure transparency of the acquired firms and to assure customers of continued presence. Once these goals were accomplished other considerations have tended to become more significant. Financial decentralization established accountability but created problems in dealing with customers who had businesses with many ABB companies and tended to result in excessive time spent on internally negotiating product and price. In 1993–4 there was a stronger emphasis on integrating and consolidating interrelated businesses and a drive to strengthen the role of business area management ('the product logic') at the expense of the national entities ('the socio-cultural logic'). The original 65 business areas were consolidated into 50 and the role of the executive board strengthened. One case of such a consolidation is the merger of Process Automation and

*ABB* 329

Drives to form the much larger business area ABB Industrial Systems, at one stroke doubling the workforce to 15,000.

To understand the dynamics of the corporate giant it is necessary to study selected business areas, how they attempt to achieve integration and economies of scale without resorting to traditional hierarchical coercion, how they organize cross-border learning and knowledge transfer, and use the TBM concepts to drive performance and change. The next section presents Power Transformers. In this business ABB has accomplished a central goal in the M&A strategy and is the world's premier producer. Transformers are built on a basically mature technology and ABB/ASEA has a tradition going back one century. The next case, the business area Process Automation, is a young business, and competitive conditions, strategy and structure very different from Power Transformers.

## Power Transformers – the Power of Benchmarking

ABB Power Transformers is a multinational in its own right, comprising 24 plants in 17 countries, with a total employment of 8,000 people. On average, this business area commands 35 per cent of the world market. According to ABB, local manufacture contributes very significantly to a high share in national markets. The restructuring which has accompanied the acquisitions is mainly focused on consolidating plants within each country, for example Norway, Spain and English-speaking Canada, rather than consolidating on a global or continental level.

The plants in this global network vary considerably. A core group of plants was part of ASEA's transformer operation. Historically, the Swedish transformer centre in Ludvika enjoyed a strong position, supported by world-class technological capabilities in areas such as high-voltage direct current transmission (HVDC). Engineers and managers in Ludvika still pride themselves on working at the 'Mecca of transformers'. The German plant in Bad Honnef, which also belonged to the historical part of ASEA, has a reputation for manufacturing excellence. These 'old stars' have played an important role as teachers. Other plants in the industrialized world, such as the Canadian operation in Guelph or the Australian in More-bank outside Sydney, used to belong to Westinghouse. Acquired by ABB in 1989, they are now in the midst of catching up. A third group of plants is located in the industrializing countries. They are 'late developers', but several of them have proved to be quick learners.

To avoid the various national subsidiaries competing with each other in third markets, the business headquarters in Mannheim, Germany exercises control of export market allocation. The norm is that plants should primarily serve their national market; domestic customers should account for 70 per cent of the output. This applies for general products. Ludvika, the other Nordic plants, and Germany's Bad Honnef export a significantly higher proportion, in Ludvika's case 85 per cent (1993). Of Ludvika's production, however, a major share consists of special products. For the traditional export plants, niche products are of crucial importance for maintaining a significant manufacturing base as well as preserving a technological advantage within the group.

In order to integrate the business area, foster internal competition (increasingly important when ABB has come to dominate the market) and drive organizational learning, the international management has introduced a comprehensive set of metrics, measuring quality conformance, on-time delivery, customer satisfaction, productivity, inventory and manufacturing through-put time, as well as total through-put time from order to delivery. The measures of through-put time are central tools for enforcing time-based management. Business area management has a truly globalist approach. Countries certainly differ, but that does not mean that companies must reflect those differences. An important task for the co-ordination office is to identify a 'best practice' for every process, be it German, Finnish or Canadian, and then try to diffuse that in the whole network. To avoid nationalist deadlocks, it is crucial to be very specific in this process of identification.

A potentially powerful tool for achieving integration and economy of scale is technology. Because of the many acquisitions, several different transformer technologies exist within the business area. The business has started projects to develop a common technology supported by common processes in design and assembly. This, however, has not been easy to accomplish. A pilot run of the new standard technology was carried out in 1993, but the results were disappointing, and the project had to be restarted from scratch. A complete commonization of the transformer technologies is not likely to be realized until the turn of the century. The experience testifies to the difficulties in consumming mergers and in fully achieving the potential economies

*ABB* **331**

of scale. None the less, the benchmarking exercises and the stress on cross-border learning have triggered substantive improvements in newly acquired plants. One most impressive case is the Canadian Guelph plant.

*ABB Guelph: learning at a brownfield plant*

Guelph was opened as a General Electric plant in the early 1950s. In 1986, Westinghouse bought the plant. According to managers who worked at Guelph in this period, GE had been fairly progressive, re-flecting the CEO Jack Welch's new approach, whereas Westinghouse management was a clear step backward. The two cultures were very difficult to integrate. In close-by Hamilton, Westinghouse had another plant with its own streams of suppliers and managerial hierarchy. In 1989 ABB acquired both operations. This was an all-time low for Guelph. Market share was rapidly falling as customers grew suspi-cious of the repeated changes of owners. They were familiar with American technologies but not with ABB. Westinghouse had been driving very hard for volume and sales, but not paying attention to costs and throughput. According to the supply manager, 'the plant was crammed with transformer jobs in different stages of process-ing. Lead times and overtime were excessive. We were eating like an elephant but shitting like a mouse. Westinghouse had no real respect for the customers; volume was the important thing' (interview with the author, October 1993).

ABB approached the Canadian operation with a comprehensive change programme. This involved technological modernization, con-solidation of plants and staff reduction, management screening and selection, infusion of an international perspective, aggressive per-formance goals and systematic benchmarking. When the new man-agers, including the general manager from Sweden, arrived in early 1990 they were appalled by the disorder in the plant. In spite of serious problems with belated deliveries, they ordered an immediate production stop and a two-week clean-up of the plant. That was a powerful symbolic message. In the next year the facility was modern-ized and the production equipment upgraded to international stand-ards. These investments proved to employees that ABB was going to stay in business. That was important for morale since the com-pany also took several hard decisions. The Hamilton plant was closed. Soon after ABB acquired Guelph, the market deteriorated rapidly and half the workforce was made redundant. At the management level, too, there was a shake-out. All managers were assessed based on an evaluation of past performance, complemented by formal test procedures. This measure was a crucial part of the change programme, but painful for the affected employees, as one of the interviewed managers observed: 'People who had been working at the plant for 25 years now had to re-apply for their jobs, and that was very hard for them. Those who failed were sent out the door.'

New, demanding goals were a distinctive component of the new management style. These goals were not about 4–5 per cent improvements, but 40–50 per cent gains in productivity, lead times, quality costs and inventories. In order to change the outlook and culture of the plant, a series of visits to other ABB plants was organized, including Secheron in Switzerland and Bad Honnef in Germany. The programme started with managers in order to convince them first, then supervisors and people from the shopfloor were brought over. These visits were very important eye-openers and introduced the Guelph people to a completely different manufacturing culture. A veteran manager from the Westinghouse time was particularly impressed by the cleanliness at Bad Honnef where 'you could eat on the floor'. One year after the takeover, considerable progress could be registered at Guelph. From 1989 to 1991 throughput time was cut by 58 per cent and inventories as percentage of revenues reduced from 74 per cent (sic!) to 35 per cent. New quality systems were put in place in order to build quality into the process, instead of the traditional practice of 'fighting fires'. Comparisons with other plants in the business and the relative position of Guelph are now communicated through the entire organization, even on the shopfloor. Customer reviews and regular reporting of customer complaints are emphasized. Also 'non-complaints', such as customer enquiries, and presumably the length of the response time, are to be documented and analysed. Previously this kind of information was only handled by individuals, and never documented, which meant that it was not dealt with as an issue for organizational improvement.

The 1990–2 period witnessed a crash effort to bring a run-down plant up to reasonable performance. In 1993 further big improvements had become much more difficult to accomplish. The market was still depressed. That was a potential threat to morale – after all these efforts, changes and pains, there might still be more layoffs. In spite of these problems, Guelph continued to improve at an impressive rate in the first quarter of 1994.

*ABB* 333

*The problem for the old stars*

The old core operations in the business area are in a different position from the turn-around plants. Whereas sites like Guelph and the Brazilian company have used the business area network to progress on a steep learning curve, and rapidly approach the performance of their role models, the 'teachers' cannot play a similar catch-up game. For the Swedish manufacturing operation in Ludvika the business area structure has meant losses of autonomy as well as market potential. Business area management in Mannheim determines the strategic capacity of each operation, and plants are not allowed to ship general products to countries where ABB has local manufacture. Because of the small and stagnant home market, export opportunities are a crucial issue for Ludvika. In the early 1990s the plant received huge orders from China and adjacent countries, but these markets may be gone in five or ten years because of saturation and the up-grading of local capabilities. One solution for the old 'Mecca of transformers' is to pursue its niche strategy further. Another is to increase vertical integration and collaboration with its customers, mostly other ABB companies selling complete power plants. Ludvika also seeks to develop its manufacturing competence and invest in specialized machinery. This takes advantage of the overall manufacturing strategy of the business, which is to preserve local manufacture in every important market but concentrate capital-intensive processes in a few centres. A multi-year project is to develop a new computerized design process which will support a comprehensive re-use of components and documents and is expected to reduce the design time by an order of magnitude. Whereas the autonomy of the Ludvika plant is circumscribed by the business area, its development and engineering departments are profiting from the international operation and its broad manufacturing base.

The plant has embarked on an ambitious programme of rationalization. Suddenly it has discovered that the 'teachers' also have to learn and improve. As in Guelph, aggressive goals have been set up at the old 'Mecca'. From 1991–3, Ludvika reduced average throughput-time by 30 per cent and the failure rate by almost 50 per cent. The targets for 1995 include a further reduction of throughput times by 50 per cent and a breakthrough in design efficiency. The turn-around at Guelph is impressive but theoretically easy to explain as the results of a focused catch-up effort. The goals and results at Ludvika seem to testify to the impressive potential for improvement even at supposedly mature and rational plants.

Power Transformers probably belongs to ABB's most well-managed and well-structured business areas. There are few direct economies of scale and integration flowing from ABB's far-flung merger strategy, however. The programme to consolidate its several different transformer technologies into one common technology is advancing slowly. In this respect, ABB's insistence on decentralization and local presence render speed and scale more difficult to accomplish. The most powerful lever of its international organization is the process of organizational learning which is unleashed by the emphasis on benchmarking, knowledge transfer and internal competition.

## Process Automation

ABB Automation supplies integrated and distributed control and supervision systems for process automation. This comprises general systems ('automation platforms') and industry-specific optimization packages as well as highly dedicated control technology such as the AccuRay system for paper machine control. In 1991 ABB Automation had 6,400 employees world-wide, with a concentration in four countries, Germany, Sweden, Switzerland and the US.

In late 1993 Process Automation was merged with Drives and some other businesses to form Industrial Systems. This roughly doubled the size of the business area and also changed the organizational structure. In this section I will focus on the operations of Process Automation.

ABB/ASEA is a relatively new contender in the industrial-control business. Whereas Power Transformers is the market leader, Process Automation faces stiff competition, both from electrotechnical giants such as Siemens and from established rivals in the instrumentation business, where Honeywell enjoys a very strong position. ABB's control systems are marketed to a range of industries. In pulp and paper applications ABB Automation is one of the world leaders. Another substantial market segment is the metallurgical industry. As in pulp and paper, ABB has the advantage of a strong Nordic cluster in this sector. World-wide, the most important segment is the chemical industry. There is a broad movement from proprietary hard- and software to open control systems, where customers can combine packages and components from various vendors. ABB's new automation platform, the Advant series, released in 1992, is built on workstations from Hewlett-Packard and software from several different specialists, such as a real-time Unix operating system and a database system

*ABB* 335

delivered by Oracle. Customer requirements are changing rapidly, too, especially in the European paper industry. In Sweden and Finland the industry has completely converted its traditional bleaching processes by introducing new processes such as oxygen bleaching, or totally chlorine-free bleaching. The conversion started by regulatory pressures but is now driven by market demands, especially in Germany. As a result of this and other changes, pulp mills face a much larger product variety. Where they used to have two grades, they now sometimes have to produce 20 different grades, and this requires more advanced control systems.

ABB Process Automation has to cope with these changes in the environment while at the same time taking care of the internal complexities resulting from its M&A history. In 1987, when ASEA and BBC merged, there were two competing systems, ASEA's Master and BBC's Procontrol. After hard arguments (according to participating managers 'there was blood on the floor'), it was decided to halt further development of the Procontrol system and focus on the Master concept. In 1989 ABB acquired Combustion Engineering, itself a loosely organized conglomerate, which only a few years earlier had acquired a company in the industrial control business, Taylor Instruments in Rochester. Its basic system, MOD Taylor 300, was complementary market-wise with a stronger position in chemicals than the Swiss–Swedish constellation enjoyed. ABB Automation decided to keep both systems but to merge them in future product generations, and eventually market only one system world-wide. This was an expensive solution, but was seen as the only one possible to avoid losing more market share as otherwise it would be very difficult to retain any of the MOD Taylor customers. In this aspect Process Automation resembles Power Transformers: both have to devise long-term strategies to integrate a cumbersome mixture of technologies which is a result of the M&A strategy.

The international business area management of ABB Automation was first located in Mannheim, then moved to Stamford and in 1994 was relocated to Zürich. It is functionally organized with executives responsible for marketing, system product management and manufacturing. By contrast to Power Transformers, manufacturing is highly centralized. Västerås, Sweden produces all printed circuit boards and cabinets for the automation platform, whereas Columbus, Ohio, is responsible for the AccuRay line of dedicated control and measuring devices for paper machines. The development of new system products is distributed, however, and takes place in three centres: Västerås,

Rochester and Mannheim. At the customer end of the business area, the organization is highly distributed with a global net of sales and engineering operations. The majority of the competing vendors of control systems are ethnocentric, not multi-domestic. North American companies tend to develop both basic products and custom software at central locations, one in the United States and one in Europe, for example, and deliver from the centre to local industry sites. ABB is distinguished by its large network of local sales and engineering companies, which develop applications in close contact with their customers. At an intermediary level there is a structure called Business Units (BU). This is an industry-oriented organizational dimension which supports the sales and engineering offices by developing and servicing specific applications, including optimization packages for reheat furnaces in rolling mills, pulper control programmes, bleachery control packages, and so on. For local sales and engineering centres it is not possible to develop the necessary expertise in these specialized areas.

Several issues in this complex business are highly industry-specific. ABB's endeavours to create an effectively working international network raise themes common to other business areas, however. Such issues are local accountability versus integration and economy of scale, the importance of cross-border learning, and the problems of joint international efforts in product development or, more generally, the dilemma of trying to be at the same time participative and effective in the time-based competition.

### Manufacturing – international consolidation

ABB decided to consolidate and specialize the manufacturing operations shortly after the mergers. According to production managers in Västerås, there was no real choice. Compared to computer manufacturers, the company is still disadvantaged by its suboptimal volumes of PCBs. The consolidated structure means there is little competition between different plants. Several performance metrics are used to measure particular processes as well as plants, but they do not play the same driving role as in Transformers. For Process Automation, external benchmarking is of more vital importance. In 1990 ABB Sweden launched a highly publicized, corporate-wide programme called T50, signifying the goal of a 50 per cent reduction of all lead times from order to delivery within a period of three years. The manufacturing department responded immediately to the challenge.

*ABB* 337

In less than two years lead times from order to delivery were compressed from 12–16 weeks to 7–8 weeks. According to the head of manufacturing, the emphasis on lead times was a powerful driver for overall improvements. When throughput times were cut by half, quality and delivery morale improved and late deliveries became much less frequent. In 1993, the goal at Process Automation was to compress the process by another 50 per cent. The actual trend was different, however. In that year order intake and capacity utilization started to increased steeply, and so did delivery times. The T50 programme had been launched when Sweden was in a deep recession and capacity utilization was low. In 1994 the central unresolved challenge was to continue to shorten response and delivery times when production was booming.

## *T50 in design – parallel local efforts*

In late 1993 ABB Process Automation in Sweden was awarded the prestigious status 'T50-company', as an official confirmation of its comprehensive strategies to compress lead times and increase responsiveness and customer focus. When at the same time there was a meeting of designers and engineers at the development department, nobody could explain why the company had obtained that status. T50 was seen as the concern of the manufacturing department, in spite of the repeated stress that the programme should encompass the total delivery process, from design to customer installation. However, by that time a management team had already spent considerable efforts in mapping the current design methods for PCBs and trying to devise a faster and more controllable process. In the existing process, lead times were not only lengthy but also very difficult to predict, the development span stretching from several months to several years. At the start of the project the Swedish CEO of Process Automation advocated a reduction of design lead time to one third of the current average. The immediate reaction was defence. Various participants in the team spent months arguing why it was impossible to reduce lead times that much. Finally, they arrived at a more positive track, started to map the current process and outline a more compact, 'concurrent' and team-based process. Four strategies were devised: cross-functional teams; a measurable process; new methods of testing; and synchronized daily plans instead of sequential weekly plans. The programme is currently in the state of implementation. Logical and physical designers and test engineers form teams and for the first time ever they plan the process together. The introduction of daily plans requires them to work in a more disciplined manner than before, to be careful to document every step in the prototype testing, for example, and to involve everybody in the planning process early on. Since specialist knowledge is still perceived as vital, the basic functional structure of the organization has not been affected. This makes the team-based process strongly dependent on the support of functional managers. The bonus for these managers is a much speedier process; on the downside they lose control. They cannot assign their subordinates to different tasks the way they did before since these engineers do their own cross-functional, horizontal planning. A critical question is what happens when management changes.

The most difficult design process is the development of new automation platforms involving a large amount of both new hard- and software. ABB Process Automation has been an innovative player in this field and an early proponent of the Open Control Systems (OCS). From a management perspective, however, there are numerous problems with its platform development. Lead times tend to be very long and, to make things worse, extremely difficult to plan and schedule. Products are released involving a lot of new technology, and when a new product generation is released, sales and services departments have to spend years on so-called 'after-sales development', before quality is acceptable to customers.

One of the problems in launching the T50 initiative was that there existed no tradition of measuring efficiency in product development. Bolstered by strong management commitment (defined as allocation of executive time, and not mere 'support'), the change project was initiated. A working party started by conducting a detailed mapping of the existing process in order to identify the current workflow. This effort included structured interviews with nearly all 200 engineers about problems in the current process and the obstacles to a more rapid design flow. The guiding idea is to define the product development process rigorously in terms of input data, process characteristics and definitions of output data. Such process characteristics include: decentralized decision making; controllable and measurable process; flexibility to develop alternative solutions; customer involvement; and customer focus. Decentralization is both a means and an end. When the new product development model is implemented, it will be possible for engineers and project managers to take all relevant decisions

*ABB*  **339**

themselves within the project. A crucial problem is to make the process measurable, to define relevant metrics and monitor them in a consistent way. How is productivity to be measured, for example? The ABB managers are not content with measuring lines of source code per engineer and time, a traditional productivity measure in software engineering used extensively by Japanese software factories (Cusumano, 1991). For the change project it is vital to use metrics that are really perceived as relevant by the design engineers.

The efforts to improve the design processes at ABB Automation are basically local efforts operating in parallel. The German research centre in Mannheim started its improvement activities with an assessment using the Capability Maturity Model (CMM) approach. This is a method developed by the Software Engineering Institute for the American Department of Defence in order to evaluate software vendors before buying any programme development from them. As a result of this assessment the German organization has identified a number of weak spots, including process measurement. There is an ongoing exchange of experiences between Germany and Sweden, but no co-ordinated business area effort. The US organization, burnt by a previous failed attempt to redesign the design process, has opted not to participate at all. The development department in Västerås is the dominant design centre in the business area but has no command and control of the other design centres. In the current process, this is a disadvantage.

*Project delivery – common tools for the internationally dispersed sales structure*

Automation systems are normally sold in the form of project deliveries. In the case of paper machine control (AccuRay), the company offers specified process capabilities in terms of paper thickness, moisture and opacity. Project deliveries comprise repeated customer interaction, applications engineering, project management and, sometimes, operator training. Average lead times are 9–12 months. Traditionally, the all-important performance parameter for account managers is gross profit. Their goal is to improve the calculated gross profit margin, and the secret of project management is how to do that. Timely delivery is crucial, since the customer normally shuts down the process, for example a paper mill, for only a short time. But this parameter is reflected in the profit margin, since delivery delays will result in fines. There are benefits in a short delivery process, such as reduced cost of project management and of capital tied up in inventory, but there are no incentives for account managers to compress these times. Even worse, there is little organizational learning. There are few standards; project engineers work in individualistic ways, and many of them are safeguarding their autonomy. The company has developed computerized sales tools but no overall computer support. World-wide, Process Automation employs several thousand project and applications engineers. If the business area could construct an effective system for global information sharing and re-use of tested solutions there would be a huge rationalization potential. Such information sharing could also be used to identify and diffuse 'good practices', which could serve as a further basis for organizational learning.

To tap into that potential several change projects have been launched, with the aim of establishing common core processes in project management and designing appropriate computer tools to support these processes. The company has gone to great lengths to secure cross-border commitment to these projects. An effort to develop Computer Aided Project Support (CAPS), for example, has been supported by an international group involving participants from Sweden, the UK, Germany, Switzerland, Norway and the US. In 1994, pilot versions of the 're-engineered' processes of bid and proposal as well as project management were tested by an international team in the 'neutral' territory of Britain.

One Swedish account manager interviewed in this study previously worked with AccuRay projects for Combustion Engineering, Europe. They had a centralized project and applications site in Ireland. From this centre, engineers were sent all over Europe to negotiate contracts and participate in the commissioning of delivered equipment ('a typical job for bachelors'). In this way Combustion developed a strong engineering competence and effective information and learning among project managers, but they had severe difficulties in fostering customer rapport and in servicing complicated equipment. ABB is committed to maintain a local presence and local engineering competence. Effective cross-border flows of information and structured efforts to improve engineering learning are key to the success of this strategy. The Business Unit centres are responsible for supporting local engineering offices in specific deliveries, but also for the development of common methods and tools. Another vehicle for cross-border learning is the use of international teams designated for business area projects,

*ABB* **341**

for example the effort to define a new common process for bid and proposal in 1994. A third approach is to develop new tools based on modern information technologies, such as CAPS, computer-aided project support, common databases and common libraries for re-use of solutions. In 1994 the business area markedly increased its investments in business-wide tools and processes. Technology was seen as an important enabler; organizational practices and individual incentives determine if these resources are actively utilized.

## Conclusion

One goal of ABB's acquisition strategy is to establish dominant market positions. As the business area cases presented here demonstrate, this does not mean a vision of complacent oligopoly. Power Transformers has indeed become the market leader in its industry, but that has only intensified its efforts to build international plant metrics which foster internal competition and cross-border learning. The approach has been successful in turning around old brownfields and stimulating late developers. The difficult task of implementing common technologies and design processes across the business area remains to be accomplished, however. In the Process Automation business the dynamic character of the technology and the markets precludes the emergence of any dominant player. In this business, local manufacture would entail substantial diseconomies of scale without providing any market advantages. ABB Automation therefore combines centralized manufacture with a highly distributed network of local application and project management offices. This structure facilitates customer interaction but makes it more difficult to develop consistent approaches and upgrade engineering methods. Effective cross-border co-operation and learning are of vital importance for the competitiveness of ABB's distributed, multi-domestic strategy across its business areas.

## Questions

1   What does ABB's slogan 'being local world-wide' mean? Using evidence from the case, illustrate how it operates in practice. What are the main advantages and disadvantages of this approach?

2  What does this case tell us about new emerging forms of organization structure and control? In particular, what does it tell us about decentralization?

## References

Bartlett, C. and Ghoshal, S. 1990: Managing innovation in the transnational corporation. In Bartlett, C., Doz, Y. and Hedlund, G., *Managing the Global Firm*, London and New York, NY: Routledge.

Björkman, T. 1993: ABB – performance improvement in a 'multidomestic' corporation. In North, K. (ed.), *Improving Enterprise Performance: International Transfer of Approaches*, Geneva: ILO (forthcoming).

*Business World* (Affärsvärlden): ABB förskönar men behåller förtroendet 1994: 16 March, p. 46. Högre värdering trots sämre lönsamhet i ABB 1993: 5 May, pp. 57–61. ABB har en bra position men GE ligger i täten 1994: 13 April, pp. 38–49.

Carroll, P. 1993: *Big Blues*. New York: Crown Publishers.

Caulkin, S. 1993: GEC – Alsthom: A marriage à la Jack Sprat. *Management Today*, July, pp. 36–40.

Chandler, A. 1969: *Strategy and Structure*. Cambridge, MA: The MIT Press.

Cusumano, M. 1991: *Japan's Software Factories – A Challenge to U.S. Management*. New York, NY and Oxford: Oxford University Press.

Evans, P., Lank, E. and Farquhar, A. 1989: Managing human resources in the international firm – lessons from practice. In Evans, P., Doz, Y. and Laurent, A. (eds), *Human Resource Management in International Firms*. London: Macmillan.

Evans, P. and Lorange, P. 1989: The two logics behind human resource management. In Evans, P., Doz, Y. and Laurent, A. (eds), *Human Resource Management in International Firms*. London: Macmillan.

Hofheinz, P. 1994: ABB's big bet in Eastern Europe. *Fortune*, 2 May.

Kapstein, J. 1990: Preaching the Euro-gospel. ASEA Brown Boveri redefines multinationalism. *Business Week*, 23 July.

Perlmutter, H. V. and Heenan, D. A. 1979: *Multinational Organization Development: A Social Architectural Perspective*. Reading, MA: Addison-Wesley.

Peters, T. 1992: *Liberation Management. Necessary Disorganization for the Nanosecond Nineties*. New York: Macmillan.

Peters, T. and Waterman, R. 1982: *In Search of Excellence*. New York: Harper and Row.

Rapoport, C. 1992: How Percy Barnevik makes ABB work. It's Europe's best cross-border merger since Royal Dutch and Shell. *Fortune*, 29 June.

*ABB* **343**

Stalk, G. and Hout, Th. Jr 1990: *Competing Against Time.* New York, NY: The Free Press.

Taylor, W. 1991: The logic of global business. Interview with ABB's Percy Barnevik, *Harvard Business Review*, March–April.

# 25

# Indian Snacks

*Change and continuity*
GRAEME SALAMAN

## Background

The company, Indian Snacks, is based in the Indian subcontinent. It has two factory sites some 100 miles apart and a head office in the nearby town. The two factories manufacture products in the food, drinks and snacks market. The company is owned by a UK-based multinational which owns factories manufacturing similar products in almost 40 other countries. The products are largely for consumption within the subcontinent, but there is also a small export production for the Gulf and the former Soviet Union.

Before the changes described in this case study there were in factory A: 36 managers, 17 supervisors, 1,400 permanent workers and 322 temporary workers. In factory B, there were 24 managers, 14 supervisors and 1,278 workers.

Work was organized on a three-shift basis. There was a small head office staff. Local conditions within the subcontinent had a number of features that were relevant to the performance of the company. Labour legislation covers many aspects of Indian Snacks management and was seen by them to tie their hands on many issues where in the West managers could act unilaterally – there are, for example, restraints on the adoption of labour-saving technologies; on the ability of management to make workers redundant; and wage raises were decided unilaterally by the Government. Also on a national level there were problems of poor levels of mass education, of high illiteracy, of low-level or indeed an absence of social benefits – unemployment benefits, social security, public housing, health provision, and so on.

The company had been in existence for many years – since before independence. And its origins in imperial conditions was still evident in minor ways: the layout and maintenance standards of the sites; the guest house and associated conventions, the factory clubs. There are those who argue that the legacy is still alive in important ways.

Head Office in the UK (HOUK) was prepared to leave detailed management to local managers, and national restraints made it impossible to have any more than one senior manager post filled by an expatriate. In this case this was the chairman who was a senior HOUK manager with many years experience of the multinational and of Indian Snacks. HOUK laid down certain requirements – for example concerning safety – and demanded certain levels of financial contribution.

## Performance

HOUK compiles annual figures on all 40-odd companies on a number of key performance measures. These were available to management of all the companies. They supplied a public statement of relative performance – a public benchmarking. On these figures, Indian Snacks was one of the largest employers in the group and had one of the highest levels of output of units per year, but was bottom on units per man-hour, which was the way efficiency was measured and was one of the poorest (that is, highest) in terms of 'conversion cost' – the cost of producing a million units. Furthermore, worryingly, these conversion costs were showing a long-term tendency to rise steadily: from 18.00 rupees per million in 1992 to 20.54 rupees in 1993 and 21.97 rupees in 1993. Fifty per cent of conversion costs were due to labour costs, a higher proportion than in other companies despite the relatively low cost of labour in the country.

Indian Snacks' annual contribution to HOUK was below expected guidelines. A further and serious problem associated with Indian Snack's low and declining profitability was the inability of the company to raise prices because of strong price pressure from competitor brands of superior quality. These brands were already eroding Indian Snack's market share, and any increase in price of Indian Snack brands would certainly result in further loss of market share to competitor products.

There were other problems that were recognized: quality was poor at a time when consumers were increasingly demanding quality products – and was very poor by the group's own measurements; levels of inflation in the country were in excess of tolerable price increases.

## Need for Change?

There was widespread recognition that change was necessary. Among Indian Snacks senior and middle management and HOUK staff there was recognition that something had to be done. The company faced a combination of long-term decline in market share; rising costs; rising rates of inflation which led to cost increases but inability to raise prices; poor efficiencies; and poor quality at a time of rising customer expectations. Internal pressures for change were also identified: the worker-management divide was very strong; communications were poor; relations between functions, disciplines and shifts were poor; the power of the union meant that management freedom to manage was significantly reduced; there was serious overmanning. In many respects management had allowed the union elected to represent the workforce (the Collective Bargaining Agency, or CBA) to take over many functions more conventionally seen as management's responsibility: workers took their problems to their CBA representative; most internal communication was from senior management or employee relations specialists to CBA representatives, not via management; all discussions of job redesign, redundancies, and so on, were negotiated through ER staff and CBA staff. The role of management was highly restricted – to the fire-fighting management of the production process – and even this was limited, for the serious problems caused by absenteeism were also seen as being the proper province of ER/CBA relations.

## Solutions

This was the situation in 1995 when HOUK decided to encourage Indian Snacks' management to introduce team working in the manufacturing plants. HOUK had considerable experience of team working, having introduced it, after considerable initial resistance, in its UK plants. In late 1995 team working was introduced in ABC. The claimed advantages of team working were obvious and clear: the objective was to reduce unit production costs and to improve quality through installing more effective ways of working. More specifically, the move to team working was seen to lead to:

delegating greater authority to working teams;

- requiring the establishment of realistic and negotiated work targets which would be 'owned' by the teams;
- establishing team monitoring of output, waste and quality, and thus ensuring these were 'owned' by the teams;
- delegating maintenance, electrical and fitting work to the teams, thus reducing down times and improving output;
- establishing a greater degree of monitoring and management of individuals' performance by team leaders and team members;
- improving communication from management to teams and within teams;
- achieving a greater degree of flexibility within the manufacturing process with multiskilled team members being able and prepared to replace each other on any task.

In both factories it was anticipated that reduction in manning levels by 1996 would be of a scale of approximately 25 per cent.

The traditional organization of production at Indian Snacks in both factories involved a highly differentiated and specialized division of labour with the total process of unit manufacture divided into shifts and into a number of interdependent functions, and with specialist maintenance services operating independently of the manufacturing management. This led to great inflexibility. With a tendency to high levels of absenteeism, especially during harvest seasons or religious festivals, the result was seriously interrupted output when key staff were absent and other functions were consequently lacking materials or maintenance. Targets were previously imposed without consultation; therefore workers felt no responsibility for them, and simply saw their role as contributing their specialist input to a process that was, as a totality, someone else's responsibility. Quality was the responsibility of a specialist team. Under these conditions crisis was constant. Blockages, delays, breakdowns, all had serious knock-on effects on a highly interdependent process and required constant heroic, frenetic intervention by management. Inflexibility led to overmanning as shift managers attempted to cushion themselves against variations in absenteeism rates and bottle-necks.

## Planned Implementation

The initial impetus came from HOUK. An HRS specialist with experience of team working and training within HOUK arrived from the UK. During this visit he discussed the principles of team working with senior managers, including: teams have defined tasks and targets against which they are measured; teams have the necessary skills, and broadly defined work roles; team leaders will work flexibly; team leaders, selected by management, will have a say in selection of team members; and team leaders will be responsible for team communications, discipline and grievance.

It was agreed that the introduction of team working would be phased: a pilot application, then spreading it to an entire function then to all other departments, over a time-scale of a year and a half.

## *Project management*

The visiting specialist discussed the composition of the teams with Indian Snacks' managers and agreed that initially teams should consist of 19 members including a team leader, and two technical roles (maintenance, fitting, and so on) and 16 operators. This would produce a saving of approximately 19 workers.

The machine layouts were discussed and agreed, including the location of storage space, team boundaries, and so on. The timetable for the introduction of team working was developed and new management structures agreed. With the new role of team leader taking some of the responsibilities of current shift managers, there was a planned reduction of the middle management cadre of approximately 50 per cent.

It was agreed that the project would require two project managers to be responsible for the project design and implementation. The introduction of team working was recognized as a major event with considerable implications. The project would need careful management, co-ordination and administration. It would probably also arouse resistance and cause confusion and stress, for example for the team leaders. Therefore there was a need for someone to whom the team leaders could go for advice and support.

## *Communication*

Communication was seen as central to the success of the project. It was agreed that a formal briefing process be introduced to ensure that employees were aware of, and understood, what team working was and why and how it was to be introduced. The role of the team leader in the communication process was also recognized as critical.

Issues to be communicated to employees would be principally those of performance, including company results, individual factory performance and progress against team targets. Information about company projects should also be included. Since there was no such communication system in place a new structure would have to be designed to ensure competent, regular, formal, systematic communication in company time using the team leaders. It was recognized that the explicit commitment to the project of all the senior managers was essential, and that senior management must ensure that the unions and workforce were fully informed of the project and were also supportive.

*Training*

Training was also identified as critical. At a senior and middle management level it was recognized that managers should be thoroughly familiar with the nature and background of the team working project. The visiting consultant worked with senior managers but also agreed to organize three team-working seminars for all middle managers (including actual or potential team leaders) to discuss:

- the need for change;
- the objectives of team working;
- the impact of team working on existing practices;
- the roles and responsibilities of managers in implementing the change;
- possible problems in implementation;
- the price of failure.

The team leader role was a new one to Indian Snacks and was obviously central to the success of the project. The specification for the role was devised and the selection process launched. It was recognized that incumbent managers at the equivalent level would not necessarily make suitable team leaders. Some would be recruited from outside. The most professional methods of selection should be used, not least because it was important that the selection process should be seen as fair, objective and demanding by prospective candidates – for example an assessment centre. The team work project managers would be involved in the training and management of selection processes.

A structured development programme was devised. First there was a two-day team working induction course which addressed the nature and benefits of team working, team leader accountabilities and the practical issues arising from the implementation of team working within Indian Snacks. After this a team leader development programme would be devised which would run over a 12-month period. It would include modules on team working; management; communication; interviewing; health and safety; finance; quality; and so on.

Team members too would need training. This would start with a one-day event (a Team Day) which would cover the reasons for, nature of, and practical implications of, teamwork.

ABC management then initiated a process of planning and consultation. The union and the workforce were formally briefed about the project (which was presented in terms of quality and efficiency).

## Actual implementation

About a year into the team working project, when some pilot teams had begun work, a review of progress through discussion with middle and senior managers revealed a number of issues requiring attention.

*Team leaders* This was a very demanding role, and required a form and type of management that was new to the Indian Snacks factories. The role was still not entirely clear in terms of authority levels, and the salary scales applying to the role had not been clarified. In particular there had been difficulties establishing the division of authorities between the new team leaders and shift managers. In fact the role of shift manager was now quite unclear – and it was not obvious that it was truly necessary. There were difficulties with the financial and authority levels of team leader, particularly with regard to ordering spares.

*Management* It was clear that the success of the team working project depended on the emergence of a radically new conception of what management is about, a conception in which managers would have to develop new sorts of relationships with the workforce. Managers would have to stop being fire-fighters and become professional man managers, concerned with directing, motivating, supporting – even developing – their teams. It was also clear that senior and middle management would have to alter their conception of their management role, and the vigour with which they confronted issues of performance management and staff costs (that is, confronted the CBA).

*Union relations* Under the previous regime managers had focused on resolving production crises and administration and had in effect abdicated many management functions to the unions. Communications to the workforce, for example, tended to be through the union representative, which supported the officials' authority. Previously workers took their problems to their union representative. But under team working managers would have to regain their authority *vis-à-vis* the workforce and communicate with them directly, dealing themselves with workers' problems. It was recognized, in short, that a major implication (and prerequisite) of team working was for managers to establish a new sort of relationship with the workforce regarding the allocation of work, work targets and standards, skill development, flexibility arrangements, and so on.

*Communications* While communications were seen as essential to the success of the team working project there were still problems apparent. While a great deal of effort was spent on external marketing communications relatively little systematic effort went into internal communications. Staff were not sure where the project had got to, how various developments related to each other – indeed *if* they were related to each other. While the project managers and some senior managers could see the overall pattern behind the various events, the workforce often could not see these patterns. This followed managers' abdication of responsibility for communications to the union, or to employment relations staff.

*Team working project management* The team working project managers were two young, eager individuals. A number of people felt that while they were entirely suitable to manage the project, their youth and relative lack of seniority gave the wrong impression: there was a need to demonstrate more clearly the involvement and support of senior management – preferably through the establishment of a steering group.

## Outcomes of the Project

By late 1995 there were some data available on the outcomes of the change project. In all some 11 teams had been introduced and were seen to be working well. Twelve new team leaders had been recruited and the vast majority were seen to be working well in this key role.

The team leaders had experienced a training programme in the requisite skills of the role.

As a result of the introduction of team working it had been found necessary to flatten the organizational structure (for the new team leader role made some managerial and supervisory positions unnecessary) and to change the entry point for new graduate recruits, who now entered at the team leader grade and were expected to be able to take on the role of team leaders. This incorporated the team leader role in the career structure and ensured that graduates required to become team leaders did not experience a change or drop in status. The team leader role began to assume a central role within the management area.

The introduction of 12 new team leaders from outside the company, allied to changes in the entry point of graduates and delayering, had resulted, it was claimed, in a significant and important change in management attitudes towards a more performance-focused conception of the role.

With respect to the key indicators of company performance, however, the picture was less rosy. At the beginning of the change project Indian Snacks was one of the largest employers in the group; it still was. It had one of the highest levels of output of units per year, and output had actually increased by about 7 per cent. But on the key productivity measure (output per employee hour) Indian Snacks was still very near the bottom of the group league: 35th out of 38. Similarly, with respect to quality, which is measured against a maximum of 100 with marks being deducted for any quality defects, Indian Snacks in 1995 showed a slight improvement, to 52 per cent from 48 per cent in 1994, but was still a long way off the desired level – around 80 per cent was expected. With this score, Indian Snacks was second to bottom within the group.

The most encouraging single improvement was in the reversal of the long-term increase in conversion costs, which were now dropping, if slowly.

Senior management argued that the company was now poised for a striking improvement in productivity, but since this was measured in terms of the relationship between staff numbers and output, this would clearly require either a very significant increase in production – and the company was already top of the league in absolute terms, without any increase in staff numbers; or a significant decrease in staff. And this was the problem. Although the introduction of team working had resulted in a number of employees being rejected for team membership because of their lack of relevant skills for team working, these people had not been discharged. Surplus staff were still on the payroll, not only adding to costs but also acting as a source of discouragement and disgruntlement to the newly formed teams.

Senior management attributed its unwillingness, or inability, to get rid of surplus staff to the power of the union – the Collective Bargaining Agency (CBA). This agency was chosen by the workers from among all the unions present in the plants. Each factory elected its own CBA. In order to win this election the unions outbid each other in their promises, and once installed the CBA's clout was greatly enhanced by statutory restrictions on management action and government-initiated nationwide wage increases. But even more important in accounting for the power of the union was management's unwillingness to act firmly and to confront them. A policy of gradualism, of negotiated incrementalism, was so deep-rooted in managers' conception of their role and their allocation of key areas of decision making to ER/CBA specialists that most managers took for granted a situation where their freedom of action, and specifically their ability to reduce manning levels in order to achieve the output targets established for team working, were significantly constrained.

## Implications

The process of change discussed here was externally driven and imposed as a result of comparative performance benchmarking. However, this initial cause was closely related to other HOUK concerns: concern about the 'toughness' of local management, the determination to impose a particular management style, and the determination to apply solutions developed elsewhere. This case therefore says something about the origins of change, about the relationship between multinational head office management of regional companies.

However, the local management were not fully aware of the need for change; they were not clear about the vision of the future; they lacked many of the resources necessary to make the change effective; and they had not fully broken down the change into small incremental steps. Some of these deficiencies were rectified during the course of the programme. The initial change which was focused on the shopfloor was very obviously dependent on the achievement of other key changes, many of which had not been fully recognized and some of which went to the heart of the existing culture and ways of doing things: communications systems; the nature and definition of management; attitudes towards the union. In other words, it is possible to argue that the ultimate source of the problems of productivity and quality and costs (management attitude and robustness, and managers' conception of their role *vis-à-vis* the management of the workforce) were not directly and immediately changed by the introduction of team working – at least as far as senior managers were concerned. The progress of the change revealed deep-seated attitudes and practices (about management and towards the CBA, or workforce) that were incompatible with the proposed change; but these were not apparent to the participants: they were seen as natural, and were taken for granted. The initial problems then reappeared as obstacles to the achievement of the full potential of the change process.

The project was designed to introduce new ways of behaving and communication. But to some degree it also relied on new ways of working and managing. Managers and workers had to let go of established ways of working and thinking – ways which in many cases were institutionalized in procedures and historic patterns of behaviour, for example the normal ways of thinking about and relating to the unions or ways of communicating with workers. The success of the change relied on the very changes it seeks to achieve. It thus puts pressure on these traditional ways which are now less comfortable, and work less well (or else the change works less well). These tensions and discrepancies need careful identification and analysis. The change project has to be broken down into a personal agenda for everyone involved so that they can see how they should now go about a simple operation that might have been altered radically by the new system.

It seems it is more important – and more difficult – to unlearn than to learn. It may be that the most important outcome of the change project is that through its relative failure to meet expectations it has highlighted with unmistakeable emphasis the real sources of inertia within the company and therefore made them more exposed to direct confrontation.

---

## Questions

1  What were the main factors that caused senior management to seek to initiate a programme of change at Indian Snacks?

2  What were the perceived benefits of teamwork in this company?

3  How was the implementation of teamwork planned?
4  What implementation issues and difficulties arose in the installation of teamwork at Indian Snacks?

## Further reading

Beer, M., Eisenstadt, R., Spector, B. 1990: Why change programmes don't
produce change, *Harvard Business Review*, November/December, pp. 158–
66.
Mabey, C. and Salaman, G. 1995: *Strategic Human Resource Management*,
Blackwell: Oxford.
Pettigrew, A., Ferlie, E. and Lee, L. 1992: *Shaping Strategic Change*, Sage:
London.
Tichy, N. 1983: *Managing Strategic Change*, Wiley: New York.

## 26

# Food and Drink International

*International staffing: policy and practice*
HUGH SCULLION

During the 1990s there was a surge of interest in international human resource management (HRM). This can be explained by the rapid increase in global activity and global competition and the growing recognition that the effective management of human resources internationally is a major source of competitive advantage in international business (Dowling et al., 1994). Also, there is evidence that many companies underestimate the complex nature of HRM problems in international business (Tung, 1984).

The particular focus of this case study is on the key issue of international staffing. One feature of the case was the exclusive focus on managing 'international managers'. The main theme of the case is to illustrate the key influences on international staffing decisions. In particular the case explores the links between international staffing and the international evolution of the firm.

A case study dealing with international staffing is appropriate for the following reasons:

1 The international staffing process is of considerable importance to an international firm. 'Virtually any type of international problem, in the final analysis, is either created by people or must be solved by people. Hence, having the right people in the right place at the right time emerges as the key to a company's international growth. If we are successful in solving this problem, I am confident we can cope with all others' (Duer, 1968 p. 43).

2   The staffing problems facing international firms are more complex than in domestic firms and inappropriate staffing policies may lead to difficulties in managing overseas operations (Tung, 1984).

3   The international literature indicates that expatriate failure continues to be a problem for many international firms and that business failures in the international arena may often be linked to poor staffing decisions (Dowling et al., 1994).

4   Shortages of international managers are becoming an increasing problem for international firms and recent research suggests that the successful implementation of global strategies depends to a large extent on the existence of an adequate supply of internationally experienced managers (Scullion, 1993).

5   The advent of the Single European Market and the rapid growth of British direct investment abroad since the early 1980s mean that issues of international staffing are increasingly important concerns in a far wider range of organizations than the traditional multinationals.

## Organizational Setting

Food and Drink International (FDI) is a UK-owned international food and drinks group. In the mid 1990s the group employed over 160,000 people world-wide, of whom approximately 100,000 (60 per cent) were employed outside the UK. Food and Drink International concentrates its activities in Western Europe, North America, Japan and the Far East. Yet in the late 1970s FDI was basically a UK organization with relatively few international activities. The rapid growth of foreign employment in FDI reflects the rapid and successful internationalization of the group's activities and the development of the group as a leading competitor in world markets.

Wholly-owned subsidiaries (foreign direct investment) had been the principal form of the group's involvement abroad but more recently there has been a significant growth in international joint ventures and strategic alliances due primarily to the globalization of the drinks industry.

When the group was founded in the early 1960s it was run very successfully by entrepreneurs as totally disparate businesses. There was little strategic synergy between the businesses. The company gained a reputation as a buy-and-sell company and, in the absence of a strategic approach, acquisitions were made on the basis of sound underlying property values.

In the early 1980s a more structured approach to business emerged. A new strategic approach developed which had several key elements:

Copyright John Storey 1996, Blackwell Cases in Human Resource and Change Management

1   The group would seek to develop through organic and acquisitive growth.

2   There would be a focus on high-quality businesses.

3   The group would seek to internationalize in related market areas (food and drink) primarily through acquisitions in the United States and Europe.

4   The strategy was to achieve a more even spread of earnings across the major geographical areas (the UK, the US and the rest of the world).

While the group continued to operate in a highly decentralized way the new strategic approach of the early 1980s was in sharp contrast to the approach of the late 1970s when the group comprised a series of stand-alone companies and was still basically a highly decentralized holding company.

The late 1980s saw a further major development in the international business strategy of Food and Drink International. The group made several acquisitions of giant food and drink businesses in the United States and Europe. As a result of these acquisitions the international character of the group was fundamentally altered and for the first time in their history the group had more business (by turnover) and profit in the US than in the UK.

These changes reflected a further development of the group's internationalization strategy. The strategy of Food and Drink International was now to become a global company in order to compete effectively in industries which were increasingly becoming global in character. In the late 1980s the global drinks industry was consolidating into four major global players. The rationale behind the strategy of acquiring large US drinks companies was to acquire the global brands which came with them. In the global drinks industry of the late 1980s and early 1990s, global competitive advantage was gained either by acquiring global brands or securing control of distribution on an international basis. The strategic motivation underlying the acquisition of a very large US international food company in 1988 by Food and Drink International was primarily to give the group 'critical mass' in the world foods market and control over some of the strongest brands in the world's richest food market.

Currently, Food and Drink International has an established strategic focus as an international food and drinks group, and recent acquisitions and divestments reflect this strategy. The international brand marketing skills are seen as a major source of competitive advantage for the group and as key to strengthening the position of global brand leaders and other brands in the group's portfolio.

## International Staffing Policy and Practice

International firms face three alternatives with respect to the staffing of management positions abroad: the employment of parent country nationals (PCNs), host country nationals (HCNs) or third country nationals (TCNs). In the 1970s in the early stages of the internationalization of Food and Drink International, the staffing policy of the group was largely ethnocentric in character (all key positions at the centre and locally being filled by parent company nationals). This approach is relatively common in the early stage of internationalization where a company is setting up a new business process or product in another country and knowledge of the company's culture and reporting systems is considered essential (Zeira, 1976).

International staffing policy, like HRM strategy generally, however, must be linked to the strategic evolution of the firm (Schuler et al., 1993). As Food and Drink International moved beyond the early phase of internationalization and adapted a highly decentralized approach to international business operations a number of the disadvantages of an ethnocentric approach became increasingly significant.

1   The effective adaptation of PCNs to some host countries frequently took longer than anticipated.
2   There were limited promotion and development opportunities for local managers. This made it more difficult to attract and motivate high-calibre local staff.
3   Problems sometimes emerged when PCN and HCN compensation packages were compared.

Given the disadvantages of an ethnocentric staffing policy outlined above and the highly decentralized approach adopted by Food and Drink International, it is not surprising that the firm shifted towards a polycentric staffing policy (which is one where HCNs are recruited to manage subsidiaries in their own country and PCNs occupy senior positions in corporate headquarters).

Food and Drink International identified a number of advantages of operating with a polycentric approach which are consistent with findings in the literature (Dowling et al., 1994):

1   It removed the adjustment problems of expatriates and their families.
2   Local managers were more sensitive to local culture and local market trends.

3 Host country national managers generally cost less than parent company nationals.

4 A polycentric approach allowed greater continuity of management within the foreign subsidiaries.

5 A polycentric approach was a better fit with the highly decentralized business approach.

6 This approach enhanced the ability of the group to recruit, motivate and develop local staff.

Yet while Food and Drink International adopted a formal staffing *policy* which favoured using host-country managers to run their foreign operations, in *practice* there had been a very significant increase in the use of expatriates to run their foreign operations. The explanation of this paradox is at the heart of the case study.

There were a number of principal reasons given by Food and Drink International to explain their increased use of expatriates over the previous decade. The first was simply the lack of availability of management skills in some less-developed countries. Second, the performance of foreign subsidiaries was a significant factor influencing the use of expatriates (Scullion, 1992). This is well illustrated by the two largest international acquisitions made by Food and Drink International in the late 1980s. The first acquisition was a global drinks business with its headquarters in the US, and the second was a large US food business. The staffing policy differed sharply in the two acquisitions. In the former case, the existing management team (comprised entirely of host-country national managers) continued to run the business. In the words of a corporate HR executive: 'In this case, we inherited an excellent management team who were achieving first-class results. Why change a winning team and upset morale by introducing expatriates?'

In the second case, by contrast, the entire US management team was replaced by UK expatriates, 'mainly due to poor financial results and weak managerial performance'. The third major reason given for using expatriates was the objective of control of local operations (Brewster, 1991). Expatriates were felt to be more familiar with the corporate culture and control system of headquarters. A key role for senior expatriates was to train local managers to understand corporate financial and control systems to ensure more effective communication and co-ordination between subsidiary companies and headquarters. The fifth principal reason for using expatriates (usually very senior expatriates) was to maintain trust in key foreign business, following the increasing number of very large international acquisitions. The emergence of trust as a major factor in international staffing decisions in UK companies is related to the rapid growth in the number and scale of international acquisitions by British firms in the late 1980s (Scullion, 1995). In the present case, Food and Drink International was not willing to have a very large strategically important foreign investment being run by host-country national management. This was for two main reasons. First, the HCN managers were not known to headquarters management. Second, the loyalty of the HCN managers to 'the business' was not proven. The Food and Drink International case also highlighted that expatriates are more likely to be used in the early stages of new foreign operations. Control and trust, the two factors mentioned above, are particularly important in the early stages of internationalization (Zeira, 1976).

This factor also helps to explain the contrast between the staffing practices of Food and Drink International in Europe and the US. In Europe the majority of foreign operations had been established for some time. The senior management of the European companies mainly comprised HCNs. The new European companies which had been recently established were in contrast usually run by UK expatriates. Similarly, in many of the newly established or recently acquired US companies the tendency was to bring in senior UK expatriates to run the businesses.

The sixth principal reason for using expatriates in Food and Drink International was for management development purposes. This in part reflected a recognition of the two major disadvantages of the polycentric approach (Kobrin, 1988):

1   the need to bridge the gap between host country national managers and parent country managers; and

2   problems concerning the career paths of HCN and PCN managers. It also reflects the group's recognition that international management development activities were regarded as strategic and vital to the group's ability to develop as a global company. While Food and Drink International was a highly decentralized group with a rather limited corporate HR role, in practice succession planning and management development were operating on a global basis for the top 250 managers in the group. These managers were regarded by the centre as a group resource and were managed at group level.

The use of expatriates for management development purposes was also linked to the recent trend in Food and Drink International to

Copyright John Storey 1996, Blackwell Cases in Human Resource and Change Management

identify young, high-potential managers and give them international experience much earlier in their career than previously. In addition to the cost advantages of sending younger managers abroad, this strategy was also related to the problem of finding international managers and reflected also the increasing concern about the international mobility and repatriation of older managers.

## Current Position

Notwithstanding the very significant increase in the use of expatriates *in practice* to run Food and Drink International's foreign operations, the *intention* was to use senior UK expatriates for only a relatively short-term transitory period. The international human resource strategy was to localize management in the operating companies by developing host-country national managers to take over the running of foreign businesses and withdrawing the expatriates. The implementation of the localization strategy is a major challenge for Food and Drink International given that many international firms have tended to neglect the training and development needs of their host country managers and focus virtually all their management development efforts on their parent country nationals (Shaeffer, 1989, p. 29).

Food and Drink International were responding to this challenge by increasing significantly the practice of developing host-country managers through developmental transfers to corporate headquarters. The corporate management development manager outlined four major advantages arising from this type of international transfer:

1. HCN and TCN nationals obtained first-hand experience of the corporate culture and headquarters control systems.
2. Bringing HCN managers to the corporate centre helped the HCN managers to develop a broader corporate perspective.
3. The process helped to identify high potential HCNs and supported career and succession planning activities.
4. This approach to international development was seen as vital in helping to build global management teams and global firms.

The present case study is a good example of a multinational which passes through various stages of internationalization between evolution from a domestic to a truly global organization (Negandhi, 1987). This is a typical pattern of multinational development. The case has highlighted that international staffing strategy must be linked to the strategic evolution of the firm. It also suggests that, for multinationals, staffing and development issues will be key challenges in the late 1990s.

## Postscript

Food and Drink International attributed its rapid international growth and success in global markets to three main factors:

1  the success of the national and global brands;
2  the recruitment of high-calibre people and their development to the highest possible standard;
3  a highly decentralized approach.

## Questions

1  Explain the growth of interest in staffing issues in international firms.
2  Identify the key elements of Food and Drink International's strategy in the early 1980s.
3  What was the rationale underlying the strategy of acquiring large US Food and Drinks businesses in the late 1980s?
4  What are the main advantages/disadvantages of an ethnocentric staffing approach?
5  What are the main advantages/disadvantages of a polycentric staffing approach?
6  Why do firms pursuing a broadly polycentric approach to international staffing continue to use expatriates to manage their foreign operations? Identify and discuss the main reasons.
7  Identify the most important roles for corporate human resource management in a highly decentralized international firm.
8  Outline the benefits of seeking to develop host-country managers through developmental transfers to corporate headquarters.

## References

Brewster, C. 1991: *The Management of Expatriates*. London, Kogan Page.
Dowling, P. J., Schuler, R. S. and Welch, D. 1994: *International Dimensions of Human Resource Management*. (2nd edn), Belmont, CA: Wadsworth.

Duerr, M. G. 1968: *International Business Management: its Four Tasks*. Conference Board Record, October.

Kobrin, S. J. 1988: Expatriate control and strategic control in American multinationals. *Human Resource Management*, **27**, 63–75.

Negandhi, A. N. 1987: *International Management*. Newton, MA: Allyn and Bacon.

Schuler, R., Dowling, P. J. and De Cieri, H. 1993: An integrative framework of strategic international human resource management. *International Journal of Human Resource Management*, **4**(4).

Scullion, H. 1992: Strategic recruitment and development of the international managers: some European considerations. *Human Resource Management Journal*, **3**(1), 57–69.

Scullion, H. 1993: Creating international managers: recruitment and development issues. In Kirkbride, P. (ed.), *Human Resource Management in Europe*, London: Routledge.

Scullion, H. 1995: International human resource management. In Storey J. (ed.), *Human Resource Management: A Critical Text*, London: Routledge.

Shaeffer, R. 1989: Managing international business growth and international management development. *Human Resource Planning*, March, 29–36.

Tung, R. L. 1984: Strategic management of human resources in the multinational Enterprise. *Human Resource Management*, **23**(2), 129–43.

Zeira, Y. 1976: Management development in ethnocentric multinational corporations. *California Management Review*, **18**(4), 34–42.

# Index